The material in this book is restricted. This book may be read only by those who have received a highest yoga tantra empowerment and the oral transmission of the instructions.

The Guru Yoga of Jé Tsongkhapa

The Guru Yoga of Jé Tsongkhapa

A Commentary

by H. E. Chöden Rinpoché

translated and edited by

Ian Coghlan and Voula Zarpani

Wisdom

Wisdom Publications
132 Perry Street
New York, NY 10014 USA
wisdom.org

Library of Congress Cataloging-in-Publication Data
Names: Chöden Rinpoché, 1930–2015, author. | Coghlan, Ian, translator. | Zarpani, Voula, translator. | Tsong-kha-pa Blo-bzang-grags-pa, 1357–1419. Srad brgyud phugs kyi bla ma'i rnal 'byor Dga' ldan lha brgya ma bzhugs so. English. | Pha-bong-kha-pa Byams-pa-bstan-'dzin-'phrin-las-rgya-mtsho, 1878–1941. Zab lam Dga'-ldan lha brgya ma'i rnal 'byor nyams su len tshul snyan brgyud zhal shes lhug par bkod pa'i man ngag rin chen gter gyi bang mdzod ces bya ba. English.
Title: The guru yoga of Jé Tsongkhapa / a commentary by Chöden Rinpoché; translated and edited by Ian Coghlan and Voula Zarpani.
Other titles: Dga' lha rgyas pa'i bshad pa byin rlabs kyi sgo 'byed ces bya ba. English
Description: First wisdom edition. | New York: Wisdom Publications, 2024. | Includes bibliographical references and index.
Identifiers: LCCN 2024005217 (print) | LCCN 2024005218 (ebook) | ISBN 9781614298366 (paperback) | ISBN 9781614298571 (ebook)
Subjects: LCSH: Guru worship (Rite)—Buddhism. | Tsong-kha-pa Blo-bzang-grags-pa, 1357–1419. Srad brgyud phugs kyi bla ma'i rnal 'byor Dga' ldan lha brgya ma bzhugs so. | Pha-bong-kha-pa Byams-pa-bstan-'dzin-'phrin-las-rgya-mtsho, 1878-1941. Zab lam Dga'-ldan lha brgya ma'i rnal 'byor nyams su len tshul snyan brgyud zhal shes lhug par bkod pa'i man ngag rin chen gter gyi bang mdzod ces bya ba. | Dge-lugs-pa (Sect)—Rituals
Classification: LCC BQ7699.G87 C46 2024 (print) | LCC BQ7699.G87 (ebook) | DDC 294.3/438—dc23/eng/20240511
LC record available at https://lccn.loc.gov/2024005217
LC ebook record available at https://lccn.loc.gov/2024005218

Translated from Tibetan.
Dga' lha rgyas pa'i bshad byin rlabs kyi sgo 'byed. Commentary on Pabongkha Rinpoché's *Zab lam dga' ldan brgya ma'i rnal 'byor nyams su len tshul snyan brgyud zhal shes zab bshad lhug par bkod pa'i man ngag rin chen gter gyi bang mdzod / Bountiful Advice Clarifying the Oral Transmission and Explaining the Deep Meaning of How to Practice the Profound Path of Yoga of the Hundreds of Deities of Tuṣita, Called "A Treasury of Precious Jewels"*

ISBN 978-1-61429-836-6   EBOOK ISBN 978-1-61429-857-1

Designed and typeset by Gopa & Ted2, Inc. Cover painting copyright © 2012 by Richard Wehrman
29 28 27 26 25   5 4 3 2 1

Printed on acid-free paper that meets the guidelines for permanence and durability of the Production Guidelines for Book Longevity of the Council on Library Resources.

Printed in the United States of America.

MIX
Paper | Supporting responsible forestry
FSC® C005010
FSC www.fsc.org

Please visit fscus.org.

Contents

Foreword by Gyalten Khen Rinpoché ... xi
Translators' Acknowledgments ... xiii
Translators' Introduction ... 1

Extensive Explanation of
THE HUNDREDS OF DEITIES OF TUṢITA,
Called OPENING THE DOOR OF BLESSINGS

A Commentary on Jé Pabongkha Dechen Nyingpo's
Bountiful Advice Clarifying the Oral Transmission and Explaining the Deep Meaning of How to Practice the Profound Path of Yoga of the Hundreds of Deities of Tuṣita, Called "A Treasury of Precious Jewels"

1. INTRODUCTION ... 11
   1. Explaining the Meaning of the Title 11
   2. Homage and the Pledge to Compose 12

2. PRELIMINARIES ... 23
   1. Visualizing the Field of Refuge and Merit 23
   2. Actual Refuge 30
   3. The Awakening Mind 32
   4. The Four Immeasurables 34
   5. Contracting the Field of Refuge and Merit 38

3. The Seven-Limb Prayer 41
1. Visualizing the Merit Field 41
2. The Seven-Limb Prayer 63
1. Requesting to Remain 63
2. Prostration 63
3. Offering 66
4. Confession 72
5. Rejoicing 78
6. Urging to Turn the Wheel of Dharma 82
7. Dedication 86
3. Maṇḍala Offering 89

4. Requesting the Four Empowerments as a Blessing 95
1. Making Requests to One Whose Illumination Equals External [Space] 97
2. Making Requests to One Who Possesses Those Internal Qualities 102
3. Making Requests to One Who Is Indivisible in Nature from the Secret Special Deity 106

5. Requesting the Blessings of Special Wisdom 113
1. Vast Wisdom 118
2. Clear Wisdom 120
3. Swift Wisdom 121
4. Profound Wisdom 122
5. Wisdom of Explanation 123
6. Wisdom of Debate 124
7. Wisdom of Composition 125

6. The Visualization for the Miktsema Praise 131

1. First Round of Visualization 131
2. Second Round of Visualization 137
3. Third Round of Visualization 140
4. Fourth Round of Visualization 141
5. Fifth Round of Visualization 143

7. Requesting the Blessing of the Entire Path, Collectively 149

1. First Round of Explanation 149
2. Second Round of Explanation 171
3. Third Round of Explanation 174
4. Blessings of the Four Initiations 174

8. Concluding Practices 179

Condensed Explanation of The Hundreds of Deities of Tuṣita, *Called* Opening the Door of Blessings

1. Motivation 201

2. The Six Preliminaries 215

1. First Preliminary: Cleaning Your Room 215
2. Second Preliminary: Arranging Offerings 219
3. Third Preliminary: The Seven-Point Vairocana Posture 220
4. Fourth Preliminary: Visualizing the Merit Field 227

5. Fifth Preliminary: The Seven-Limb Prayer 233

1. Requesting Not to Pass into Paranirvāṇa 234

2. Prostration 236

3. Offering 240

4. Confession 243

5. Rejoicing 245

6. Urging to Turn the Wheel of Dharma 247

7. Dedication 248

6. Sixth Preliminary: Offering a Maṇḍala 249

3. ACTUAL PRACTICE AND CONCLUSION 251

1. Actual Practice of Reciting the Miktsema Praise 251

2. Conclusion 256

Appendix:
The Full Text of *The Hundreds of Deities of Tuṣita* 261

Notes 265

Glossary 277

Bibliography 289

Index 295

About the Contributors 303

About Awakening Vajra 307

Foreword by Gyalten Khen Rinpoché

In the practice of guru yoga, the guru—or in Tibetan, *lama*—is not simply a teacher or philosopher, but one who awakens the student from the sleep of confusion. According to oral tradition, each syllable can be seen as imbued with special significance: *la* denotes "the highest," here referring to the highest state of existence, enlightenment; *ma* refers to the "mother" giving birth to this enlightened state, the guru. In guru yoga the teacher introduces the student to the nature of their own mind, leading them to recognize their innate inner light. In this spiritual union, disciple truly meets master.

In these teachings, adeptly translated by Ian Coghlan and Voula Zarpani, one of the greatest lamas of our time offers, from his own direct experience, a profound method of spiritual transformation. In doing so, he opens the gate through which we, too, can enter into the city of eternal joy and bliss.

Gyalten Khen Rinpoché,
co-founder with
H. E. Chöden Rinpoché of Awakening Vajra International

Acknowledgments from the Gyalten Translation Group

Initiated by Rinpoché's close disciple Gyalten Khen Rinpoché, the Gyalten Translation Group of Awakening Vajra International is dedicated to preserving and spreading Chöden Rinpoché's intellectual and spiritual legacy. The members of the GTG (Jeff Seipel, Gyalten Tsondue, Sue Bartfield, Timothy Brown, and Ven. Gyalten Jigdrel) wish to thank Ian Coghlan and Voula Zarpani for helping to make the works of Chöden Rinpoché available to an English-speaking public. Their vivid translation of *The Guru Yoga of Jé Tsongkhapa* makes possible the first of several revised translations of Rinpoché's works to be published by Wisdom Publications in partnership with the GTG. We also wish to thank Laura Cunningham at Wisdom Publications for her untiring editorial support.

We also express our deep appreciation for Chöden Rinpoché's students from around the world, whose steady support of Awakening Vajra International makes the GTG's work possible. Above all, the group offer our heartfelt thanks to Gyalten Khen Rinpoché for his role in protecting and spreading Chöden Rinpoché's teachings, and most importantly, to Chöden Rinpoché himself—now reincarnated as Gyalten Tenzin Rinpoché—for his authoritative spiritual guidance and inspiration.

Gyalten Translation Group

Translators' Acknowledgments

We wish to express our deep gratitude for the broad support we have received in the publication of this book. In particular we would like to acknowledge the generosity of Lee Oi Loon and her family for sponsoring the original publication of this book in Tibetan. We wish to extend a heartfelt thanks to the following benefactors of the English edition of this book: Anonymous (71), Alan Carter, Alec Franklor, Andreah Da Costa, Brian Li, Chandrakirti Meditation Centre, Chen Kuan-Ju, Chen Yun-Tso, Cheng Hong Lee, Cheryl Chase, Chee Soon, Chiu Ming-Chen Family, Ven. Chonyi Taylor, Chris Kang, Claudia L'Amoreaux, Daniel Yeoh, Don Irwin, Douglas Matthews, Doug Tallman, Eric Tan, Gary Freeman, Graeme Magruder, Guy Parish, James Parratt, Jaroslava Kubalcik, Jeff Starrs, Jennifer Kim, Jim Lewis, Joakim Opostolas, John Whaite, Jose Manuel Gonzalez, Kala Dostal, Kathleen Wansey, Li Guan-Yu, Li Liao Mei-Jui, Li Si-Xian, Li Yi-Ju, Liao Jen-Chieh Family, Lin Ying-Chun, Llysse Velez, Lucy Bresichsich, Majola Oosthuizen, Min Li Chong, Nga Nguyen, Oi L Lee, Owen Cole, Phillipa Rutherford and Bruce Farley, Preston Cox, Rosa Shen, Robert Bloor, Rosanne Park, Seah Koon Tay, Sean Gonzalez, Sergio Gouvea, Shen·Shou-Chen Family, Simone Dowding, Sherrill Kratenstein, Stuart Parish, Tai Yu-Lien, Tang Sau-Ying Family, Tania Duratovic and Phil Hunt, Tom Forsyth, Tony

Steel, and Zac Parish. In memory of Ang Song Kang, a loving father who made every provision for his child's life. All merit is dedicated to his swift enlightenment.

Translators' Personal Acknowledgment

We wish to convey our deep appreciation to H. E. Chöden Rinpoché for composing this important work and suggesting it be translated into English for Western students. The initial translation was skillfully edited by Victoria Scott and published in 2012. The current revised translation has been edited by Laura Cunningham and Ben Gleason, and we express our heartfelt gratitude for their amazing work. Finally, we express our appreciation to Wisdom Publications for republishing this work, so that this important explanation of guru yoga remains in print and available to students.

Translators' Introduction

GURU YOGA is a term widely used in Tibetan Buddhism to indicate how the mind of the student should be trained so that it may harmonize or link (yoga) with the mind of the preceptor (guru). It is the method by which you actualize the state of your guru. This practice was prominent in Indian Buddhist tantra and, faithful to the Indian tradition, Tibet has embraced and preserved guru yoga in its many forms. In Buddhism guru yoga is the realization that one's spiritual friend, or guru, has the essential nature of all the buddhas. Guru yoga shows how a person can best interact with his or her spiritual guide to purify the mind at its deepest level and develop inspired realizations of the path. Because of its importance, guru yoga is emphasized throughout Mahāyāna Buddhism.

The Guru Yoga Text and Its Extensive and Condensed Commentaries

This work consists of two texts. The first is an extensive commentary of *The Hundreds of Deities of Tuṣita* based on the tantric oral tradition as presented by Pabongkha Dechen Nyingpo in his *Treasury of Precious Jewels*. The second is a condensed commentary to the same work based on the sūtra tradition. Each explains the guru yoga practice of Jé Tsongkhapa from a different perspective and emphasizes different meditative practices.

Tsongkhapa's *Hundreds of Deities of Tuṣita*

It is said that the original form of the guru yoga practice presented here was imparted by Jé Tsongkhapa (1357–1419) to select students during his lifetime. One of his students, Gyalwa Gendün Drup (1391–1474), later known as the first Dalai Lama, taught it to his own students, and it was collated by Dülkarwa and written down by Dülnakpa Palden Sangpo (1402–73), who is often named as its author. Later, more extensive versions appeared and doubt arose about the original author, but it is clear that the practice itself was inspired by Jé Tsongkhapa.

The ten verses of the original version are not ostensibly related to mantra. The first verse introduces the central figure of this guru yoga—Jé Tsongkhapa—who is visualized in Tuṣita heaven, abiding among the retinue of Maitreya, the future buddha. A white cloud issues from Maitreya's heart, and at its crest is Jé Tsongkhapa and his two spiritual sons, Gyaltsap Jé and Khedrup Jé.[1]

The next seven verses explain the proper means of interacting with the guru, for each verse explains a limb of the seven-limb prayer.

The ninth verse teaches the five-line Miktsema[2] praise:

> Avalokiteśvara, great treasure of nonreifying compassion,
> Mañjuśrī, master of stainless wisdom,
> Secret Lord, destroyer of hordes of māras,
> Tsongkhapa, crown jewel of scholars of the Land
> of Snows,
> Losang Drakpa, I make requests at your feet.

Originally this verse was composed by Jé Tsongkhapa in praise of his teacher Jé Rendawa (1349–1412), but Rendawa changed the wording and offered it back to Jé Tsongkhapa. The tenth verse is a concluding prayer.

The ten verses are numbered ||1||, ||2||, and so forth up to ||10|| in the translation that follows. Verse 10 of the original version has been replaced in Pabongkha's commentary with verses from the oral tradition. All ten verses of the original version are set out and explained in H. E. Chöden Rinpoché's condensed commentary .

The Extensive Commentary

The practice of the hundreds of deities of Tuṣita is explained at length by Pabongkha Rinpoché (1878–1941) in his commentary called *A Treasury of Precious Jewels*, which adds detailed instruction from the oral tradition on yogic or tantric practices. Pabongkha's commentary (described in more detail below) is indented, boldface, in either non-italic or italic type. Non-italic type—corresponding to the large letters in the Tibetan text—indicates words to be recited or contemplated. Italics—corresponding to small letters in the Tibetan text—generally marks instruction on how this guru yoga is to be practiced.

Pabongkha Rinpoché's Commentary, *A Treasury of Precious Jewels*

Pabongkha's commentary is called *Bountiful Advice Clarifying the Oral Transmission and Explaining the Deep Meaning of How to Practice the Profound Path of Yoga of the Hundreds of Deities of Tuṣita, Called "A Treasury of Precious Jewels."* Since it adds instruction from the oral transmission, it transforms the hundreds of deities of Tuṣita into a work related to tantra.

Pabongkha Dechen Nyingpo Rinpoché, Jampa Tenzin Trinlé Gyatso (1878–1941), was recognized at an early age as an emanation of Jangkya Rolpai Dorjé (1717–86). He trained at Sera Mé College, where he completed his geshé degree, and later became the revered teacher of Ling Rinpoché (1903–83) and Trijang Rinpoché (1900–81), tutors of the Fourteenth Dalai Lama. Regarded as a brilliant orator, learned exponent of tantra, and charismatic teacher of *lamrim* (the stages of the path), he famously taught *Liberation in the Palm of Your Hand* in Lhasa in 1925 at the request of the Thirteenth Dalai Lama, Thubten Gyatso (1876–1933). His collected works, in fourteen volumes, remain an important source for clarifying points of sūtra and tantra.

The Structure of Pabongkha's Commentary

The subdivisions of Jé Pabongkha's commentary are to be found in bold numbers within the body of his text. There are three major sections: the preliminaries, the actual practice, and the conclusion.

The preliminaries cover the standard topics: refuge, bodhicitta, the four immeasurables, and the merit field, and these are explained in chapter 2.

The actual practice deals with visualizing the merit field, offering the seven-limb prayer plus a maṇḍala, and the main practice itself. Visualizing the merit field and offering the seven-limb prayer (verses 2 through 8 of the ten verses of *The Hundreds of Deities of Tuṣita*) teaches the way, common to both sūtra and tantra, that one should engage in guru yoga. This corresponds to chapter 3.

The main practice has three sections, in which the blessings of the four empowerments, the seven types of special wisdom, and finally the entire path are serially invoked. Receiving the blessings of your guru's enlightened mind is at the heart of guru yoga, and here the blessings are enhanced by the addition of essential elements of the tantric path from the oral tradition.

In the first section, the blessings of the four empowerments—vase, secret, wisdom, and word—are merged with Jé Tsongkhapa guru yoga. Here the three lineage protectors—Mañjuśrī, Avalokiteśvara, and Vajrapāṇi—and their external, internal, and secret forms are visualized at the crown, throat, and heart of Jé Tsongkhapa. Then they serially confer the blessings of the four empowerments. This corresponds to chapter 4.

In the second section, requesting the blessings of special wisdom, five rounds of visualization are also explained. First, detailed instruction is given on how to generate seven types of wisdom: vast wisdom, clear wisdom, swift wisdom, profound wisdom, and the wisdoms of explanation, debate, and composition. This corresponds to chapter 5.

Then, in the five rounds of visualization, five different visualizations are applied to five rounds of Miktsema praise in order to purify the negativities of body, speech, and mind and to receive the blessings of the vajra body, vajra speech, and vajra mind, as well as the blessings of the four empowerments. This corresponds to chapter 6.

In the third section, requesting the blessings of the entire path, Pabongkha Rinpoché gives a broad overview of the path to enlightenment, dealing first with guru yoga and then with the practices of small, medium, and great scope. It is only by constantly bringing to mind all the practices leading to enlightenment, which are themselves incontrovertibly related in a causal sequence, and nurturing their generation, that one can actually attain enlightenment. This corresponds to chapter 7.

The final section is the conclusion, in which Pabongkha

gives extensive instruction on how to properly conclude meditation on guru yoga. This corresponds to chapter 8.

H. E. Chöden Rinpoché's Extensive Commentary

His Eminence Chöden Rinpoché adds clarifying instruction to Jé Pabongkha's inspired commentary. By doing so he brings out the deeper meaning of the text, revealing how ordinary practitioners can understand and apply Pabongkha's instruction on the tantric oral tradition. H. E. Chöden Rinpoché's words appear in regular type in the translation that follows.

The Condensed Commentary

In this section, H. E. Chöden Rinpoché explains the practice of *The Hundreds of Deities of Tuṣita* from the perspective of sūtra. He explains all ten verses of the original version, which are reproduced in the appendix. His commentary has three parts: motivation, the six preliminary practices, and the actual practice and conclusion.

Chapter 1, "Motivation," presents a brief discussion on the entire path, including the precious human rebirth, death and impermanence, karma and its result, the causes of refuge, the Mahāyāna, and guru yoga in order to incite a virtuous motivation.

In chapter 2, that virtuous motivation is applied to the six preliminary practices (*sbyor chos drug*). First the practitioner cleans his or her room, then arranges offerings, and then sits in the seven-point Vairocana posture. The fourth preliminary—visualizing the merit field—focuses on the first verse of *The Hundreds of Deities of Tuṣita*, which establishes the focal object of this guru yoga. The fifth preliminary—offering the seven-limb prayer—corresponds to verses 2 to 8 of *The Hundreds of Deities of Tuṣita*. In the sixth or final preliminary—offering a mandala—a symbolic universe is offered to the merit field.

Chapter 3, "Actual Practice and Conclusion," has two sections. The first explains the actual practice of the Miktsema praise, comprising verse 9 of *The Hundreds of Deities of Tuṣita*, in which requests are made to the three lineage protectors—Avalokiteśvara, Mañjuśrī, and Vajrapāṇi—embodied by Jé Tsongkhapa. The second section is the conclusion, where the merit field dissolves into one's crown, blessing one's body, speech, and mind. Sometimes certain material covered in this work is restricted, but Chöden Rinpoché's wish was to make this material available to the wider community of qualified tantric practitioners.

The Author

His Eminence Chöden Rinpoché, Losang Gyalten Jikdrel Wangchuk (b. 1931), taught the essential meaning of this practice in a series of lectures at Sera Monastery in 2004. His words were then transcribed, and the manuscript was edited and then published in Tibetan under the title *Dga' lha rgyas pa dang bsdus pa'i bshad pa blo dman las dang po ba la 'khyer bder spel ba byin rlabs kyi sgo 'byed* (*Opening the Door of Blessings of the Extensive and Abbreviated Explanation of* The Hundreds of Deities of Tuṣita *to Enhance the Practice of Beginners with Limited Intelligence*).[3] This work is the English translation of the Tibetan edition.

His Eminence Chöden Rinpoché is a renowned yogi, scholar, and teacher of Tibetan Buddhism. He was born in far eastern Tibet to a devout family renowned for their contemplative practice. Early in life he was recognized by Reting Rinpoché as the reincarnation of Lama Chöden of Rongpo Rabten Monastery, a highly revered lama who had been recognized as a candidate in the search for the reincarnation of the Twelfth Dalai Lama. At the age of seven H. E. Chöden Rinpoché took novice ordination from Pabongkha Rinpoché, who named him Losang Gyalten Jikdrel Wangchuk. Then, following the advice of Pabongkha Rinpoché, he joined Sera Jé Monastery at the age of 15. During this period his main teachers included Trijang Rinpoché, Pabongkha Rinpoché, and other prominent lamas from whom he received empowerments and oral transmissions, as well as pith instructions that enabled him to develop realizations of the teachings. He completed his study of the five major topics at the age of 28, and despite being urged by Trijang Rinpoché to sit his final exams quickly, he followed the advice of the then-abbot of Sera Jé to continue his studies. Soon thereafter, the Tibetan uprising against the Chinese occupation of Tibet disrupted his studies, and he entered retreat in a small and secluded room in Lhasa for more than nineteen years, relying on texts he had already memorized. In 1985, H. E. Chödon Rinpoché escaped to India and, at the request of the Dalai Lama, began teaching at Sera Monastery in south India. Later he established his own center in California and taught at various centers around the world. Chöden Rinpoché passed away in Sera Monastery on September 11, 2015.

Extensive Explanation of
The Hundreds of Deities of Tuṣita, *Called* Opening the Door of Blessings

A Commentary on Jé Pabongkha Dechen Nyingpo's
Bountiful Advice Clarifying the Oral Transmission and Explaining the Deep Meaning of How to Practice the Profound Path of Yoga of the Hundreds of Deities of Tuṣita, Called "A Treasury of Precious Jewels"

1. Introduction

1. Explaining the Meaning of the Title

It is called "Profound Path" because those who gain the state of union obtain union in dependence on the practice of such guru yoga. This practice of guru yoga called "yoga of the hundreds of deities of Tuṣita" was secretly imparted to some in the lifetime of Jé Rinpoché, and Gendün Drup selectively taught this instruction in statements such as "From the snow-capped eastern peak . . ." and so on. A student of Gendün Drup called Dülkarwa collated this material on the hundreds of deities of Tuṣita, and another student, Dülnakpa, whose full name was Dülnakpa Palden Sangpo, acted as the scribe. There are many brief and extensive versions of "how to practice the yoga of the hundreds of deities of Tuṣita," [11] and from among them this is an extensive version [by Pabongkha Rinpoché] called *Bountiful Advice Clarifying the Oral Transmission and Explaining the Deep Meaning, Called "A Treasury of Precious Jewels."*

> **If you practice impure view and conduct, the three types of oath-bound protector will impose a heavy vajra punishment.**

Since this is bountiful advice clarifying the oral transmission, it is said that if you do not uphold the view and conduct of the

Ganden oral transmission, if you deprecate the Geden[4] tradition, or if you practice such impure view and conduct, then the three types of oath-bound guardians will impose a heavy punishment. In terms of seals (*mudrās*) of secrecy,[5] there are the vajra seal, the essence seal, and so forth. This is a vajra seal.

2. Homage and the Pledge to Compose

> **Solitary father, your youthful smile, like ten million suns,**
> **is fully concealed amid robes of morning clouds.**
> **You are the Lord of Speech with a melodious voice;**
> **I bow to Tsongkhapa who is Mañjuśrī.**

These are words of homage. You are called "solitary father" for you are Venerable Mañjuśrī, who appears as the father of all the conquerors, as their son, and as their mother. Since the body of Venerable Mañjuśrī is orange in color, [12] it is said that "your youthful smile of ten million suns is fully concealed amid robes of morning clouds." You should understand that the orange-hued morning clouds refer to the youthful marks and signs of Mañjuśrī, which are concealed amid the orange outer robe, or Dharma robe, of Jé Rinpoché. "You are the Lord of Speech with a melodious voice" since you are the Lord of Speech with a voice capable of imparting instructions on any sutric or tantric treatise. "Lord of Speech" is the name of Mañjuśrī. The body of Venerable Mañjuśrī remains concealed amid these robes, but since his speech emerges and manifests as Mañjuśrī, it is said: "I bow to Tsongkhapa who is Mañjuśrī."

> **In the land of āryas, all that remains is the name of Śākyamuni,**

and the northern region is filled with counterfeit explanations.
Even when influential teachers analyzed the profound meaning,
they mistook the extreme of nihilism for the Middle Way.

Now the teachings have degenerated in the land of āryas, and all that remains is the name of Śākyamuni. The Bhagavān himself said that when the teachings declined [in India] they would spread to the north, and in accordance with his words they [13] spread to the northern region of Tibet after they declined in India. The verse states, however, that [now Tibet] became filled with counterfeit explanations, for though the earlier period of the Dharma kings was propitious, later the land became filled with wrong explanations. And even when influential teachers analyzed the profound meaning, they mistook the extreme of nihilism for the Middle Way, for when the influential scholars who had proclaimed the teachings delineated the profound meaning of emptiness, they did not recognize the extreme of nihilism and mistook it for the Middle Way.

Alas, those of the mountainous region
were adorned with the jewel-like qualities
of scripture and realization, but what use are they
when saturated with the poisonous waters of evil view?

This is an expression of sadness for what has happened in Tibet. In earlier times there were many who upheld the teachings in the Land of Snow. Though they were adorned with jewel-like ornaments such as bodhicitta and internal qualities of realization, what use are they? To sever the root of saṃsāra, you must generate the mind realizing emptiness that directly opposes the mode of apprehension of self-grasping ignorance. You must settle [the view of] emptiness exactly as it is, but if you do not do that, what use [are good qualities]? Even if you have [other good] internal qualities, they will not benefit you if you lack [perfect] view and [your good qualities] are saturated with the poisonous waters of evil view. It is like wholesome food [14] that is soaked in poisonous water not benefitting us. Therefore, when affected by evil views, [other qualities] cannot benefit us.

> **When they investigated the profound meaning,**
> **their mind's eye was completely blinded.**
> **Thus former scholars labored in vain since they were confused**
> **about the path in the darkness of the two extremes.**

Although scholars prior to Jé Rinpoché investigated the profound meaning, they did not properly identify the object of negation. Some said that without placing the mind on anything in particular everything should be negated, but by making the object of negation too broad they fell into the extreme of nihilism. Others made the object of negation too narrow, and due to that they were unable to negate it. Thus their mind's eye was completely blinded, and since they were not able to resolve the meaning of emptiness exactly as it is, they fell into the extreme of eternalism or of nihilism. Since they were like newcomers confused about the path, they did not know how to proceed in the darkness of the two extremes. Thus when such former scholars analyzed the meaning of emptiness, they labored in vain.

At this time, Mañjuśrī Tsongkhapa appeared,
and due to the light of the sun of his elegant explanation
of the profound state and dependent origination just as they are,
he universally took care of reincarnating beings.

At just this time Jé Tsongkhapa appeared in the snowy region of Tibet, and due to the light of the sun of his elegant explanation of the mutual compatibility of emptiness and dependent origination, where emptiness does not negate dependent origination [15] and dependent origination does not negate emptiness, he universally took care of reincarnating beings. The words that, "due to the light of the sun" eliminating the collective darkness of grasping at extremes, "he universally took care of reincarnating beings" express his quality of resolving the view [of emptiness] and dependent origination.

He brought to completion the wish-fulfilling jewel of the Sage's teachings
with the purifying agent of the threefold examination
and placed it on top of the victory banner of the Sage's teachings and practice,
producing hundreds of precious treasures in this land.

It is said if that if you pray to a wish-fulfilling jewel at the pinnacle of a banner of victory after you have made offerings to it, the siddhi you desire will be conferred upon you. So too, it is said that Jé Rinpoché brought to completion the entire teachings of the Sage, which are like a wish-fulfilling jewel, with the purifying agent of the threefold examination, like cleaning a wish-fulfilling jewel by washing, rubbing, and polishing it. Then he placed it on top of the victory banner of teaching and practice, producing hundreds of precious treasures in this land. Many became scholars in the snowy land of Tibet, graced with numerous qualities of scriptural and realizational [Dharma], and [their appearance] was similar to a rain of jewels from a wish-fulfilling gem. [16]

In former times, lotsāwas, paṇḍitas, scholars, and siddhas
could not discern the tradition of the Sugata.
Through evaluating treatises with fair-minded analysis,
have faith that he is the second Nāgārjuna.

In the snowy land of Tibet, in former times or prior generations, many lotsāwas, paṇḍitas, scholars, and siddhas appeared, but they could not discern reality as it is. It was Jé Rinpoché who discerned the tradition of the Sage, and he was thus known in the Land of Snows as "the One who Discerned the Tradition [of the Sugata]." Jé Rinpoché composed the *Essential Explanation of Interpretive and Definitive Meaning* and differentiated the interpretive and definitive meanings of the treatises exactly as they are. Through evaluating them while maintaining fair-minded analysis, he is not different from Protector Nāgārjuna himself. Have faith that he is the second Nāgārjuna.

Therefore he is Lord of All the Conquerors and manifests as a human

> **possessing three secret qualities unfathomed in depth or limit,**
> **caring for us with kindness that exceeds myriads of conquerors,**
> **and we should strive in this yoga with heartfelt recollection.**

Question: What qualities should a practitioner of the profound path of this yoga have?

Reply: Jé Rinpoché is Vajradhāra, Lord of All the Conquerors, and he manifests as a human or appears in the aspect of a human being. It is said that he has "qualities unfathomed in depth or limit" since it is difficult to measure the depth or limit of the three secret qualities of his body, speech, and mind. It is said that he "exceeds myriads of conquerors" since [he acts] through combining both faith and [17] kindness. "With heartfelt recollection . . . and so on" is stated since we should strive in this yoga with faith that is heartfelt faith in one who possesses these three secret qualities difficult to measure, and who manifests as a human though he is all the conquerors; and by means of faith that recalls in general the one who has brought to completion the teachings of the Sage in this snowy land of Tibet, and in particular the one who has clarified profound dependent origination.

> ***Through a hundred lines of faultless scripture and reasoning, followers of Dharma establish strong conviction that without doubt Jé Rinpoché is the Lord of All the Conquerors by means of the path of valid cognition.***[6]

Although Conqueror Vajradhāra is understood to be the Lord of All the Conquerors, here it is more pertinent to take

Venerable Mañjuśrī as Lord of All the Conquerors. Jé Rinpoché is established to be Venerable Mañjuśrī through a hundred lines of faultless scripture and reasoning since this is proven by citations in the *Mañjuśrī Root Tantra*, [Maitreyanātha's] *Ornament of Mahāyāna Sūtras*, [the works of] Machik Labdrön,[7] and the *Collected Works of the Kadam*, and so on.

> ***The banner of his renown as the bodhisattva Mahāsattva unfurls ever more [widely] in myriad buddha-fields in every direction.***

In a previous life, when he made his pledge in the presence of [Buddha] Indraketu, he was called Bodhisattva Mahāsattva, [18] and the conqueror and his children praised him and declared "May the teachings of Conqueror Losang spread" due to the power of truth."

When the Sage [Buddha] Indraketu appeared, this bodhisattva joined his retinue. And at that time, Indraketu asked: "Who is capable of spreading the Mantric Vehicle in conjunction with the profound Middle Way view in the border regions?" But from among his retinue only the one who possessed the same mindstream as the great Jé Tsongkhapa stood up and stated: "I will spread these teachings in conjunction with the profound Middle Way view in the border regions." Thus Indraketu, along with all the buddhas and bodhisattvas in every direction, called him "Mahāsattva" [Great Being], and it is said that the banner of his renown unfurls ever more [widely].

> ***You alone revealed the tradition in the Land of Snow.***

In the snowy region of Tibet, Jé Rinpoché alone is called "Tsongkhapa who revealed the tradition in the Land of Snow." Earlier scholars and siddhas were unable to clearly reveal the meaning of sūtra and tantra exactly as it is. But you alone revealed the tradition and thus set apart the intention of sūtra and tantra exactly as it is.

> ***Placing just a drop of the nectar of your fame as Losang Drakpa, Tsongkhapa, king of the Dharma in the three realms,*** [19] ***in my heart of faith plants the seed of liberation.***

It is said that merely hearing the name of Jé Rinpoché plants the seed of liberation. [Tsongkhapa's] *For As Long As* states:

> By merely pronouncing or remembering my name,
> may those tormented by the effects of negative karma
> attain the glory of perfect happiness and
> ascend the steps of the supreme vehicle.

Reciting this prayer made by Jé Rinpoché not only benefits through planting the seed of liberation and pacifying diseases and spirits, but also [ensures that] "the good fortune to enjoy vast and lasting well-being" will arise, and not just in this life.

> ***You are the great being who has obtained the good fortune to enjoy vast and lasting well-being. In striving in this yoga, I do not observe any other fortunate outcome to be greater than this noble festival of supreme fortune.***

Striving in the guru yoga of Jé Rinpoché in this way is supreme good fortune. Do not observe any other fortunate outcome to be greater than this.

> ***Therefore I will earnestly strive in the yoga of the inseparability of my root guru and Mañjunātha Tsongkhapa, for this will establish the root of my future prosperity and well-being, and I will progress in the essential points of study, contemplation, and meditation.***

Since from among these you have the advice on the practice cycle for accomplishing wisdom, you will progress in the essential points of study, contemplation, and meditation.

> ***Obstacles will not take root,*** [20] ***and it will protect me against obscurations and the harm of kings, violent spirits, and nāgas. It will establish my desired aims, according to my wishes.***

"Obstacles will not take root" refers to the harm of kings, violent spirits, and nāgas, which are removed in dependence on reciting the Miktsema praise. "Protect against" refers to rain, frost, and so forth. In the past, there were 108 activities [or feats] reliant on the recitation of the Miktsema praise, but these days, due to decline, only twenty-one remain.

> ***In particular, [it establishes] the transmission of enlightened activities for vast, clear, swift, and profound wisdom, and so forth.***

Venerable Mañjuśrī and Jé Rinpoché are inseparable, and since Venerable Mañjuśrī is the deity of wisdom,

> *Whatever you seek to accomplish, such as swift or clear wisdom, you will experience enhancement after just one month of practice.*

Kyabjé Dechen Nyingpo [Pabongkha Rinpoché] stated from his own experience that there was enhancement "after just one month." It is also reported he said that when he recited the Miktsema praise in the [Sera] Mé College debate grounds, he experienced an extraordinary increase of wisdom by applying this visualization.

> *In this and future lives there are limitless benefits, such as without doubt meeting the teachings of Guru Mañjunātha and taking birth in the field of Tuṣita and so forth.* [21]

There are limitless benefits such as taking birth in the field of Tuṣita, since we set our minds on the field of Tuṣita.

His pledge to compose this work:

> *Therefore I have composed this work on the essence of the oral tradition*[8] *with supplementary verses, so that [practitioners] may easily enter the practice of the* Hundreds of Deities of Tuṣita, *which is the guru yoga of the inseparability of my guru and Mañjunātha Tsongkhapa; clearly highlighting the subtle and profound points of the oral transmission; elegantly supplementing that with other appropriate works; ensuring that the meaning to be contemplated is covered by the recitation; and supplementing that with a concise review of the path.*

The meaning to be contemplated follows the word order.

2. Preliminaries

1. Visualizing the Field of Refuge and Merit

This work has three parts:

1. *Preliminary practices*
2. *Main practice*
3. *Concluding practices*

1. Preliminary practices

[Könchok Jigmé Wangpo's] *Six Preliminary Practices* states:

> ***In a place that has been cleaned and made attractive, set out objects representing the body, speech, and mind.***[9]

Set out objects representing [the Buddha's] body, speech, and mind, such as a statue of Jé Rinpoché.

> ***Arrange any offerings that you have obtained*** [22] ***without deceit, in an appealing manner.***

"Deceit" refers to deceit in terms of the material or motivation. If you make offerings of materials established by wrong livelihood[10] or derived from those with impure samaya (vows), there will be no benefit. This is *deceit in terms of motivation.* Making offerings of inferior quality even though you possess fine objects (but don't offer them), or making offerings of impure samaya substances, inappropriate offering materials, or poisonous substances is *deceit in terms of the material.* Thus it is said that you should arrange any offerings you have obtained without deceit, in an appealing manner.

> ***[Sit] on a comfortable seat, in the eight-point position or any comfortable posture.***

The eight-point position of the body is the seven attributes of Vairocana plus counting the breath. Alternatively, this means that you should arrange yourself in any comfortable posture such as the vajra position, but it does not mean you should sit in a disrespectful posture such as stretching your legs out and so forth.

> ***First, go for refuge with a heightened virtuous mind and visualize the [refuge] objects according to the verses [on refuge].***

If you have the thought to benefit your future lives, this is called "a virtuous mind," and "heightened" refers to the need to take refuge influenced by the mind of enlightenment (bodhicitta). [Paṇchen Losang Chökyi Gyaltsen's] *Guru Pūjā* also states:

> From within a pure and intensely virtuous mind . . .[11]

Therefore, as one needs to understand bodhicitta, [23] you take refuge influenced by bodhicitta. First you visualize the refuge objects and intone and recite [the refuge formula] according to the verses [on refuge].

In the space directly in front of me, on a broad and high throne made of precious substances supported by eight great lions, upon a variegated lotus, moon, and sun maṇḍala seat, sits the essence of my own root guru in the aspect of the conqueror Buddha Śākyamuni.

[The refuge object] is at the level of your eyebrows in "the space directly in front of me," and when you prostrate, your head reaches the point directly below his feet. The height of the visualization is such that you don't need to look up or bend down to see it, and you visualize [the refuge object] as something you can see directly in front of you.

There are eight lions, since there are two lions at each corner. The throne is "supported by eight lions" because the eight lions symbolize [the refuge object] who possesses the eight sovereign qualities[12] in his mindstream.

The lion throne is covered by a variegated lotus at whose center is a small throne. On that [throne] is another lotus, a moon, and a sun maṇḍala. The three [components of the seat]—the lotus, moon, and sun—symbolize the three principal aspects of the path.[13] The lotus grows from mud yet remains untainted by it, symbolizing the mind of renunciation, the method for [achieving] liberation from saṃsāra. The moon is by nature cool, and like that, bodhicitta is by nature that which solely benefits [beings]. The sun powerfully matures the crop for harvest and eliminates darkness, and so too does wisdom realizing emptiness. These three therefore symbolize renunciation, [24] bodhicitta, and correct view. Above the throne:

The color of his body is like refined gold, he possesses a protrusion at his crown, and he has one face and two

> **arms. His right hand is in the mudrā of subduing the earth, and his left in the mudrā of equipoise, holding an almsbowl full of nectar.**[14]

First, when applying [attributes] to Buddha Śākyamuni, it is said that the color of his body is like refined gold since the color of gold has a luster different from any other, and is held in high esteem. His right hand is in the mudrā of subduing the earth, symbolizing that he has subjugated the four māras.[15] His left hand is in the mudrā of equipoise, symbolizing that he remains in single-pointed equipoise on emptiness. In his left hand he holds an almsbowl full of nectar.

> **His body is clad in robes of a saffron hue, he is adorned with major and minor marks that possess the nature of clear light. He is seated with his legs in the vajra posture within a mass of light radiating from his body.**

"[Robes] of a saffron hue" refers to that which is not ostentatious but the color of something that could be discarded. If it is yellow, it is not a gaudy [shade of yellow]; if it is red, it should not be something like vermilion.

His body, which is adorned with thirty-two major and eighty minor marks, is translucent and not made of solid matter. [25] He is seated with his legs in the vajra posture within a mass of light radiating from his body, which itself possesses the nature of clear light. Though the light of Lord Buddha's body extends beyond measure, to ordinary beings he appears to be seated with his legs in the vajra posture within [an aura of] light radiating one armspan.

Direct and lineage gurus, yidams, buddhas, bodhisattvas, dākiṇīs, Dharma-protectors, and guardians are seated surrounding him.

Though there are many ways to visualize the objects of refuge, some extensive and some brief, here you should follow the *Guru Pūjā* merit field because it is easy to practice. In the *Guru Pūjā*, [the merit field] arises from a lotus stem, and you may generate it in this way, for it is not clearly stated in this text. In the center is Śākyamuni, the main figure, and [below him] there are eleven broad levels of lotus petals. To his right is the lineage of extensive conduct, to his left is the lineage of profound view, and above him is the lineage of blessed practice.[16] You may visualize that [deities] of the four classes of tantra, buddhas, bodhisattvas, dākiṇīs, Dharma-protectors, and guardians are seated upon the terraced levels of lotus petals [below].

In front of each figure of that [merit field], upon a fine throne, is the scriptural Dharma proclaimed by each, which has the aspect of a sacred text (*poti*) and the nature of light.

The scriptural Dharma proclaimed by each figure has the nature of light, and to [receive their] purifying and cleansing nectar you must rely on all three objects of refuge. [26] Even though the Dharma Jewel is the [truth of] cessation and the[truth of] path existing in their mindstreams, in order [to receive] the purifying descent of nectar [one visualizes that:]

The scriptural Dharma stated by each of them exists as treatises with the nature of light. The merit field shows

that it is pleased with me, and I myself possess great faith that recalls the qualities and compassion of the merit field.

Although in general, from the perspective of our practice and conduct, we lack a basis that would please the merit field, it is said that when you begin to practice such guru yoga, the [merit field] becomes pleased with you. For example, if a student who [normally] did not study his texts one day studied them properly, his teacher would think, "Today my student has studied well," and that would make him happy. From the perspective of the three poisons, we lack the ability to please [the merit field], but when we begin to practice such guru yoga, those [who make up the merit field] are pleased. Then you yourself should focus on the objects of refuge with great faith, recalling the qualities and compassion of the merit field.

I and all mother sentient beings, from beginningless time until now, have experienced the general sufferings of saṃsāra and the specific sufferings of the three lower rebirths. [27] **Still, it is difficult to comprehend the depth of suffering.**

Since you experience suffering that is inexhaustible, it is difficult to comprehend the limit of your suffering. The causes of taking refuge are fear and faith. Regarding fear, the mind of fear and terror arises through thinking of the various types of suffering you will necessarily experience. Reflect that the objects of refuge exist in front of you and you are surrounded by all mother sentient beings. To your right is your father of this life, representing all reincarnating beings who are male. To your left is your mother of this life, representing all those who are female. In front of you are the three: enemies, spirits, and unfortunate beings. Behind you are those who are dear to you, your circle of friends, and so on. Such beings cover the earth like dust. Indeed, all six types of reincarnating being are present and each experiences its specific type of suffering according to its nature, but in the aspect of a human being. Visualize that they go for refuge.

Visualize the objects of refuge and their causes:

Now, at this specific time, I have obtained this precious human body with freedoms and endowments that are rare and full of meaning. Now I have met the precious teachings of the Buddha, which are hard to meet. If now I do not obtain the state of a perfect, complete buddha—the supreme liberation that has abandoned all samsaric suffering—I will have to repeatedly experience [28] the suffering of saṃsāra in general and various types of suffering of the three lower rebirths in particular. Since my Guru and the Three Jewels who abide in front of me have the capacity to protect from such suffering, I will take refuge in the Three Jewels in order to attain the state of a complete buddha for the sake of all sentient beings.

As you recite these words, in this way you visualize that all sentient beings also recite loudly with you, as though you are leading them from bondage [in saṃsāra].

2. Actual Refuge

Taking actual refuge:

I and all reincarnating beings, equal to the vastness of space,
from now until we reach the essence of enlightenment
go for refuge to the glorious and immaculate gurus,
go for refuge to perfect bhagavān buddhas,
go for refuge to the immaculate Dharma,
go for refuge to the Ārya Saṅgha.

Repeat three or seven times.

If time permits, when reciting "I go for refuge to the glorious and immaculate gurus," you should visualize the five classes of guru: (1) the central figure of the five classes of guru is your glorious root guru, who is by nature inseparable from Conqueror Śākyamuni; (2) in front of him are the immaculate gurus who possess actual attainments and with whom you have a Dharma connection; to his right are those of [29] the lineage of extensive conduct; (4) to his left are those of the lineage of profound view; and (5) above him are those of the lineage of blessed practice. While focusing on the five classes of guru you take refuge, and from the bodies of the five classes of guru streams of nectar descend, purifying all negativities and obscurations you have incurred from beginningless time. In particular, all obscurations and negativities incurred in relation to your guru—such as endangering his body, disobeying his word, and disturbing his mind—are purified and cleansed. Reflect that you have attained all the blessings of your guru's body, speech, and mind.

When reciting "I go for refuge to the perfect bhagavān Buddhas," such as the thousand buddhas of the fortunate eon, nectar flows from however many buddhas you have assembled, purifying you.

"The immaculate Dharma" refers to the truths of cessation and path existing in the heart of the central deity. When the purifying nectars descend and purify, they descend and purify from scriptural Dharma in the form of sacred texts. Reflect that acts of abandoning Dharma and so on, and all negativities and obscurations committed in relation to such acts, are purified, and that you receive blessings.

When reciting "I go for refuge to the Ārya Saṅgha," you go for refuge to all those who possess the eye of pristine wisdom, such as bodhisattvas, hearers, and solitary realizers, as well as Dharma-protectors. You go for refuge to the Ārya Saṅgha three times. The instruction [in italics] states three or seven times. [30]

A stream of five-colored nectar descends from the objects of refuge,
entering the bodies and minds of myself and others,
purifying the mass of fault [incurred in] relation to them,
and all their blessings enter our mindstreams.

Recite once.

At that time you can visualize that five-colored nectar-light radiates from the objects of refuge, or that first light radiates and then a stream of nectar descends, coiled around the rays of light. You may practice whichever is easier to visualize. A stream of light descends, entering your body and mind as well as the bodies and minds of the other beings surrounding you.

Up until now you have visualized each separately, but if you combine them, then you purify the mass of faults [incurred] in relation to each of the Three Jewels, and all the blessings of the Three Jewels enter the mindstreams of yourself and others. Visualize that all sentient beings, both yourself and others, come under the protection of your Guru and the Three Jewels, as you recite the verse "A stream of five-colored . . . enter our mindstreams" once.

Focusing on the Three Jewels as the resultant refuge and central object, and seeking to obtain that [resultant] state for the sake of all sentient beings, is uncommon Mahāyāna refuge and visualization of the focal object and aspect of the awakening mind.

Taking refuge in the resultant refuge is taking refuge while focusing [31] on the Three Jewels, which is the state you shall obtain in the future. Reflecting "I will obtain that state for the sake of all sentient beings" is to visualize the focal object and aspect of the awakening mind.

3. The Awakening Mind

I go for refuge until I am enlightened
to the Buddha, the Dharma, and the Supreme Assembly.
By my practice of generosity and so forth,
may I become a buddha to benefit reincarnating beings.

Recite this verse as many times as you can and strongly generate this aspiration: "I will engage in all actions of the victors' sons and daughters, such as generating the awakening mind and practicing the six perfections."

Having already gone for refuge before, you visualize the focal object of uncommon Mahāyāna refuge with this [verse]. The statement "By my . . . generosity and so forth" invokes many different points. By "practice of generosity and so forth," the six perfections of generosity, ethics, patience, effort, absorption, and wisdom are understood. By "practice," practice or action is understood. The purpose of stating "Due to this merit"[17] is to visualize the focal object and aspect of the awakening mind through reflecting: "May I obtain the state of a buddha to benefit all reincarnating sentient beings in dependence upon the force of whatever root of virtue I have established."

> **From Guru Munīndra[18] who resides in front,** [32]
> **a replica separates and dissolves into me.**
> **I transform into Munīndra's body, which radiates light,**
> **establishing all reincarnating beings in supreme enlightenment.**

Due to strongly generating the awakening mind that reflects that "I will attain buddhahood for the sake of all sentient beings," a replica or a second image separates from Munīndra, who resides in the space in front [of you], and [this second image] dissolves into you. Thus, your [body] transforms into Munīndra's body and light radiates from it. You should visualize that at the tip of each ray of light is the body of the Sage, which proceeds to the crown of [the head of] every sentient being who surrounds you. Moreover, reflect that [when] these rays of light strike [every] sentient being, their suffering and its causes are purified merely by the light striking them, and they are established in the state of Munīndra. Alternatively, reflect that Munīndra resides at the tip of each ray of light; each

Munīndra comes to reside at the crown of each sentient being; and due to the stream of nectar flowing from his bodies, their negativities and obscurations as well as their imprints are purified, and they are established in the state of Munīndra.

> ***Recite once, and meditate on the awakening mind, taking the result as the path. The potency of bodhicitta greatly increases.***

Reflect: "I have established all sentient beings in the state of buddhahood and have accomplished their purpose." An important point is then to cultivate joy. Thus, convinced that you have established all sentient beings in the state of buddhahood, [33] you cultivate joy thinking that "I have accomplished the great purpose of [all] sentient beings," and maintain [that thought] for some time.

4. The Four Immeasurables

Next you should focus on the four immeasurables. Some may think that all sentient beings are already enlightened, but to my mind sentient beings comprise the six types of beings who currently experience their specific types of suffering.

> ***Practicing the four immeasurables to eliminate interferences and enhance practice:***

Immeasurable equanimity

> **Why shouldn't all sentient beings abide with equanimity,**
> **free from**

> **[holding others] as close through attachment and distant through hatred?**
> **May they abide [in equanimity].**
> **I will cause them to abide [in equanimity].**
> **Guru-deity, please bless me to achieve this.**

When you train your mind, you must first train in equanimity; thus, here you initially practice equanimity. Aspiration beyond measure is to [generate] the aspiration reflecting "Why shouldn't [they abide in equanimity]?" and this is called "immeasurable aspiration." Praying, "May they abide [in equanimity]" is immeasurable prayer. Immeasurable special intention is "I will cause them to abide [in equanimity]," for the thought "I will do this" is special intention. "Guru-deity, please bless me to achieve this" is the immeasurable request. Each immeasurable includes the four immeasurables of aspiration, prayer, special intention, and request. [34]

The words "Why shouldn't sentient beings abide in equanimity free from [holding others] as close through attachment and distant through hatred?" refer to all sentient beings accumulating karma by the power of attachment and hatred, and cycling in saṃsāra due the power of that. Therefore the root is karma and affliction, and from those, [others are held] as close through attachment and distant through hatred. Through reflecting "Why shouldn't they be free from that?" you should meditate on immeasurable [equanimity].

Immeasurable love

> **Why shouldn't all sentient beings possess happiness and the cause of happiness?**

May they possess [happiness].
I will cause them to possess [happiness].
Guru-deity, please bless me to achieve this.

This is also complete in the four types of immeasurable. To possess happiness, you must establish virtue that is the cause of happiness.

Immeasurable compassion
[Then reflect:] Why shouldn't they be separated from nonvirtue that is the cause of suffering?

Why shouldn't sentient beings be separated from suffering and the cause of suffering?
May they be separated [from suffering].
I will cause them to be separated [from suffering].
Guru-deity, please bless me to achieve this.

Immeasurable joy
Then, after this [verse], there is immeasurable joy:

Why shouldn't all sentient beings not be separated from the pure happiness of higher rebirth and liberation?
May they not be separated [from happiness].
I will cause them to not be separated [from happiness].
Guru-deity, please bless me to achieve this.

Recite each three times.

You should recite each verse beginning with "Why shouldn't sentient beings . . ." three times. If you have time to visualize this, it is good to focus on these focal objects until they appear clearly. Then you should reflect, "Guru-deity, bless me to achieve this." [35]

> ***You should understand the general focal object and aspects of the unique awakening mind of highest yoga mantra,*** [19] ***and in particular the special focal object and aspects of the profoundly swift Ganden oral transmission, which is capable of establishing complete enlightenment in just twelve human years, or three years and three months.***

When the words "I will quickly and even more quickly obtain the state of a perfect, complete buddha"[20] are applied to highest yoga mantra, "quickly" refers to sūtra and "even more quickly" refers to highest yoga mantra. In sūtra, the state of a perfect, complete buddha is obtained "quickly." But in mantra, the state of buddhahood is obtained "even more quickly," in just three years and three months; therefore you state, "I will quickly and even more quickly" obtain the state of a perfect, complete buddha. This is the focal object and aspect of the unique awakening mind of highest yoga mantra.

In terms of the "profoundly swift Ganden oral transmission," when the words "quickly and even more quickly" are applied to the Ganden oral transmission, "quickly" refers to attaining enlightenment in a single lifetime through highest yoga mantra, while the second "quickly" refers to the profound oral transmission, which has the potency to establish [enlightenment] in just twelve human years, or three years and three months. You should practice with an understanding of these attributes.

Repeat three times:

I will cultivate profound guru yoga
to quickly and even more quickly attain the state
of the guru-deity who is the primordial protector of great bliss, [36]
for the sake of all sentient beings who pervade the limits of space.

When it is said, "I will attain the state of buddhahood for all sentient beings, and I will attain it in this life, within twelve years, or within three years and three months," this is the special awakening mind.

5. Contracting the Field of Refuge and Merit

There are various ways to contract the merit field, such as contemplating nonreified [emptiness], contemplating the figures departing to their residences, or contemplating them dissolving into you. Here, you contemplate that they dissolve into you.

Then, contract the merit field:

The entire merit field, which is like a peaceful bank of clouds
within the expanse of space, contracts into Munīndra.
He too dissolves between my eyebrows,
and through that I obtain every blessing without exception.

Reflect on this.

You cannot say where the banks of clouds disappear to within the expanse of space, for they disappear of their own accord. The lion throne of the previously visualized merit field dissolves into the lotus, and the outer figures of the merit field dissolve into Munīndra. Here the words ". . . contracts into Munīndra. He also dissolves . . . and I obtain every blessing without exception" are related to mantra. Visualize that he dissolves between your eyebrows at the upper opening of the central channel, [37] and at this time you should meditate on the path, [focusing on] the salient point of dependent origination. This [completes] refuge and the awakening mind.

3. The Seven-Limb Prayer

1. Visualizing the Merit Field

The main practice

1. *Visualizing the merit field and dissolving the wisdom beings*
2. *Offering the seven-limb prayer and a maṇḍala*
3. *Reciting prayers and requesting blessings*

Here you visualize Jé Rinpoché and his two spiritual sons in front of the merit field; the wisdom beings dissolve into them, [and] you offer the seven-limb prayer and a maṇḍala, and having recited these prayers, request blessings.

Blessing the offerings

1. Visualizing the merit field and dissolving the wisdom beings

The profound points of the oral transmission appear mainly to be related to mantra, therefore here also, you generate yourself as the deity and purify the environment and its inhabitants. You bless and arrange the offerings as related to mantra, following the advice of Jé Gungthangpa.[21]

In general, *The Hundreds of Deities of Tuṣita* that is commonly recited is not related to mantra at all; however, here when you apply the instructions of the oral transmission, it becomes related to mantra. Therefore, here you generate yourself as the deity, then Guru Munīndra dissolves between your eyebrows, and thus you dissolve into light from above and below until you become a nonreified state. This is not merely a "nonreified state" but it is recalling emptiness, which is the state empty of inherent existence. [38]

> **From the expanse of reality, naturally pure and free from elaboration,**
> **I arise in the body of Vajrabhairava.**
> **My three sites are marked with three syllables. HŪṂ radiates light,**
> **striking the environment, its inhabitants, and the offering substances.**

We recall emptiness, and the mind realizing such emptiness purifies the coarse aggregate of our body of flesh and blood. Then, since the part of that mind that is the object-aspect[22] is generated as the deity, "I arise in the body of Vajrabhairava" with one face and two arms, in the mode of instantaneous generation. "My three sites are marked with three syllables" means that you visualize that your crown is marked with the syllable OṂ, the nature of vajra body; your throat is marked with the syllable ĀḤ, the nature of vajra speech; and your heart is marked with the syllable HŪṂ, the nature of vajra mind. You cannot purify the faults and defects of the impurities of the offering substances, the environment and its inhabitants, and so on while you remain as an ordinary being, so you generate yourself as a deity. At your heart "the syllable

HŪṂ radiates light, [striking] the environment, its inhabitants, and the offering substances." The syllable HŪṂ is the seed syllable of Akṣobhya, vajra mind. Akṣobhya appears as the deity, in essence the pristine wisdom of the expanse of reality from among the five types of pristine wisdom. Further, it is said: "The syllable OṂ makes it blaze, the syllable ĀḤ blesses it as nectar, and the syllable HŪṂ purifies its faults and defects." In accordance with that, when it is time to bless the environment and its inhabitants and purify their faults and defects, the syllable HŪṂ is both the seed syllable of Buddha Akṣobhya and the essential element that purifies faults and defects.

Therefore, "the syllable HŪṂ radiates light" [39] refers to light radiating from the syllable HŪṂ [at the heart of yourself] visualized as Vajrabhairava, which strikes the environment and removes every fault, such as shards of stone [and so forth], so that the ground becomes "soft when pressed and rebounds when released." Visualize that it becomes a jeweled foundation, free of all environmental faults and defects, like the pure land of Sukhāvati. As the light strikes the sentient beings who inhabit [the purified environment], it purifies their negativities, obscurations, and potent imprints, and they appear as male and female deities. Next, it purifies the faults and defects of all offering substances, [both] those actually arranged and those not owned in these mundane realms.

This purifies all the faults of impure mistaken appearance,
the pure supported and supporting [maṇḍalas] clearly appear,
and clouds of Samantabhadra offerings arise
possessing the three properties of all offering substances.

Stating this blesses the offerings.

All environments appear as celestial mansions, and all inhabitants appear as male and female deities. "Clouds of Samantabhadra offerings" possess three properties: (1) their nature is bliss and emptiness, (2) in aspect they are individual offering substances, and (3) their function is to powerfully generate the pristine wisdom of uncontaminated great bliss. "Clouds of Samantabhadra offerings arise" for they are just like the jewel that Bodhisattva Samantabhadra holds in his hand, from which two jewels emanate, and from each of those, two [more] emanate so that each emanates two until they fill the realm of space. [40] We should visualize making offerings similar to how Bodhisattva Samantabhadra made offerings, so that even though we offer a single flower, we visualize that it multiplies until the realm of space is filled. And just this is described as "arising as clouds of Samantabhadra offerings."

Visualizing the merit field of the main practice

Visualizing the merit field:

In the midst of an ocean of Samantabhadra offerings in front
is a jeweled throne, radiating light, supported by lions.
It possesses a variegated lotus, sun, and moon as seats.
In the center, upon a slightly higher [seat] above those three . . .

This is the same as the *Guru Pūjā*, where it states that [the nature of offerings is] indivisible bliss and emptiness. You visualize that the pristine wisdom of bliss and emptiness becomes like form in space, and in its midst generate yourself as a deity. Imagine immeasurable Samantabhadra offerings, and in their midst generate a jeweled throne, radiating light, supported by lions. Its height and width should be visualized as before. This is the seat of Jé Rinpoché, which is elevated.

> **. . . my own guru, who is the miraculous emanation of pristine wisdom,**
> **of one taste with all the conquerors in the expanse of reality,**
> **appears as Mañjunātha Tsongkhapa, king of the Dharma,**
> **but they are not differentiated as one or many.**

As it is stated in various texts, such as [Maitreya's] *Ornament of Mahāyāna Sūtras*, all conquerors are of one taste within the expanse of reality. [41] For example, in this world there are many different types of water above ground in terms of their place, time, size, and so forth, but when they merge in the ocean they become of one taste. So too, as sentient beings they have distinct mindstreams, but when they become enlightened it is as though all merge in a single mindstream. It is very helpful to consider this when we rely on one's spiritual friend. The pristine wisdom, of one taste with all conquerors in the expanse of reality, appears one in nature with Guru Mañjunātha Tsongkhapa, and since they are one, they are not differentiated.

> **In aspect, his body is white with a red hue,**
> **a youthful, miraculous body, the union of method and wisdom.**

The mudrā of turning the wheel of Dharma demonstrates that causal and
resultant vehicles, emptiness and interdependence, are not contradictory.

Stating "his body is white with a red hue" symbolizes the union of method and wisdom. He is called "youthful Mañjuśrī" for he is youthful due to not being defiled by the duties of a householder, and his vitality has not declined. Stating that his body "is white with a red hue" indicates that his bodhicitta has not declined. Since he possesses the red component that gives the white component its red hue, it is said that this symbolizes the union of method and wisdom.

He physically performs the mudrā of turning the wheel of Dharma.[23] What does this symbolize? Jé Rinpoché demonstrates that the meaning symbolized by the mudrā of turning the wheel of Dharma exists. [42] Previously in Tibet, disciples who took Vinaya as their main practice would abandon mantra, while those who took mantra as their main practice would abandon Vinaya. Seeing sūtra and mantra to be contradictory—like hot and cold—those who practiced sūtra disparaged mantra, and those who practiced mantra disparaged sūtra. Those who practiced the union [of sūtra and mantra] and the means of practicing that union almost completely disappeared. So too, when they sought to establish both emptiness and dependent origination, they were unable to refute the object of negation. When they refuted the object of negation, they refuted everything and were unable to establish dependent origination. It was as though there was no one able to posit the noncontradictory nature of emptiness and dependent origination. But Jé Rinpoché demonstrated how to practice the causal

Perfection Vehicle and the resultant Vajra Vehicle in a noncontradictory way, and how to practice emptiness and dependent origination in a noncontradictory way, and this is symbolized by the mudrā of turning the wheel of Dharma.

> **He holds at his heart stems of the utpala flowers**
> **of love and compassion to his right and left ear,**
> **supporting a sword severing the snare of ignorance and**
> **a text proclaiming the perfect, pure path.**

Just as the hand implements of Mañjuśrī are a sword and a text, so too Jé Rinpoché demonstrates the mudrā of turning the wheel of Dharma while holding the stem of an utpala flower to his right [that supports] a brandished sword. Since we need wisdom to sever the snare of ignorance that binds [us] to saṃsāra, the sword of wisdom is brandished. [43] The text is a volume teaching the entire path. The text does not merely remain inert but proclaims its subject matter as it abides on an utpala flower. With [his hands] in the mudrā of turning the wheel of Dharma, he holds the stems of utpala flowers, whose flowers fully open at the level of his right and left ear. Above the right [flower] is a sword and above the left [flower] is a text proclaiming the entire path like the roar of thunder. The utpala symbolizes love and compassion. Jé Rinpoché wears the three Dharma robes, symbolizing that he has completed the aggregate of ethics and is not sullied by the least fault.

> **His paṇḍita hat has the color of refined gold**
> **since he has resolved the meaning of scripture**
> **through the three types of valid analysis. It has a high peak**
> **since he has reached the expanse of highest view.**

You should reflect that his hat is a paṇḍita's hat with a high and sharp peak. It also possesses the color of refined gold, for just as gold must be examined by burning, cutting, and rubbing it, so too [the meaning of] scripture should be settled through the three types of valid analysis. To symbolize this, his hat is gold in color. Having a high peak symbolizes that he has reached the expanse of highest view. He sits with his legs in the vajra posture, [44] which is also symbolic.

He sits in the vajra position to demonstrate
that he has actualized union through the four types of position.
At his heart the solitary father, the central deity Mañjuśrī,
is seated within a blazing mass of orange light.

The four types of vajra position are stated in relation to mantra. He sits in the vajra position to demonstrate that he has actualized (1) the vajra position of the channels, (2) the vajra position of the winds, (3) the vajra position of the drops, and (4) the vajra position of bliss and emptiness. At the heart of Jé Rinpoché, visualize Venerable Mañjuśrī, with an orange-colored body, holding a sword in his right hand and a text in his left. He is the same as a commitment being.

At his heart is the wisdom being Vajradhāra,
shining with sapphire [light]. At his heart
is the concentration being, the blue syllable HŪṂ,
like an immense, eternally burning butter-lamp.

At Mañjuśrī's heart is Vajradhāra with a body of shining blue light, similar to a brilliant sapphire. At his [Vajradhāra's] heart is the blue syllable HŪṂ, radiating light in order to destroy the darkness of ignorance, like an immense, eternal butter-lamp. Thus visualize Jé Rinpoché with the three levels of being.[24] [45]

> **Upon the throne to his right is the Supreme Ārya Protector of the World,**
> **[Gyaltsap Jé] Darma Rinchen,[25] advanced in age, with a gentle and peaceful countenance.**
> **At his heart is four-armed Avalokiteśvara, and**
> **as before he possesses the three levels of being.**

Jé Rinpoché is an emanation of Mañjuśrī, and to his right is Gyaltsap [Darma Rinchen] Rinpoché, the Supreme Ārya Protector of the World. "Lord of the World" is another name for Avalokiteśvara, and Darma Rinchen is inseparable in nature from him. He is advanced in age, gentle and peaceful, and seated in a manner that shows respect to Jé Rinpoché. At his [Gyaltsap Rinpoché's] heart, visualize four-armed Avalokiteśvara as the commitment being, and at [Avalokiteśvara's] heart, the wisdom being Vajradhāra. At [Vajradhāra's] heart, meditate on a dark-blue syllable HŪṂ.

> **On the throne to his left is the Secret Lord in the guise of a human.**
> **He is the Sun of Speech, with a youthful and imposing countenance.**
> **At his heart is the Secret Lord, blue in color.**
> **He possesses three levels of being, as before.**

On the throne to the left is the Secret Lord Vajrapāṇi, the Sun of Speech, in the guise of a human. Khedrup Jé,[26] the Sun of

Speech, is youthful, and since he rebukes and reprimands those who misconceive the teachings of Jé Tsongkhapa, his countenance must be imposing. These days there is a trend, when making statues of Jé Rinpoché and his two spiritual sons, for [the practice of] *The Hundreds of Deities of Tuṣita* [46] to depict Khedrup Jé showing a respectful expression to Jé Rinpoché, in the same way Gyaltsap Jé is depicted. [But] in the past when such statues were constructed, the trend was to depict Gyaltsap Rinpoché with a respectful countenance, advanced in age, gentle and peaceful, while Khedrup Rinpoché was [depicted] seated, with an imposing countenance [ready to rebuke any who misconceive the teachings of Tsongkhapa].

At his [Khedrup Jé's] heart is the commitment being Secret Lord [Vajrapāṇi]. At [Vajrapāṇi's] heart is the wisdom being Vajradhāra. At [Vajradhāra's] heart is the concentration being, the dark-blue syllable HŪṂ. As before, he possesses the three levels of vajra being.

Both disciples' right hands show the mudrā of explaining Dharma;
their left hands show the mudrā of equipoise holding a text.
They wear three Dharma robes, and paṇḍit hats the color of refined gold.
They sit with their legs in the vajra position.

I am never sated by looking at the handsome bodies of
the father and his spiritual sons, complete in major and minor marks.
I am never sated by listening to their pleasant speech,
which is endowed with the sixty types of melody.

Their bodies are endowed with the glory of major and minor marks. Therefore, when you view them, you do not tire of looking at them and desire to keep looking at them. However much you listen to their speech, [47] you are never sated.

> **Their minds are profound and vast, unfathomable in depth,**
> **possessing twenty-one types of uncontaminated pristine wisdom and so forth.**
> **They are free from the stains of fault and complete in good qualities.**
> **Merely recalling them removes the torment of saṃsāra and nirvāṇa.**

These represent the qualities of a buddha. Further, when you visualize them, they do not just sit idly:

> **They enact the twelve deeds in limitless fields and so forth,**
> **revealing various amazing emanations according to disciples' [needs].**
> **They manifest buddha-fields in the pores of their bodies.**

Their bodies emit rays of light and enact the twelve deeds [of a buddha].[27] As stated in [Candrakīrti's] *Entering the Middle Way*, [those who have achieved] the resultant ground are capable of manifesting a buddha-field in each pore of their body, each of their bodies also pervades all fields, all such fields contract to the pores of their body, and their body [expands to] pervade all fields and so forth. These are qualities of the state of union.

Their bodies pervade all fields, emanating, absorbing, and so on.
They have inconceivable secret biographies
and maintain the appearance of being pleased with me.

While engaged in such activities, they maintain the appearance of being extremely pleased with you. This is said to be the generation of commitment beings. [48]

Next, invite the wisdom beings. It is necessary to properly visualize the design of the field in order to place imprints [in your mind] to be born in the field of Tuṣita in future. Therefore use appropriate words that make it easy to visualize the focal object and aspects.

When you invite the wisdom beings, [first] visualize that Jé Rinpoché currently abides in Tuṣita with the essential form of Mañjuśrī, and that you must invite him from the abode of Tuṣita. In order to invite him from that abode and place imprints in your mind for taking rebirth there, you must contemplate the design of the field of Tuṣita.

The words "To the north of my abode" [given below] refer to the six types of gods of the desire realm who reside on the levels of Mount Meru, including [the Heaven of] the Four Great Kings on the first level, [the Heaven of] the Thirty-Three on the second level, [the Heaven] Free of Conflict in space [on the third level], and Tuṣita on the fourth level. The Tuṣita mentioned in the words "from the heart of the Protector of the hundreds of deities of Tuṣita" refers to the city of Tuṣita, which exists elevated in space above Tuṣita Heaven where [ordinary] gods of the desire realm reside. The "Delightful Dharma

Abode" exists above that, like a monastery. It is called "abode" since 1,002 buddhas of this fortunate eon [will demonstrate] the act of actually taking rebirth in Tuṣita [49]. Further, by nature it is [composed of] precious substances and is smooth and blissful, like the palm of your hand. If you repeatedly contemplate the layout of Tuṣita field, you shall be reborn there in the future, and for this reason you should contemplate it thoroughly using these words:

> **To the north of my abode, at the peak of the fourth level of Mount Meru, is the Heaven of the Thirty-Three, and in space above that, at a higher level, is the Heaven Free of Conflict. Above that is the expansive abode of joyous sons and daughters of the gods, like a city. Set apart from it, like a monastery at a higher level in space, is the abode from which the one thousand buddhas of this fortunate [eon] come. It is the precious field relied upon by all bodhisattvas who will attain enlightenment in their next life. [The ground] by nature is even and blissful, like the palm of one's hand, free of stone shards and so on. It is soft when pressed and rebounds when released. The golden foundation possesses a checkered inlay of lapis. It has pleasure groves with lakes and ponds, and wish-fulfilling trees that provide whatever is needed or desired. The lake[bed]s are covered with sands of precious substances, and various plane birds continuously proclaim the sound of Dharma with their melodious voices, while sweet fragrances permeate the environment. Merely bringing it to mind generates joy. [50] In the midst of this field of purity, perfectly endowed with such qualities, is the Vijaya Palace, which**

cannot be rivaled in any way, a noble residence elevated by Dharma and a hermitage [graced] by tall victory banners. In front of it is a pleasant grove where Venerable [Maitreya] teaches Dharma.

In the center of this Delightful Dharma Abode is a throne made of precious substances, supported by eight great lions, upon which is seated the regent Ajitanātha [Maitreya]. His body resembles the color of refined gold, possessing the splendor of a hundred thousand suns. He has one face and two hands that are in the mudrā of turning the wheel of Dharma as he holds the stem of a nāga-tree flower, a wheel, and an anointing vase. He wears jeweled ornaments and silk robes, and his crown is adorned with a stūpa of enlightenment, the essential nature of Buddha Śākyamuni. Being seated in the noble posture confirms in this very moment that he will come to this world, and with an air of utter purity he looks at me with a radiant smile of delight. To his right is Jowo Jé Lord Atiśa, who is the divine youthful emanation Stainless Sky, and to his left is Jé Rinpoché, who is the divine youthful emanation, the victors' son Mañjuśrīgarbha. An immeasurable assembled retinue gathered from limitless fields in the ten directions, [including] the great siddha of Lhodrag, who is the divine youthful emanation Stainless Light and so forth, distinctly proclaims the melodious tones of the Perfection of Wisdom sūtras. Even the wind that stirs the trees [51] and the birds of various types melodiously proclaim the pure Dharma. My ears clearly hear these sounds, and their meaning becomes evident to my mind. My nose registers the sweet fragrances, and my

eyes directly perceive the extraordinary array of qualities of this environment and its inhabitants. I visualize this abode clearly, as though I am actually there.

It was previously stated: "In the center of this Delightful Dharma Abode . . . ," yet the noble residence of Indra, lord of the gods in the Heaven of the Thirty-Three, is also called the "Vijaya Palace." It was also said: [Tuṣita's] "Vijaya palace . . . cannot be rivaled in any way, a noble residence elevated by Dharma and a hermitage [graced] by tall victory banners." The palace of Venerable Maitreya in this Delightful Dharma Abode of Tuṣita is said to be "elevated by Dharma and [graced] by tall victory banners," and the palace of Indra, lord of gods, cannot rival it in any way. It is said that even if the [monetary] value of just one solitary palace of the lord of gods could fill the entire world, the value of [Venerable Maitreya's] palace would be greater. If a palace like that were to exist in the world, then it would also have victory banners above it. At this time a basis for such extremely tall [banners] is the palace of Tashi Lhunpo Monastery,[28] [52] though its victory banners are placed below [Tuṣita's] victory banners, which are higher, and there is also a tradition in Ganden Monastery to say, "they are placed below [Tuṣita's] victory banners." In addition, in Lhasa they also say, "they are placed below [Tuṣita's] victory banners," and there is a tradition that says, "lharampa geshés take their pledge under the white banners of victory." The palace is also known as the "noble residence of the tall banners of victory."

In the future, when [Maitreya] demonstrates the deeds of a buddha, [then just as] our Teacher [Śākyamuni] demonstrated the way to become a buddha under the Bodhi tree, [so too] Venerable Maitreyanātha will demonstrate the way to become a buddha at the foot of a nāga-tree. Therefore even now, as his hand implements he holds the stems of a nāga-tree whose flowers [support] a [Dharma] wheel in his right hand and an anointing vase in his left. To represent the proper way to rely on one's spiritual friend and to signify that he pays respect to his guru with the crown of his head, he is adorned with a stūpa of enlightenment. He is seated in the noble posture of legs extended, since he demonstrates the deed of having taken actual birth and residing in Tuṣita. Sitting in this noble posture establishes a special auspicious connection for coming quickly in the future. Once he has appeared in the aspect of the supreme emanation body, [53] it is best that he [is depicted] seated in the full lotus position, for to be seated in a position [demonstrating] that he is about to depart is a little inappropriate. Khensur Rinpoché Losang Wangchuk[29] posed the following question: "Once the supreme emanation has extended his legs and departed [from Tuṣita], where does he need to go?" The aspect of the supreme emanation body seated in full lotus position establishes a greater auspicious connection. The reason for sitting in this noble posture [is to show that he will come] from Tuṣita to this world, for the text states: "Being seated in the noble posture confirms in this very moment that he will come to this world, and with an air of utter purity he looks at me with a radiant smile of delight. To his right is Jowo Jé Lord Atiśa, who is the divine youthful emanation Stainless Sky, and to his left is Jé Rinpoché, who is the divine youthful emanation, the victors' son Mañjuśrīgarbha."

This [confirms] that Jowo Jé Atiśa went to Tuṣita. Dromtönpa asked Jowo Atiśa, "Where will you go?" and he replied, "I will go to Tuṣita." Drom inquired, "So then, could I be reborn in Tuṣita; could I be born there?" Atiśa replied, "In the latter part of your life you will contract leprosy, the worst of diseases, then you will be able to be reborn there." There is an illness called "the wooden hand of sin and obscuration," and Dromtönpa contracted this type of leprosy in the latter part of his life and then went to Tuṣita. [54] It is also mentioned in the *Praise to Jowo Atiśa*[30] that after Reting Monastery[31] was built and during its consecration, flowers descended from Tuṣita. Thus Jowo Jé Atiśa proceeded to Tuṣita. The fact that Jé Rinpoché would proceed to Tuṣita was also predicted by Vajrapāṇi in response to a question put to him by the Mahāsiddha Lhodrag Namkha Gyaltsen to the mahāsiddha Lhodrag Namkha Gyaltsen,[32] for when he asked where Jé Rinpoché would be born in the future, Vajrapāṇi replied that he would proceed to Tuṣita. Also, Jé Rinpoché himself declared many times that in his next life he would proceed to Tuṣita. The mahāsiddha Lhodrag Namkha Gyaltsen and also the mahāsiddha Karmavajra have stated this. The text states: ". . . the great siddha of Lhodrag, who is the divine youthful emanation Stainless Light and so forth, distinctly proclaims the melodious tones of the Perfection of Wisdom sūtras. Even the wind that stirs the trees and the birds of various types melodiously proclaim the pure Dharma. My ears clearly hear these sounds, and their meaning becomes evident to my mind."

We visualize that we have actually reached this land of purity and we hear the melodious sound of Dharma: ". . . my ears clearly hear these sounds, and their meaning becomes evident to my mind. [55] My nose registers the sweet fragrances, and my eyes directly perceive the extraordinary array of qualities of this environment and its inhabitants. I visualize this abode clearly, as though I am actually there." If we visualize that we have actually reached this land of purity, we can establish imprints to be reborn there.

Reflecting, "May I also be cared for," recite fervent prayers.

When you recite the fervent prayer "May I also be cared for" to Venerable Maitreyanātha, it contains the crucial point [of acting as a cause] to be among his retinue when in the future he demonstrates the deeds of a buddha in this world.

This cleanses the field of purity and matures [imprints] to go [there at death].

By cleansing the field in which one achieves completion, maturation, and purification, and by maturing [imprints] to go there, you mature potent [causes] to be reborn in Tuṣita.

Next:

Clean the heart of Maitreyanātha as you would clean a golden plate, and the reflection of an endless knot appears.

It is permissible to think that cleaning the golden plate is like cleaning a mirror. Within the cleaned golden plate at the heart appears an image of a golden knot.

Vividly, in its midst, [arises] a billowing mass of white clouds [56] of pristine wisdom that cares for all beings of this world. At its center [arises] the great being Tsongkhapa, king of the Dharma in the three realms—

> **who is indivisible in nature from your kind root guru and the single essence of the realization, compassion, and power of all the conquerors—and his two spiritual sons. They possess the three levels of being and abide as though you actually see them.**

It has the nature of pristine wisdom at the heart of Venerable Maitreyanātha that cares for disciples in this world. In aspect it is a mass of billowing white clouds.

You should consider that whatever you generate exists in reality as the nature of the compassionate cloud at the heart of Maitreyanātha and abides within it. Further, you should consider that you have actually arrived at this field of purity and that you actually meet Jé Rinpoché and his two spiritual sons.

> ***Then recite melodiously the verses invoking the wisdom beings.***

Visualize that Jé Rinpoché and his two spiritual sons are invited from Tuṣita. They come to the space in front of you.

> **The five sites of the merit field in front are marked**
> **with five syllables. Light radiates from the HŪṂ at their hearts,**
> **[inviting] all gurus, yidams, conquerors, their sons and daughters**
> **from the myriad pure fields of the ten directions.**

The deities of the merit field visualized in front are marked with OṂ at their crown, ĀḤ at their throat, HŪṂ at their heart, SVĀ at their navel, and HĀ at their secret place. The merit field is marked with OṂ, ĀḤ, HŪṂ, SVĀ, and HĀ. [57]

> **All are in the form of my kind gurus.**
> **I invite my kind guru, Jé Rinpoché, and his spiritual sons**
> **from the heart of Maitreyanātha in the Delightful Dharma Abode,**
> **especially [from] myriads of fields in all ten directions.**

Visualize that rays of light radiate in the ten directions, inviting all gurus, yidams, conquerors, and their sons and daughters who reside in the ten directions—[all] in the form of our three kind gurus: Jé Rinpoché and his two spiritual sons. Jé Rinpoché resides in myriad pure fields in the ten directions, for when Khedrup Jé, who had five visions of Jé Rinpoché, asked him,[33] "Where do you reside at present?" he replied "In general my emanations are everywhere, such as Tuṣita, Kachö,[34] Śambhala,[35] and so forth, but just now I am residing at Wutaishan in China, explaining mantra to eight hundred vajra holders. If you request me to come, you should invite me from the myriad pure fields of the ten directions, since I reside there. Furthermore, I am of one taste with the dharmadhātu of all the conquerors." Therefore, we should not invite just Jé Rinpoché from those pure fields, but should invite all the conquerors of the ten directions and their sons and daughters to come in the form of Jé Rinpoché's body.

An ocean of bodhisattvas of the ten directions indicates a very large number. Also,

> **From the heart of the Protector of the hundreds of deities of Tuṣita [58]**

comes a cloud resembling a mass of fresh white curd.
At its crest is Omniscient Losang Drakpa, king of the Dharma,
and his spiritual sons. Please come to this abode. ||1||

The words "hundreds of deities of Tuṣita" indicates a great number [of deities]. From the heart of Venerable Maitreya, who is the protector of a great number of deities of Tuṣita, "issues a cloud resembling a mass of fresh, white curd," which means that at the heart of Maitreyanātha there is a cloud resembling a mass of fresh, white curd. "At its crest is Omniscient Losang Drakpa, king of the Dharma, and his spiritual sons. Please come to this abode." When you recite the words of invocation, ". . . Omniscient Losang Drakpa, king of the Dharma, and his spiritual sons. Please come to this abode," [visualize that] from the heart of Venerable [Maitreya] a white cloud like stretched wool extends as an unbroken thread of cloud to the space in front of you, where Jé Rinpoché and his spiritual sons dissolve into the generated images.

Though you do not move from the pure expanse of reality,
you observe beings in the ten directions with immeasurable compassion
engaging in the extensive enlightened actions of all the conquerors.
Gurus of the three times with your retinues, I request you to come here.
JAḤ HŪṂ BAṂ HOḤ. The wisdom beings dissolve into each commitment being.

If you offer a ritual bath, you should do so here.

Although they do not move from the expanse of the Dharma body, they proceed in the form of emanation bodies for the sake of the disciples. The words "You observe beings . . . with immeasurable compassion" and so on indicate that the conquerors of the ten directions [59] and all their sons and daughters are invited in the aspect of Jé Rinpoché and his two spiritual sons from myriad fields in the ten directions. In particular, the myriad conquerors of the ten directions who are invited in the aspect of Jé Rinpoché and his two spiritual sons dissolve into Jé Rinpoché and his two spiritual sons who were invited from the heart of Protector Maitreya.

You should arrange images of Jé Rinpoché and his two spiritual sons in front of you and meditate on them. By stating JAḤ, [they approach] like one man above another; by stating HŪṂ, they begin to merge; by stating BAṂ, they merge inseparably; and by stating HOḤ, they are bound indivisibly in a state of delight.

When you state, "the wisdom beings dissolve into each commitment being," the wisdom beings of Jé Rinpoché and his two spiritual sons dissolve into their [respective] commitment beings. Thus, regarding Jé Rinpoché and his two spiritual sons, [the wisdom being of] Jé Rinpoché dissolves into Jé Rinpoché, and those of Gyaltsap Jé and Khedrup Jé dissolve into each [spiritual son], respectively.

It is stated that "if you offer a ritual bath, you should do so here." If you offer a ritual bath after inviting these deities, then just as stains are cleansed through washing, so you also experience the purification of negativities since this functions as the compatible cause [of both]. [60]

2. The Seven-Limb Prayer

2. Offering the seven-limb prayer and a maṇḍala, with all salient points of accumulation and purification

1. Requesting to remain

Usually when we offer the seven-limb prayer, the request not to pass into paranirvāṇa occurs after the request to turn the wheel of Dharma. However, here the request to remain [in saṃsāra] comes first:

> **Venerable gurus with your white smiles of delight,**
> **seated on lion thrones, lotus, and moon in the space**
> **before me,**
> **please remain for hundreds of eons in order to spread**
> **the teachings**
> **as the supreme field of merit for my mind of faith. ||2||**

Next is prostration

2. Prostration

> **Your intelligent minds comprehend the full extent of**
> **objects of knowledge.**
> **Your eloquent speech is the ear ornament of the**
> **fortunate.**
> **Your beautiful bodies blaze with the glory of renown.**
> **I prostrate to you who are meaningful to see, hear, and**
> **recall. ||3||**

This verse expresses the qualities of body, speech, and mind. I think that the words "to see, hear, and recall" indicate that we prostrate to their bodies, which are meaningful to see; their speech, which is meaningful to hear; and their minds, which are meaningful to recall. On the one hand, not only does their realization universally pervade both the qualities of a buddha and objects of knowledge, it is also superior realization. On the other hand, superior objects of knowledge do not belong to those who are unenlightened, [61] nor could [their minds] encompass them. Therefore the words "Your intelligent minds comprehend the full extent of objects of knowledge" express the qualities of a buddha.

The words "Your eloquent speech is the ear ornament of the fortunate" are similar to the words "the ear ornament of the fortunate" or "the necklace of the fortunate" found in the titles of certain works. But since the speech of Jé Rinpoché is free from all stains of misunderstanding, misconception, and doubt, it is solely the ear ornament of the fortunate. Since it could never not be an ear ornament, it is called "the ear ornament."

The words "Your beautiful bodies blaze with the glory of renown" principally refer to the body of Jé Rinpoché, which is an emanation of Mañjuśrī. However, to ordinary appearance he [possesses] the perfected aggregate of ethics, unsullied by any fault. That being so, whoever sees him is not sated [by merely that], and even though [you are] intimidated as you first meet him, when you come near to his body you lose interest in external pursuits. These are said to be physical qualities. Thus "I prostrate to you who are meaningful to see, hear, and recall."

I prostrate reverently with my body, speech, and mind,
recalling the unmixed attributes exclusive to buddhas

and the three secret states distinguished in the Dharma body
so that I may attain the three vajras.

Recall the qualities of the buddhas' three secret states distinguished in the Dharma body, such as the eighteen unique qualities of the buddhas[36] and so forth. [62] Prostrate with your body, speech, and mind so that in the future your ordinary body, speech, and mind will become a vajra body, vajra speech, and vajra mind through the three vajras. You will become enlightened with the nature of vajra body that is Buddha Vairocana, the nature of vajra speech that is Buddha Amitābha, and the nature of vajra mind that is Buddha Akṣobhya.

At this point, if you intend to accumulate a certain number of prostrations, recite:

OṂ NAMO MAÑJUŚRĪYE/ NAMAḤ SUŚRĪYE/ NAMO UTTAMA ŚRĪYE SVĀ HĀ//

which is the multiplying mantra for prostrations. First recite the mantra three times while making full-length prostrations, then accumulate prostrations while reciting the verse: "Your intelligent minds comprehend the full extent of objects of knowledge . . . and so on."

You generate the merit field with Jé Rinpoché in front, and while focusing on it you accumulate prostrations, and your prostrations are increased by using the multiplying mantra for prostrations. It is also said that if you prostrate at this point, you obtain a benefit equal to reading all the scriptures. Thus, having recited the mantra for multiplying prostrations, you accumulate prostrations while reciting the verse: "Your intelligent minds comprehend the full extent of objects of knowledge . . . and so on."

3. *Offering*

3. The limb of offering

Visualize that countless vajra offering-deities are emitted from your heart, who offer boundless clouds of offerings. [63]

The limb of offering is related to mantra, and therefore you imagine that vajra offering-deities are emitted from your heart. They are goddesses of vajra form, vajra sound, vajra aroma, vajra taste, vajra tactile objects, and so forth. When you offer flowers, you offer them by emitting goddesses who bear flowers. There are different types of offerings, such as external offerings, inner offerings, secret offerings, and offerings of suchness.

First external offerings

I offer this ocean-like cloud of offerings actually arranged
and mentally created to you, the supreme field of merit,
such as pleasing water offerings, various flowers,
fragrant incense, light, and scented water. ||4||

When you offer external substances such as flowers, scented water, light, and so forth, it is called "external offering." In general, the Three Jewels are referred to as "the field of merit," but among them your own guru is the supreme field of merit. By taking Jé Rinpoché to be inseparable from your guru, you state that you make offerings "to you, the supreme field of merit." You offer the inner offering by transforming inner qualities into offering substance; therefore the inner offering substance is internalized.

Please accept this collection of white virtue of myself
and others,
such as instruction and practice, the three trainings,
and the two stages,
beautifully arrayed in an attractive offering cloud, [64]
and bestow on me blessings without limit.

This is offering instruction and practice, and so forth.

May you generate supreme satisfaction and delight
due to this great ocean of nectar that is purified, realized,
and blazes
through the light of the three vajras, radiating and
contracting
the pure essence of the five buddha families and four
consorts.

When [its light] radiates, it [absorbs] the blessings of the body, speech, and mind of all buddhas and bodhisattvas, and when its [light] contracts, it dissolves into the inner offering. By reciting HŪṂ any defect of color is purified, by reciting ĀḤ it is realized as nectar, and by reciting OṂ it blazes manifoldly. "Purified" refers to the purification of stains, "realized" means that it is transformed into the essence of nectar, and "blazes" means that it increases manifoldly and becomes inexhaustible. Reflect that their minds are satisfied due to such offerings. Now the secret offering:

> **The emanated assembly of field-born, mantra-born, and**
> **innately born seals dissolves into the consort of Lord**
> **Vajradhāra.**
> **Through the joy of their union, the [deities] and their**
> **retinues**
> **are satisfied with uncontaminated joy.**

There are field-born ḍākinīs, mantra-born ḍākinīs, and innately born ḍākinīs. There are different ways of explaining field-born ḍākinīs, such as field-born ḍākinīs of the twenty-four great abodes, those of the eight great cemeteries, those of Vajrāsana, and so on. They are emanations of heroes and heroines who come to these [65] special fields blessed by holy beings of the past. Emanations of heroines are called "field-born ḍākinīs," "ḍākimas," and "field-born seals." Those who abide in the three isolations of mantra[37] and possess the illusory body are called "mantra-born ḍākinīs." Those who have attained the realizations of clear light and the state of union are called "innately born seals." Since Jé Rinpoché has the aspect of an ordained monk in the merit field, we visualize Vajradhāra and his consort at the hearts of Jé Rinpoché and his two spiritual sons, and the emanated assembly of such ḍākinīs dissolves into the consort of Vajradhāra. Vajradhāra and his consort abide in union, which means that their mindstreams are the same. Once they enter such union they generate the pristine wisdom of bliss and emptiness in their mindstreams, and you reflect that the pristine wisdom of bliss and emptiness is also generated in the mindstreams of Jé Rinpoché, his two spiritual sons, and their entire retinue.

The words "the [deities] and their retinues are satisfied with uncontaminated joy" refer to the secret offering, while the external offerings mentioned earlier are called "external offerings related to the vase empowerment." When the vase empowerment is conferred, it is conferred in dependence upon external empowering substances such as the vase water, crown, bell, and so forth. Here external substances refer to flowers, incense, and so on, and [66] they are called "external offerings related to the vase empowerment."

Those called "inner offerings related to the secret empowerment" refer to the red and white bodhicitta [produced] from the union of the guru [in the aspect of the] male deity with his consort, which you visualize giving rise to bliss when tasted during the conferral of the secret empowerment. Also, here you offer the five types of meat and five types of nectar, through generating them in the nature of nectar. When they are offered, you should reflect that these inner offerings related to the secret empowerment give rise to the pristine wisdom of bliss and emptiness in your mindstream.

Regarding "offerings related to the secret empowerment and the wisdom empowerment," you visualize that you enter into union with a knowledge consort when you obtain the pristine-wisdom empowerment. Here also, visualizing that the pristine wisdom of bliss and emptiness has arisen due to entering into union with the emanated assembly of seals is the secret offerings related to the wisdom empowerment.

Regarding the offering of suchness related to the word empowerment, [first] the offering of suchness [should be understood in relation to] the generation of the pristine wisdom of great bliss in the mind that is generally posited as the secret offering, and the ascertainment of emptiness by that [wisdom] is posited as the offering of suchness. But merely that is insufficient to be [posited as] the offering of suchness associated with the word empowerment. The word empowerment introduces [the student to] the state of union, and the word empowerment is obtained when it is recognized. That which is called "the offering related to the word empowerment" is visualizing offering your understanding of union to your guru, or [67] otherwise visualizing that you arise in the guru's body of union.

Therefore, here also,

> **Within a state where all phenomena are free from elaboration, like space,**
> **any rainbow-like form body may appear.**
> **The union of body and mind is innate great bliss.**
> **May you be pleased by the offering of the vajra of enlightenment.**

When the clear light dawns, the all-empty space-like state appears. From within that space-like state, [the deities of the merit field] arise in bodies of union from within the state of clear light, just like a rainbow appears in the sky. Therefore it is said: "any rainbow-like form body may appear." This union must be a union of body and mind because it is established from a basis of extremely subtle wind and mind, which are one in nature but distinct conceptual isolates. Since the body also is fabricated from that mind, the body and mind are one in nature and are called "a union."

Once you generate an understanding of the state of union, you visualize that you offer your root of virtue from the generation of that understanding. You also visualize that the deities of the merit field have arisen in bodies of union. This is called the "offering of suchness related to the word empowerment." [68]

When you consolidate such offerings,

In brief, I offer external and internal [offerings]—
enjoyments and desire objects—
and an offering maṇḍala related to the four empowerments,
motivated by the mind of respect.
Please accept them through the force of your great compassion.

External offerings refer to enjoyments and desire objects, and internal offerings refer to enjoyments and desire objects. External offerings called "enjoyments" refer to offering flowers, incense, light, scented water, food, and music. Internal offerings called "enjoyments" refer to inner scented water, since it is said that "conquerors have bodies of supreme qualities possessing the scent of pure morality." [This refers to] inner flowers, since it is said, "beautifully adorned with flowers of the requisites of enlightenment." [It also refers to] the internal offering of the clear flame of a butter-lamp, since it is said that "fragrant flowers decorate the palace of pristine wisdom, and the darkness of ignorance is removed by the light of pristine wisdom." Such internal enjoyments exist. External desire objects pleasing to the senses are forms, sounds, aromas, flavors, and textures. Internal desire objects pleasing to the senses are explained with respect to the knowledge consort, and are said to be "the blue aspect of the seal" and so forth.

"An offering mandala related to the four empowerments" is stated in relation to external [offerings] related to the vase empowerment and inner [offerings] related to the secret empowerment. The offering maṇḍala is offered "motivated by the mind of respect." Even though the substances that we offer [69] are next to nothing, the recipients of our offerings have thoroughly completed the two accumulations and therefore enjoy these offerings through their compassion. It is said that if a bhagavān were to eat horse feed, he would experience more than a hundred delicious flavors; therefore the text states, "Please accept them through the force of your great compassion."

4. *Confession*

4. *The limb of confession*

Strongly generating intense regret and invoking compassion:

Alas, the mass of negativity I have accumulated in saṃsāra
from beginningless time is like a king's treasure.
It seems that I have only exerted myself
in various types of negativity for hundreds of millions of eons.

Our lives are beginningless, and when we look at the mass of negativity we have accumulated over lifetimes without beginning, it is similar to looking at the treasure of a king. There is every kind of possession in the treasure of a king, and one could not say anything is missing. In addition, each item is of the best quality. Similarly, when our negativity is accumulated, every kind [of negativity] is included, and we could not say that anything is missing. In addition, it is negativity that is complete in terms of the preparation, the actual act, and the conclusion. Therefore, looking at our accumulated negativity is similar to looking at a king's treasure. Looking at the virtue that we have established is similar to looking at the possessions of a beggar. The possessions of a beggar are limited in type and poor in quality, being cracked or broken and so on. Similarly, our virtue is limited in type, and that which does exist is incomplete in preparation, actual act, or conclusion, for some [virtuous acts] possess preparation [70] but lack a conclusion, and so forth.

It is as though we have engaged in nothing but various types of negativity, such as killing, for hundreds of millions of eons. This has arisen because, from beginningless time, we have been ignorant of what should be practiced and what should be abandoned.

> **In this life, despite pretending to practice virtue and discard nonvirtue,**
> **day and night negativities and downfalls continuously descend like rain.**
> **But I lack the means to purify them completely,**
> **while my enemy, the Lord of Death, approaches suddenly without warning.**

Day and night, negativities and downfalls fall like rain. Indeed, we have already taken every type of vow, such as the vows of individual liberation and so forth, and since it is difficult to safeguard tantric vows, infractions occur like rain. Also, it is difficult to protect against states incompatible with bodhisattva vows. And though vows of individual liberation are the easiest to safeguard, we are incapable of guarding them properly. Thus this statement is made. Jowo Jé Atiśa stated that he almost never experienced the taint of transgressing his vows of individual liberation. Even when tainted, he would immediately confess it, and thus he never experienced [a transgression] remaining for a day. But he said that for bodhisattva vows downfalls arose frequently, and for tantric vows downfalls occurred like a downpour. If someone like Jowo Jé made this statement, then there is no need to speak of ourselves. [71]

Therefore, even though purification can be achieved if we practice the limb of confession complete in the four opponent powers, it is difficult for us to assemble all four opponent powers. Refuge and the awakening mind are said to be the opponent power of the basis, but this is difficult to generate. It is also said that it is important to have a mind of restraint toward future [nonvirtue], but this is also difficult for us. Meanwhile, "my enemy, the Lord of Death, approaches suddenly without warning," for the time of our death is uncertain.

Alas, haven't I already fallen into hell?
My friends and companions are now roasting in hellish flames.
Won't I also be roasting there by this time next year?
Compassionate Protector, please care for this evil one.

If we die with such negativity it is as though we have already fallen to hell. Our friends, relatives, and companions who have already died are currently being cooked in the molten bronze of hell. For instance, when those who have ingested poison are oppressed by remorse, it becomes unbearable. See whether or not it is so. When [negativity] becomes [unbearable], this establishes the opponent power of repudiation. And when that is established, the opponent power of fully applying the antidote and the opponent power of never committing that fault again will arise naturally. [72]

***The acute torment of remorse incites compassion. If you desire a more elaborate practice, you could recite the* Confession of Downfalls *and the* General Confession. *If you wish to accumulate prostrations, you may do that here, related to the* Confession of Downfalls.**

Formerly, when Jé Rinpoché was accumulating prostrations in Ölkha, he accumulated 100,000 [for each buddha] related to the *Confession of Downfalls*. Since at that time he had visions of the thirty-five confessional buddhas, this practice is known as "the practice of followers and disciples." When you accumulate prostrations, you should do so either while reciting the *Confession of Downfalls* or in connection to the *Guru Pūjā*. The actual verse of confession in *The Hundreds of Deities of Tuṣita* is this:

Finally:

Whatever nonvirtuous actions of body, speech, and mind
I have accumulated from beginningless time, and
in particular this mass of transgressions of my three vows,
I confess individually, with sincere regret. ||5||

Recite at least three times.

Our gurus advise us that when we take vows, it is as though we have not taken vows but have taken downfalls instead. Since downfalls occur like continuous rain, it is as though we have accepted downfalls. Therefore, by focusing on them, you confess them and eliminate them by reciting, "In particular, this mass of transgressions of my three vows I confess individually, with sincere regret" at least three times. [73]

Here, according to the advice of the oral transmission, it is said that Vajradhāra at your heart is pacified and transforms into Vajrasattva, and that you can purify any mantra commitments that have degenerated or are broken. The means of achieving this:

The Hundreds of Deities of Tuṣita simply states:

Whatever nonvirtuous actions of body, speech, and mind
I have accumulated from beginningless time, and
in particular this mass of transgressions of my three vows,
I confess individually, with sincere regret. ||5||

However, if you supplement this with advice from the oral transmission, you can perform recitation and meditation on Vajrasattva at this point. The wisdom being Vajradhāra, generated earlier, transforms into Vajrasattva, and you may focus on recitation and meditation on Vajrasattva.

Vajradhāra at the hearts of my guru and his two spiritual sons,

who manifests a peaceful [aspect], becomes Vajrasattva. A replica proceeds to the crown of myself and others, and a stream of nectar cleanses all negativities and downfalls.

Recite the hundred-syllable mantra [of Vajrasattva], and if accumulating mantras, you may do so here.

Vajradhāra at their hearts becomes Vajrasattva, and a replica separates from each one. The replicas then proceed to your crown, and nectar flows from their bodies. When you accumulate the hundred-syllable mantra, reflect that all negativities and obscurations of your three doors are being purified, and for those who are accumulating 100,000 recitations of the hundred-syllable mantra, you may do so at this point. This practice purifies all negativity; however, if you do not confess negativity, it increases daily. [74] For example, if a single negative [action] is not confessed today, it will become two negative [actions] tomorrow. Again, if it is not confessed tomorrow, it will become four negative [actions] the day after. Therefore negativity increases manifoldly. It is said that reciting the hundred-syllable mantra each day without break twenty-one times stops any increase, while reciting it 100,000 times purifies negativity. Then, when you stop reciting the hundred-syllable mantra,

Guru Vajrasattva, who abides at the crown, dissolves into the crown of myself and others, and merges with our three sites.

At this point, visualize that you are surrounded by all sentient beings and that Vajrasattva also resides at their crowns. Your negativities, obscurations, and their imprints are purified, and you reflect that when Vajrasattva resides in your body and mind, his body, speech, and mind merge and become of one taste with your own subtle body, speech, and mind. In addition, you should reflect that you can clearly hear the voice of Jé Rinpoché telling you, "Your negativity has been purified." From your side, also, you should think that all your negativity has been purified. It is said that when done in this way, the purification of negativity is substantial. Therefore you should contemplate this.

5. *Rejoicing*

5. The limb of rejoicing

> ***The secret, inconceivable biography of Guru Mañjunātha is like an ocean. Recall it often** [75] **and meditate on it with great joy.***

The biography of Jé Rinpoché is inconceivable, since he possesses the qualities of a buddha. Jé Rinpoché himself has said, [in praise of Mañjuśrī,] "Even if I had a hundred tongues, still I could not express [your qualities]." So too, Jé Rinpoché possesses such qualities, and even though it is not possible to express all of them, recalling as many of them as we can and cultivating the joy that rejoices in them is known as "rejoicing."

> **In this time of degeneration, you studied extensively and strove to practice.**
> **And by abandoning the eight concerns, your life of freedom and endowment**

became meaningful. From the depths of my heart I rejoice,
O Protector, in the great waves of your deeds. ||6||

At first Taktsang Lotsāwa[38] opposed Jé Rinpoché, but later offered him verses of praise in which he states: "Compared to sūtra, tantra pales. Compared to tantra, sūtra pales. But you are one who practices sūtra and tantra without seeing them as contradictory. Some who emphasize study call those who practice 'ignorant meditators,' and some who practice say study has no benefit. However, you [Lama Tsongkhapa] practice through integrating study, contemplation, and meditation."

In general, the eight worldly concerns have three types: white, black, and mixed. It goes without saying that Jé Rinpoché was not affected by black worldly concerns, but he was also not affected in the least by white [or virtuous] worldly concerns. This expresses his qualities as they appear to ordinary beings. [76]

The qualities of Jé Rinpoché as they appear to ordinary beings include frequent study, exertion in practice, and never engaging in the eight worldly concerns in that life. The emperor of China sent an envoy twice, with invitations written in gold letters, inviting Jé Rinpoché to China. The first time the envoy did not even meet Jé Rinpoché. The next time Jé Rinpoché received him at the request of all Tibetan leaders, but he did not agree to visit China. Instead, he sent Jamchen Chöjé[39] as his representative. Such signs indicate that he had abandoned the eight worldly concerns.

The text states, "From the depths of my heart I rejoice, O Protector, in the great waves of your deeds." Jé Rinpoché cultivated bodhicitta from an early age, and due to this he convened a great conference on Dharma in Tölung, where he, Venerable Rendawa, Chöjé Yakpa Shuwa, and the great lotsāwa Kyabchok Palsang gave many discourses. At that time the disciplinarian criticized [the conference], while other lamas found [his criticism] inappropriate. It is said that Chöjé Losang [77] Drakpa [i.e., Tsongkhapa], who had trained in bodhicitta from a young age, offered no response. These are some of his ordinary deeds.

Who can fathom the three unique secret states of Mañjuśrī?
Even in terms of your ordinary deeds, I rejoice that you
proceeded to the highest state since you comprehended all scripture
and its commentaries, [such scripture] appeared [to you as personal] instruction, and you accomplished [that instruction].

From the perspective of his extraordinary deeds, he was Venerable Mañjuśrī, for this text states: "Who can fathom the three unique secret states of Mañjuśrī?" His biography mentions: "In the first part of his life, Jé Rinpoché strived in extensive study; in the middle part, all scriptural traditions appeared as instruction; and in the end, he practiced continuously, night and day." This passage gives the essential meaning of Jé Rinpoché's life, and you should rejoice in his deeds accordingly.

The eight black worldly concerns are to be happy when praised and unhappy when criticized, and so forth. They are "black" because they are the eight concerns that manifest for this life. The eight mixed worldly concerns include self-cherishing. The eight white worldly concerns include being bound by grasping at true existence.

Let alone the eight black or mixed worldly concerns,
you are not tainted
by the eight white worldly concerns that conceive of
entities as real.
I rejoice in your act of refining the pure gold of all the
Sage's teachings
through applying hundreds of scriptural quotations
and reasons.

Jé Rinpoché removed extraneous statements that had entered the teachings and made many amendments. It is stated in [his] *Great Exposition of Mantric Stages*:

> Extraneous statements [were analyzed] and misconceptions removed through consulting the root and explanatory tantras and texts composed by mahāsiddhas. Regarding the cycle of Hevajra from [78] Mahāsiddha Virūpa through a long lineage of Sakya scholars, there is no need to remove any misconceptions.[40]

There was a need to eliminate misconceptions about all lineages, and we rejoice in his act of refining the pure gold [of the teachings] through hundreds of quotations and reasons.

Since former scholars were confused about the profound
meaning,
all Tibet was immersed in the darkness of evil views.
I rejoice in Losang, the single sun who gave breath
with the light of dependent origination.

This is similar to the verse in [Candrakīrti's] *Entering the Middle Way*:

> The sun of pure discernment removed the thick darkness,
> and scholars understood emptiness and were liberated.[41]

The words "gave breath" refer to liberating beings tormented by sufferings from their suffering. So too, he gave breath, since he eliminated [the confusion] of all those scholars who were confused about the profound meaning by shedding light on it.

> **If someone like you, Mañjuśrī, had not come to Tibet,**
> **then in Tibet we would take refuge in a mere shadow**
> **of the Sage's teachings**
> **in terms of meditating on view, practice, and all sūtra**
> **and tantra.**
> **I rejoice in your kindness that exceeds all kindness.**

This is similar to the statement in [Khedrup Jé's] *Glorious Three Grounds*:[42]

> When all the Sage's teachings on sūtra and tantra were
> reduced to mere words, you revived them here [in Tibet].

In this way, [79] meditate on rejoicing.

6. Urging to Turn the Wheel of Dharma

> ***6. The limb of urging to turn the wheel of Dharma***
>
> ***Offering a golden wheel with one thousand spokes,***

When the Bhagavān attained enlightenment, he did not teach Dharma for forty-nine days, or seven weeks. At that time, four-faced Brahmā offered a golden wheel with one thousand spokes, and Indra offered a clockwise-spiraling white conch and requested teachings. So too, here you visualize that you offer a golden wheel with one thousand spokes. Then,

May a rain of profound and extensive Dharma fall
from the billowing clouds of wisdom and compassion
gathered in the sky of your Dharma body, venerable holy guru,
to care for disciples in any way appropriate. ||7||

When clouds form in the sky and it rains on the land, the crops flourish. The sky represents the mind of the Dharma body; the clouds represent compassion of the heart; rain represents teaching Dharma; the land represents those who need to be trained. When Dharma is taught to disciples, it resembles the flourishing of the crops when rain falls on the land. This analogy is stated so that excellent qualities, such as higher rebirth and the highest good,[43] may manifest in the mindstreams of disciples. [80]

The supreme wisdom existing in the sky of the pure Dharma body
is the pristine wisdom of emptiness conjoined with the great bliss of altruism.
May you bring us to maturity in the expanse of the maṇḍala wheel,
amid clouds of indivisible and miraculously emanated deities.

The Dharma body is similar to the form of the sky. "Supreme wisdom" is pristine wisdom comprehending emptiness. And in the statement "conjoined with the great bliss of altruism," "altruism" is understood to be compassion desiring freedom from suffering, but it is also understood as the pristine wisdom of great bliss. Here it refers to its application in mantra.

May the profound, signless, and vast deity wheel,
the profound completion stage and vast generation stage,
and the profound clear light and vast illusory bodies
send a rain of Dharma to remove the two obscurations from the root.

Reflect that your request has been accepted.

Within the state of the ultimate clear light of the Dharma body emerge numerous illusory form bodies, and that deity assembly of the maṇḍala wheel also appears in the space of clear light.

May the principal deity of the maṇḍala confer the maturing empowerment, which generates realization of the two stages of the maturing path.

From the perspective of the lower tantras, [turning the Dharma wheel] is turning the profound, signless, and vast deity wheel. If this is applied to highest yoga mantra, "the profound" refers to the completion stage and "the vast" refers to the generation stage. Or, if applied to realizations of the completion stage, [81] "the profound" refers to the clear light and "the vast" refers to the illusory body. Reflect that your request "to send a rain of such Dharma to remove the two obscurations from the root" has been accepted. When you reflect that both your request to turn the wheel of Dharma and your request to remain have been accepted, this is said to be the point of [making an] auspicious connection.

> ***Not only does the limb of requesting them to remain occur earlier, it is also offered here, in accordance with the general order of the seven-limb prayer.***

In accordance with the general order of the seven-limb prayer, the request not to pass into paranirvāṇa comes after the request to turn the wheel of Dharma.

> ***Visualize that you offer lion thrones adorned with a variegated vajra to each, and they dissolve into the lion thrones of the gurus.***

There are three gurus—Jé Rinpoché and his two spiritual sons—and you reflect that you offer a lion throne adorned with a variegated vajra to each. Then you reflect that they dissolve into the three thrones of Jé Rinpoché and his two spiritual sons. The continuum of the impure illusory body that rises from the metaphoric clear light of mental isolation is to be severed, while the continuum of the pure illusory body that rises from actual or pure clear light is not to be severed. Therefore,

> **Though the body of union that rises from the expanse of**
> **pure clear light does not appear or disappear,** [82]
> **please remain steadfast to the perception of ordinary beings**
> **in your coarse form bodies until the end of saṃsāra.**

> ***Visualize that your request is accepted.***

Although it does not pass into paranirvāṇa like the sun that rises and sets, you request that the coarse form body remains steadfast until the end of saṃsāra, without disappearing from the perception of ordinary beings. In general the body of union does not appear or disappear, but since it displays the means of passing into paranirvāṇa to the minds of ordinary beings, [you request that] it does not do this. It is said that this verse was newly inserted by Phürbuchok Ngawang Jampa.[44]

> ***If you seek a more extensive version, you may insert at this point, "I make requests to the gurus. May I be blessed by Jé Rinpoché, his two spiritual sons, and the lineage gurus" and so on, in accordance with the Ensa oral transmission.[45] Furthermore, if you wish to offer a long life pūjā to the guru with whom you have a Dharma connection and who has actual attainments, offer it here. It is said that offering long life pūjā to your guru is the supreme means for establishing your own long life.***

In the *Dākiṇī Long Life Pūjā* it is said:

> I make requests to the gurus;
> May I be blessed by Jé Rinpoché, his two spiritual sons, and the lineage gurus.[46]

It is acceptable to insert this here in accordance with the advice from the oral transmission. [83]

7. Dedication

7. The limb of dedication

With the intense aspiration to dedicate the collection of virtue of yourself and others, [to benefit] in general the teachings and reincarnating beings, and in particular to be a cause for the spread of the essential teachings of Guru Mañjunātha:

May any virtue that I have accumulated
benefit the entire teachings and all reincarnating beings.
In particular, may the essence of the teachings of
Venerable Losang Drakpa shed illumination for a long time. ||8||

You should benefit the entire teachings and all reincarnating beings through any virtue [accumulated], represented here by that accumulated from beginningless time and that accumulated in this very context. It is said that if something benefits the teachings, it benefits reincarnating beings, and that if something benefits reincarnating beings, it also benefits the teachings.

That which benefits the teachings benefits reincarnating beings, for the basis giving rise to the bliss and happiness of reincarnating beings is the teachings, and if they are benefitted, reincarnating beings are also benefitted. For something to benefit all reincarnating beings, it must benefit the teachings that are the cause of this. Therefore it is said that the dedication [of virtue] to benefit all reincarnating beings is the dedication [of virtue] to spread the teachings, and that the dedication [of virtue] to benefit the teachings is the dedication [of virtue] to be the cause of the bliss of reincarnating beings.

The teachings of Jé Rinpoché are called "the essence of the

teachings." The teachings of the Buddha are fully resolved through the proper threefold analysis,[47] [84] and since that which is fully resolved is similar to its essence, we state, "may they bring illumination for a long time." They are called "the essence of the teachings" because they possess the attribute of being able to establish the state of union in just three years and three months.

It is produced by the awakening mind over incalculable eons.
It is the means for uniting causal and resultant vehicles.
It is complete and unmistaken, possessing the heart essence.
I dedicate this as the cause for spreading myriad emanations.

Because the awakening mind increases the pure path of the Vajra Vehicle that is related to profound view over incalculable past eons, in this life, too, the awakening mind is compatible with it. It is the causal and resultant vehicle differentiated by Jé Rinpoché in Tibet, since externally it pacifies and tames through the practice of hearers, and internally it is the system of practice of secret mantra related to bodhicitta. It is the path that is not incomplete. Since others only train in specific aspects of the path, they do not achieve [the result]. But if the path is complete and unmistaken, then it should be practiced. The words "it is complete, unmistaken, possessing the heart essence" refer to that which produces the very essence of the heart of the complete and unmistaken teachings. Dedicate this as the cause for these teachings to be established through the emanation of wisdom beings from the heart of Jé Rinpoché.

[The words] "I dedicate [this] as the cause for spreading myriad emanations" are uttered since, for some, Jé Rinpoché's [85] *Stages of the Path of Secret Mantra* and *Stages of the Path of the Perfection Vehicle* appear as the form of Jé Rinpoché's realization; for some [his realization] appears as the melody of the Miktsema praise; while for others it appears in the form of the volume of the *Great Exposition of the Stages of the Path*."

In the course of all my lives, may I never be separated
from your teachings, my Supreme Guide,
and with the deep realization of its subtle and secret points,
may I quickly reach the end of abandonment and realization.

Dedicate with intense aspiration.

3. Maṇḍala Offering

Then, offer a maṇḍala. Its material, shape, method of offering, and so on are as usual.

If you have a gold or silver set, it has greater potential to accumulate [merit]. But if you generate pride through focusing on it, it becomes a fault. When Jé Rinpoché engaged in accumulating [maṇḍala offerings] and purification at Ölkha, it is said that his wrist was injured being rubbed against the stone base when making maṇḍala offerings. You may use small pebbles on a stone base to make the offering.

The maṇḍala of thirty-seven heaps is most popular.

That which [86] includes such well-known components as the Goddess of Beauty and the Goddess of Music is called the maṇḍala of thirty-seven heaps.[48]

But here you offer the unique maṇḍala of Jé Rinpoché with twenty-three heaps.

But it is said that if you offer the maṇḍala of twenty-three heaps, it is complete with all thirty-seven heaps. You offer the twenty-three heaps:

OṂ VAJRA BHŪMI ĀḤ HŪṂ.
The golden base of great might.
OṂ VAJRA REKHE ĀḤ HŪṂ.
Surrounded by a ring of external iron mountains.

If you count these two, there are twenty-five heaps. But you do not count these two.

At its center is Mount Meru, the king of mountains, in the east is Videha, in the south is Jambudvīpa, in the west is Godānīya, in the north is Kuru. In the east are Deha and Videha, in the south are Cāmara and Avaracāmara, in the west are Śāṭha and Uttaramantrin, in the north are Kuru and Kaurava. In the east is the precious elephant, in the south is the precious householder, in the west is the precious horse, in the north is the precious queen, in the southeast is the precious general, in the southwest is the precious wheel, in the

> **northwest is the precious jewel, in the northeast is the precious treasure. Inside that is the sun in the east and moon in the west.**

There are five,[49] and if you count the subcontinents there are thirteen. There are seven royal symbols and the vase, making eight, and with the sun in the inner east and the moon in the inner west, there are ten. If you add these to the former thirteen, there are twenty-three. Then, if you add both the ring of external iron mountains and the basis, there are twenty-five. By offering Mount Meru you [offer] all eight goddesses, such as the Goddess of Beauty, who exist on the terraces of the mountain. You offer the complete general wealth of the four continents, such as the jewel mountain, the wish-fulfilling tree, the wish-fulfilling cow, and the unploughed harvest. Therefore the eight goddesses, such as the Goddess of Beauty, and the four types of general wealth make twelve. If you add these twelve [87] to the twenty-five that include the iron mountains and the basis, it is complete with all thirty-seven heaps.

> **I offer the body, speech, and mind of myself and others,**
> **our enjoyments, and collection of virtue of the three times,**
> **and this precious jeweled maṇḍala with clouds of Samantabhadra's offerings,**
> **which are mentally created, to my guru, yidam, and the Three Jewels.**
> **Please accept them with your compassion and bestow on me waves of blessing.**

Pray for the three great purposes.

For a Dharma practitioner, there is no greater purpose than these three. These three are the following:

> **I prostrate and go for refuge to my Guru and the Three Precious Jewels. Please bless my mindstream. Please bless me and all mother sentient beings to quickly stop every type of distorted mind, from not respecting my virtuous spiritual friend up to generating subtle dualistic appearance during white appearance, red increase, and black near-attainment.**

Since this [prayer] is related to mantra, [white] appearance, [red] increase, and [black] near-attainment are stated.[50] If you do not relate it to mantra, you state: "every type of distorted mind, from not respecting my virtuous spiritual friend" without adding "appearance, increase, and so on," [but adding] "[… up to] grasping at the signs of the two selves." When related to mantra [88] it means, "Please bless me to quickly stop the subtle knowledge obscurations that are the dualistic appearances of appearance, increase, and attainment."

> **Please bless me to easily generate every type of undistorted mind, from respecting my virtuous spiritual friend up to generating nonlearner union. Please bless me to fully pacify all internal and external obstacles.**

In brief, it means, (1) "Please bless me to fully pacify all counter states," (2) "Please bless me to easily generate all conducive conditions," and (3) "Please bless me that no obstacles arise for that [purpose]." Since Dharma practitioners have no greater purpose than these three, they are called "the three great purposes."

Idaṃ gururatna maṇḍalakaṃ niryātayāmi.

This means "I offer (*niryātayāmi*) this (*idaṃ*) maṇḍala (*maṇḍalakaṃ*), o precious guru (*gururatna*)."

If you are accumulating maṇḍalas, at this point you should follow the tradition that counts them by combining a short maṇḍala with every [recitation] of the verse for refuge and bodhicitta.

If you are accumulating preliminary practices, then recite, "I go for refuge until I am enlightened . . ." and offer a maṇḍala. When offering the short maṇḍala, recite, "This ground anointed with perfume . . . ," and along with that recite the verse for refuge and bodhicitta 100,000 times. This completes the presentation of both the visualization of the merit field and the maṇḍala offering as part of offering the seven-limb prayer. [89]

4. Requesting the Four Empowerments as a Blessing

3. Reciting prayers and requesting blessings
   1. Requesting the blessing of the four empowerments
   2. Requesting the blessing of special wisdom that is the enlightened activity of transmission
   3. Requesting the blessing of the entire path, collectively

At the crown of the great lama Tsongkhapa are the three: the external, internal, and secret forms of Mañjuśrī; at his throat are the three: the external, internal, and secret forms of Avalokiteśvara; at his heart are the three: the external, internal, and secret forms of Vajrapāṇi, visualized as the three levels of being.

In the center of the central channel at the crown of Jé Rinpoché is the external form of Mañjuśrī. His body is orange in color, his right hand brandishes a sword, and his left holds the stem of an utpala flower at his heart, the petals of which are open at the level of his ear and support a text. This Arapatsana[51] form of Mañjuśrī is the main Mañjuśrī, while the internal and secret forms of Mañjuśrī may have different hand symbols. In this case, at the heart of orange Mañjuśrī as the *external form* is orange Mañjuśrī as the *internal form*, holding a text and a sword and embracing his consort Sarasvatī, who is similar to him and adorned with ornaments of jewels and bones. At his heart is red Mañjuśrī as the *secret form*, [90] holding a vajra and bell and embracing his consort, red Sarasvatī, similar to him and holding a knife and skullcup. These are the three levels of being.

At the throat of Jé Rinpoché is Avalokiteśvara as the *external form* in his well-known aspect, possessing four arms. The first two hands are joined in prayer at the heart, the second right hand holds a crystal mala, while the second left hand holds a lotus. At his heart is Vajradharma as the *internal form*, with left hand extended holding the stem of a lotus and right hand holding a lotus that blossoms at his heart. At his heart is Gyalwa Gyatso as the *secret form*, whose body is white with a red hue, his right hand counts [mantras on] a pearl rosary and his left holds an utpala flower. He stands upright with his right leg slightly bent and his left leg extended, embracing his consort. His consort is Secret Wisdom ḍākinī, whose white body embraces the male deity, her right hand playing a dāmaru[52] and left holding a skull filled with blood. They are both adorned with ornaments of jewels and bones.

At the heart of Jé Rinpoché is Vajrapāṇi as the *external form*, blue in color, in his well-known aspect, standing. At his heart is fierce Vajrapāṇi, [the *internal form*,] accompanied by five garuḍas similar to the external form, with garuḍas at his crown, his throat, his heart, his navel, and secret place. The five garuḍas are by nature the five buddha families. Their five right hands hold the implements of the five buddha families: a wheel, [91] lotus, vajra, jewel, and sword. Their left hands hold serpents. He stands erect in Vajrapāṇi's normal stance, with one leg slightly extended and one bent. At his heart is Vajrapāṇi Mahācakra, [the *secret form*,] with three faces and six arms. His upper two hands hold a vajra and form a threatening mudrā, and his second two embrace his consort Kāntamatī while clapping palms. His lower two hands hold two serpents mid-body, their tails pinned under his feet and their heads being devoured in his mouth. He wears a lower garment of tiger skin and stands majestically, trampling Brahmā and Indra beneath his feet. This [presentation] is found in the liturgy compiled by Kyabjé Trijang Rinpoché.

At [Jé Rinpoché's] crown are the external, internal, and secret forms of Mañjuśrī, the nature of vajra body; at his throat are the external, internal, and secret forms of Avalokiteśvara, the nature of vajra speech; and at his heart are the external, internal, and secret forms of Vajrapāṇi, the nature of vajra mind. The three levels of being [the external, internal, and secret forms for each deity] are visualized with the latter at the heart of the former.

1. Making Requests to One Whose Illumination Equals External [Space][53]

There are three ways to make requests: (1) making requests to one whose illumination equals external [space], [92] (2) making requests to one who possesses internal qualities, and (3) making requests to one who is indivisible in nature from the secret special deity.

First, the means of making requests to one whose illumination equals external [space]:

Reflect:

> **There are none among the sons and daughters of the conquerors who are equal to Avalokiteśvara in compassion, Mañjuśrī in wisdom, and Vajrapāṇi in power. Like this example, there are none among the scholars of this Land of Snows who equal the great Jé Rinpoché as a scholar of all branches of knowledge and science. Please bless me to become like you, a scholar of all branches of knowledge and science.**

Mañjuśrī is the embodiment of the realization of all the conquerors of the ten directions, Avalokiteśvara is the embodiment of their compassion, and the Secret Lord [Vajrapāṇi] is the embodiment of their power.[54] It is no exaggeration to state that there are none who equal the great Jé Rinpoché as a scholar of all branches of knowledge and science. This is similar to the statement made by the Great Fifth Dalai Lama,[55] who said that there are none who equal Jé Rinpoché in his presentation of the nature of reality in sūtra and tantra and all branches of knowledge and science. Although indeed there are scholars who match his scholarship in individual topics, there are none who can match his comprehensive scholarship. For example, though the Kadampa followers of Jowo Jé [Atiśa] may equal him in terms of compassion and bodhicitta, [93] there are none [among his followers] who can match him in secret mantra and the sciences. Thus, although there are some who match him in specific topics, there are none who can match him in every respect. Therefore you make the request: "Please bless me to become like you, a scholar of all branches of knowledge and science."

Then pray to Jé Rinpoché, reciting the Miktsema praise:

Avalokiteśvara, great treasure of nonreifying compassion,
Mañjuśrī, master of stainless wisdom,
Secret Lord, destroyer of hordes of māras,
Tsongkhapa, crown jewel of scholars of the Land of Snows,
Losang Drakpa, I make requests at your feet. ||9||

The meaning of the Miktsema praise is that [Jé Rinpoché] embodies the wisdom of Mañjuśrī. Some say that the knowledge of Mañjuśrī is embodied in syllables. It is said that in Kumbum[56] a tree grew from the ground where Jé Rinpoché's umbilical blood touched the earth, and many syllables and images of Victor Siṃhanāda appeared on its leaves. Others say that it is embodied in the melody of the prayer and the words that are the Miktsema praise. Others say that it is embodied in the sacred texts (*poti*) [94] such as the *Great Exposition of the Stages of the Path*, since it exists as speech. These embody the wisdom of Venerable Mañjuśrī.

To ordinary appearance, Jé Rinpoché himself offered this praise to Rendawa:[57]

Avalokiteśvara, great treasure of nonreifying compassion,
Mañjuśrī, master of stainless wisdom,
Secret Lord, destroyer of hordes of māras,
Rendawa, crown jewel of scholars of the Land of Snows,
Shönu Lodrö, I make requests at your feet.

When it was offered, Jé Rendawa said, "I am unworthy to receive this praise, but you are worthy," and he returned [the praise] to [Jé Rinpoché, adding], "Tsongkhapa, crown jewel of scholars in the Land of Snows, Losang Drakpa, I make requests at your feet." This means that [the verse] embodies the wisdom of Manjusri, and since to the minds of ordinary beings two holy beings offered this back and forth between them, it is said to be a unique prayer imbued with great blessings. Avalokiteśvara, Mañjuśrī, and Vajrapāṇi embody the compassion, wisdom, and power of all the conquerors of the ten directions. Therefore when you pray to them by reciting the Miktsema praise, you are praying to all the conquerors of the ten directions.

> **Please bless me to become like you,**
> **a scholar endowed with all scriptural qualities.**

> **By making such requests,** [95] **a limitless stream of white nectar-light flows from the body of Mañjuśrī at [Jé Rinpoché's] crown, entering the crowns of myself and all mother sentient beings.**

By visualizing the external, internal, and secret forms of Mañjuśrī at his crown, a limitless stream of white light and nectar flows from the body of Mañjuśrī. Visualize that all sentient beings surround you.

> **It cleanses and purifies negativities, obscurations, and their imprints accumulated through our bodies from beginningless time.**

This cleanses and purifies negativities and obscurations such as killing and stealing and their imprints.

I obtain the vase empowerment, I am authorized to meditate on the path of the generation stage, and special potent imprints to accomplish the resultant emanation body are established [in my mindstream].

Previously, we requested the four empowerments as a blessing. But now we do not receive the four empowerments through requesting them as a blessing, since the four actual empowerments must be obtained in relation to a maṇḍala.

Again recite:

Avalokiteśvara, great treasure of nonreifying compassion,
Mañjuśrī, master of stainless wisdom,
Secret Lord, destroyer of hordes of māras,
Tsongkhapa, crown jewel of scholars of the Land of Snows,
Losang Drakpa, I make requests at your feet.
Please bless me to become like you,
a scholar endowed with all scriptural qualities. [96]
I am blessed by the secret form of Mañjuśrī dissolving into me.

Then recite again the Miktsema praise [and the request]:

Again recite:

Avalokiteśvara, great treasure of nonreifying compassion,
Mañjuśrī, master of stainless wisdom,
Secret Lord, destroyer of hordes of māras,
Tsongkhapa, crown jewel of scholars of the Land of Snows,

Losang Drakpa, I make requests at your feet.
Please bless me to become like you,
a scholar endowed with all scriptural qualities.
I am blessed by the internal form of Mañjuśrī dissolving into me.

Reflect that you have been blessed.

Again make requests, as before:

Avalokiteśvara, great treasure of nonreifying compassion,
Mañjuśrī, master of stainless wisdom,
Secret Lord, destroyer of hordes of māras,
Tsongkhapa, crown jewel of scholars of the Land of Snows,
Losang Drakpa, I make requests at your feet.
Please bless me to become like you,
a scholar endowed with all scriptural qualities.
I am blessed by the external form of Mañjuśrī dissolving into me.

This is known as "making requests to one whose illumination equals external [space]" because it is making requests to Jé Rinpoché, who possesses no equal.

2. Making Requests to One Who Possesses Those Internal Qualities

Reflect:

However much compassion is possessed by Avalokiteśvara, however much wisdom is possessed by Mañjuśrī,

> **and however much power is possessed by the Secret Lord, Jé Rinpoché also possesses just those qualities. Please bless me to become like you, one endowed with realization, compassion, and power.**

Jé Rinpoché himself was the emanation of the protectors of the three lineages. And through examining the dreams of his mother and father, it can be established that he was the emanation of the protectors of the three lineages. When he was conceived, his mother dreamed that Avalokiteśvara [97] dissolved into her crown. When she was about to give birth, she dreamed that many people arrived to meet Lord Avalokiteśvara and asked where he was, and at that point a door opened in her heart and Avalokiteśvara emerged, greeting many people. Through these dreams it is established that he was an emanation of Avalokiteśvara. In terms of being Vajrapāṇi, when he was conceived, his father dreamt of a golden vajra that announced that it had been ejected from the pure land of Vajrapāṇi, and when it entered the womb it dissolved into the mother. The father thought that his wife must be pregnant with a very powerful child, and in reality he was the emanation of Vajrapāṇi. It is also clearly established by many types of scripture and reasoning that he was the emanation of Mañjuśrī. Thus he was an emanation of the three lineage protectors.

Recite:

> **Avalokiteśvara, great treasure of nonreifying compassion,**
> **Mañjuśrī, master of stainless wisdom,**
> **Secret Lord, destroyer of hordes of māras,**
> **Tsongkhapa, crown jewel of scholars of the Land of Snows,**

Losang Drakpa, I make requests at your feet.
Please bless me to become like you,
a siddha endowed with all qualities of realization.

By making such requests, a limitless stream of red nectar-light flows [98] from [the external, internal, and secret forms of] Avalokiteśvara at my guru's throat.

Previously, white nectar-light, the nature of vajra body, flowed from the external, inner, and secret form of Mañjuśrī. Now red nectar-light, the nature of vajra speech, flows:

It enters the throats of myself and all mother sentient beings, cleansing and purifying negativities, obscurations, and their imprints accumulated from beginningless time through our speech. I obtain the secret empowerment, I am authorized to meditate on the path of the illusory body, and special potent imprints to accomplish the resultant enjoyment body are established [in my mindstream].

Again recite:

Avalokiteśvara, great treasure of nonreifying compassion,
Mañjuśrī, master of stainless wisdom,
Secret Lord, destroyer of hordes of māras,
Tsongkhapa, crown jewel of scholars of the Land of Snows,
Losang Drakpa, I make requests at your feet.
Please bless me to become like yourself,
a siddha endowed with all qualities of realization.
I am blessed by Gyalwa Gyatso, the secret form of Avalokiteśvara, dissolving into me.

From among the external, internal, and secret forms of Avalokiteśvara, Gyalwa Gyatso, who is the secret form, dissolves into me.

Again recite:

Avalokiteśvara, great treasure of nonreifying compassion,
Mañjuśrī, master of stainless wisdom,
Secret Lord, destroyer of hordes of māras, [99]
Tsongkhapa, crown jewel of scholars of the Land of Snows,
Losang Drakpa, I make requests at your feet.
Please bless me to become like yourself,
a siddha endowed with all qualities of realization.
I am blessed by Vajradharma, the internal form of Avalokiteśvara, dissolving into me.

And making this prayer, I am blessed by Vajradharma dissolving into me.

Again recite:

Avalokiteśvara, great treasure of nonreifying compassion,
Mañjuśrī, master of stainless wisdom,
Secret Lord, destroyer of hordes of māras,
Tsongkhapa, crown jewel of scholars of the Land of Snows,
Losang Drakpa, I make requests at your feet.
Please bless me to become like yourself,
a siddha endowed with all qualities of realization.
I am blessed by four-armed Avalokiteśvara, the external form of Avalokiteśvara, dissolving into me.

This is making requests to one who possesses those internal qualities.

3. Making Requests to One Who is Indivisible in Nature from the Secret Special Deity

Reflect:

The supreme ārya protectors of the three lineages are the embodiment of the realization, compassion, and power of all the conquerors of the ten directions, appearing as deities. Since Jé Rinpoché is the single embodiment of these [100] three, please bless me to become like yourself, the single embodiment of the three protectors.

Recite:

Avalokiteśvara, great treasure of nonreifying compassion,
Mañjuśrī, master of stainless wisdom,
Secret Lord, destroyer of hordes of māras,
Tsongkhapa, crown jewel of scholars of the Land of Snows,
Losang Drakpa, I make requests at your feet.
Please bless me to become like you,
the vajra body of the three secret states, the nature of the three lineages.

By making this request:

A limitless stream of blue nectar-light flows from Vajrapāṇi at my guru's heart, entering the hearts of myself and all mother sentient beings. It cleanses and purifies

negativities, obscurations, and their imprints accumulated from beginningless time through our minds. I obtain the wisdom empowerment, I am authorized to meditate on the path of clear-light mahāmudrā, and special potent imprints to accomplish the [101] resultant Dharma body are established [in my mindstream].

Again recite:

Avalokiteśvara, great treasure of nonreifying compassion,
Mañjuśrī, master of stainless wisdom,
Secret Lord, destroyer of hordes of māras,
Tsongkhapa, crown jewel of scholars of the Land of Snows,
Losang Drakpa, I make requests at your feet.
Please bless me to become like yourself,
the vajra body of the three secret states, the nature of the three lineages.
I am blessed by the secret form of Vajrapāṇi Mahācakra dissolving into me.

This refers to the secret form, from among the external, inner, and secret forms of Vajrapāṇi.

Again recite:

Avalokiteśvara, great treasure of nonreifying compassion,
Mañjuśrī, master of stainless wisdom,
Secret Lord, destroyer of hordes of māras,
Tsongkhapa, crown jewel of scholars of the Land of Snows,
Losang Drakpa, I make requests at your feet.
Please bless me to become like yourself,

the vajra body of the three secret states, the nature of the three lineages.
I am blessed by the internal form of Vajrapāṇi, with the five fierce garuḍas, dissolving into me.

Again recite:

Avalokiteśvara, great treasure of nonreifying compassion,
Mañjuśrī, master of stainless wisdom,
Secret Lord, destroyer of hordes of māras,
Tsongkhapa, crown jewel of scholars of the Land of Snows, [102]
Losang Drakpa, I make requests at your feet.
Please bless me to become like yourself,
the vajra body of the three secret states, the nature of the three lineages.
I am blessed by the external form of Vajrapāṇi, blue in color, dissolving into me.

This is making requests to one who is indivisible in nature from the secret special deity.

Requesting the fourth empowerment as a blessing

Next:

May the root and lineage gurus, and in particular Guru Mañjunātha and his two spiritual sons, bless me and all mother sentient beings to generate in our mindstreams all excellent qualities of abandonment and realization, effortlessly and with ease.

While reflecting on this, recite the words of the prayer.

Again, make requests by reciting the nine rounds of the Ensa lineage:

Munīndra Vajradhāra, source of all siddhis,
Avalokiteśvara, great treasure of nonreifying compassion,
Mañjuśrī, master of stainless wisdom,
Secret Lord, destroyer of hordes of māras,
Losang Drakpa, crown jewel of scholars of the Land of Snows,
Guru Buddha, who encompasses all three refuges,
I make requests to you respectfully through my three doors:
Please mature myself and others and bless us to attain liberation;
please grant us supreme and common siddhis.

If you wish to recite the nine-line Miktsema praise from the lineage of Gyalwa Ensapa,[58] then do so here. It is said that the special deity of each guru should be added. [103] Longdol Lama[59] made prayers through inserting the name of Tārā, since he took Tārā as his main yidam.

Or make requests by reciting the nine-line praise of the Ségyü lineage, whatever is appropriate:

Sage Bhagavān, lord of the teachings,
Vajradhāra, sixth sovereign lord pervading the hundred lineages,
Avalokiteśvara, great treasure of nonreifying compassion,

Mañjuśrī, master of stainless wisdom,
Secret Lord, destroyer of hordes of māras,
Tsongkhapa, crown jewel of scholars of the Land of Snows,
Losang Drakpa, I make requests at your feet.
Please bless me to become like yourself
through your body, speech, and mind entering my body, speech, and mind.

From among the Ensapa lineage and the lineage derived from Sé Dorjé Chang, this is the nine-line Miktsema praise of the Ségyü lineage.[60]

Nectar and light of five colors simultaneously flows from the five sites of Jé Rinpoché and his two spiritual sons.

The seed syllables of the five buddha lineages—OṂ, ĀḤ, HŪṂ, SVĀ, and HĀ—exist at his crown, throat, heart, navel, and secret place. White nectar flows from his crown, red nectar from his throat, blue nectar from his heart, yellow nectar from his navel, and green nectar from his secret place. Ratnasambhava is at his navel. Also, five-colored light-nectar flows from all sites.

It simultaneously dissolves into the five sites of myself and all mother sentient beings. [104]

White nectar flows from their crowns and dissolves into our crowns, red nectar flows from their throats and dissolves into our throats, blue nectar flows from their hearts and dissolves into our hearts, yellow nectar flows from their navels and dissolves into our navels, and green nectar flows from their secret places and dissolves into our secret places, simultaneously.

> **The bodies of myself and all mother sentient beings are filled [with nectar]. This simultaneously purifies negativities, obscurations, and their imprints accumulated through my body, speech, and mind.**

Previously, during the vase, secret, and wisdom empowerments, you visualized that negativities accumulated by your body, speech, and mind were purified separately. Here you purify negativities, obscurations, and their imprints accumulated by your body, speech, and mind simultaneously.

> **I obtain the fourth empowerment [the precious word empowerment]. I am authorized to meditate on the path of union, and I become a fortunate being who will actualize the resultant state of union, the body of Vajradhāra.**

Thus you establish this capacity.

> *Next:*

> **Replicas separate from the bodies of Jé Rinpoché and his two spiritual sons and dissolve into me. My body, speech, and mind become indivisible in nature from the body, speech, and mind of the great Guru Jé Tsongkhapa and his two spiritual sons.**

The words "replicas separate from the bodies of Jé Rinpoché and his two spiritual sons and dissolve into . . . my body, speech, and mind" do not refer to your coarse body, speech, [105] and mind. Such coarse aggregates are to be discarded. Instead, they dissolve into the subtle body, speech, and mind of the fundamental wind and mind that exist from beginningless time, and proceed to the ground of buddhahood. You should reflect that they become indivisible in nature.

> ***They are the holder of the jewel treasure of the body, the sun illuminating speech, and the holder of the secret treasure of mind. Instructions on the external, internal, and secret modes of practice are precisely formulated in a single, ultimate, secret instruction.***

Previously, you made requests to bless your body by means of external, internal, and secret Mañjuśrī. He is the holder of the jewel treasure of the body. You made requests to Avalokiteśvara at his throat to bless your speech. He is the sun illuminating speech. You made requests to bless your heart through the external, inner, and secret Vajrapāṇi at his heart. He is the holder of the secret treasure of mind. Visualize that you obtain blessing from "external, internal, and secret modes of practice" [pertaining to] external, internal, and secret Mañjuśrī; external, internal, and secret Vajrapāṇi; [and external, internal, and secret Avalokiteśvara.]

They are "precisely formulated in a single, ultimate, secret instruction" since this is secret instruction precisely formulated at this time, like being granted secret instruction on the use of a hidden vajra.

5. Requesting the Blessing of Special Wisdom

2. *Requesting the blessing of special wisdom, which properly differentiates dharmas, that is the enlightened activity of transmission*

BECAUSE MAÑJUŚRĪ is the deity of wisdom, [106] there are many practices for establishing wisdom related to Mañjuśrī. Request such blessings:

> **At the heart of Jé Rinpoché is Mañjughoṣa with a youthful orange body.**
> **At his heart is a blue syllable HŪṂ marked with the syllable MAṂ.**

Similar to the previous visualization of the merit field, at the heart of Jé Rinpoché is the commitment being Mañjuśrī, and at his heart is Vajradhāra. At [Vajradhāra's] heart the syllable HŪṂ is generated. The blue syllable HŪṂ at the heart of Venerable Mañjuśrī is marked with MAṂ, since MAṂ exists within the dot (*anusvāra*) of the blue syllable HŪṂ. MAṂ is the first syllable of "mati" from Jé Rinpoché's name in Sanskrit, "Sumati" (or "Losang" in Tibetan). The letter MA is also marked with a drop (*bindu*). Therefore, when you state, "At his heart is a blue syllable HŪṂ marked with the syllable MAṂ," visualize that inside the drop of the syllable HŪṂ is the letter MA marked with a drop.

> ***The aspect of Venerable [Mañjuśrī]'s body that you prefer at his heart should accord with your specific requirement.***

The statement that at the heart of Jé Rinpoché is the youthful orange body of Mañjughoṣa was made in accordance with a specific requirement. Thus, if your main practice is *pacification*, his body should be white; if it is *increase*, his body should be yellow; if it is *power*, his body should be red; and if it is *wrath*, his body should be black. Therefore you may change the color to match your specific requirement. Regarding the syllable MAṂ within the drop of the syllable HŪṂ: [107]

> ***It is a unique instruction revealed in the "Mañjuśrī Root Tantra" to visualize at his heart a seed syllable HŪṂ marked with MAṂ.***

When the *Mañjuśrī Root Tantra* reveals the prediction of Jé Rinpoché, it states:

> The first letter of this intelligent being's [name] is MA.[61]

When it reveals the name of Jé Rinpoché (Blo bzang grags pa, Sumati kīrti), it predicts MA to be the first letter of his name: Mati [or Sumati]. Thus HŪṂ is visualized as marked with MAṂ. Then requests are made to him:

Pray:

> **Please increase my wisdom of study, contemplation, and meditation.**
> **Please increase my wisdom of explanation, debate, and composition.**
> **Please bestow common and supreme siddhis.**
> **Please bless me to quickly become like you.**

You request the supreme siddhi that is the transcendent siddhi and the common siddhis that are mundane siddhis, such as the eight great attainments[62] and siddhis of pacification, increase, power, and wrath. You also request to be blessed to attain the state of Jé Rinpoché quickly.

Now you apply this to highest mantra:

> **May the pristine wisdom of innate great bliss arise.**
> **May the stains of mistaken grasping at entities be removed.**
> **May my mind sever the web of doubt.**
> **Please bless me to quickly become like you.**

The essence of the path of highest yoga tantra is the pristine wisdom of great bliss and the illusory body. The most profound feature of mantra is the generation of innate great bliss, and then generating that innate great bliss in the nature of the mind that realizes emptiness. And you necessarily progress on the grounds and paths [of highest yoga tantra] by means of this. [108]

The words "May the stains of mistaken grasping at entities be removed" are a prayer to remove the stains of ordinary appearance and conception through understanding [the process of] grasping at entities as truly existent. The words "May my mind sever the web of doubt" indicate that you pray that all the subtle stains of [white] appearance, [red] increase, and [black] near-attainment be eliminated. You also pray to sever the web of doubt that obstructs you from directly realizing all objects of knowledge simultaneously, as they are.

Requesting the blessing of special wisdom

Now the focal objects of the practice cycle for accomplishing wisdom are taught in accordance with the root advice given by Venerable Mañjuśrī to Jé Rinpoché.

> ***As the venerable solitary father himself said:***
>
> ***Impurity is to be washed away and ignorance removed.***
> ***The body [establishes] vast wisdom, speech [establishes] clear [wisdom],***
> ***the seed [establishes] swift [wisdom], and hand symbols [establish] profound [wisdom].***
> ***Explanation, debate, and composition are established by texts, swords, and texts with swords.***

First, impurity is an object to be washed away, and [109] ignorance is an object to be removed. Establish vast wisdom by means of the body, establish clear [wisdom] by means of speech, establish swift [wisdom] by means of the seed, and establish profound [wisdom] by means of hand symbols. The wisdom of explanation is established by means of nectar, in just that form, flowing from the text one seeks to explain. The wisdom of debate is established by means of the wheel of swords when the occasion arises to debate others. The wisdom of composition is established through meditating on the hand symbols, texts, and swords in the aspect of nectar, followed by emitting and absorbing light. From this point on, the root text clearly states the practice cycle for accomplishing wisdom.

First, wash away impurities:

By making requests to the external, internal, and secret [forms] in that way,
from the hearts of Jé Rinpoché and his two spiritual sons
white light radiates as hollow tubes,
which merge as one and enters my crown.

By making requests to one whose illumination equals external [space], to one who possesses internal qualities, and to one who is indivisible in nature from the secret special deity, then, from the hearts of the three—Jé Rinpoché and his two spiritual sons—radiant white light flows within hollow tubes. When the light first radiates from their hearts, there are three streams, but then quickly they merge as one, [110] and the tip of that tube enters your crown aperture.

Visualize:

White nectar the color of milk flows through the open tube of white light, washing away every stain, illness, spirit harm, negativity, obscuration, and impurity, and my body becomes limpid and clear like crystal.

A stream of white nectar, the color of milk, flows through the tube, entering your crown aperture and filling your body. It purifies all stains accumulated from beginningless time, and your body becomes limpid and clear, like a crystal vase.

Recite the five-line Miktsema praise as many times as possible:

Avalokiteśvara, great treasure of nonreifying compassion,
Mañjuśrī, master of stainless wisdom,
Secret Lord, destroyer of hordes of māras,
Tsongkhapa, crown jewel of scholars of the Land of Snows,
Losang Drakpa, I make requests at your feet.

Regarding the five-line Miktsema praise, [in reality] there is no need to separately recite the line of the Secret Lord since Jé Rinpoché himself is the Secret Lord, and if useful you may [reduce the praise] to four lines. But as a practice establishing wisdom, you first focus on the five-line praise, and at that time you focus on eliminating the darkness of impurity and the darkness of ignorance.

1. Vast Wisdom

1. Establishing vast wisdom by means of the body

White nectar the color of milk washes away all stains of impurity, and you reflect that your body now has the nature of limpid and clear light. In the context of establishing vast [111] wisdom:

Then my body is filled with vast wisdom
in the aspect of orange nectar.

Every atom of nectar has the aspect of
Venerable Mañjuśrī clearly radiating light.

The vast wisdom in the mindstreams of Jé Rinpoché and his two spiritual sons arises in the aspect of orange nectar-light and flows in a stream of orange nectar-light through the open tube previously [established]. It enters your crown [aperture] and nectar fills your body. This is called "establishing vast wisdom by means of the body."

All the atoms of nectar filling your body are visualized as bodies of Venerable Mañjuśrī, limitless in number and size. From this nectar visualized as Mañjuśrī, which fills your body, countless rays of light radiate.

The vast wisdom of the conquerors of the ten directions, their sons
and daughters, dissolves into me in the form of deities, filling my body.
Please bless me to obtain a vast wave of wisdom
that unobstructedly discerns the meaning of myriad scriptures.

While visualizing this, recite the Miktsema praise.

[Such wisdom] dissolves into your body in the aspect of Venerable Mañjuśrī. You establish vast wisdom by visualizing that your body is filled with bodies of Venerable Mañjuśrī, limitless in number and size. In this context, you visualize that you obtain such wisdom through reciting the Miktsema praise. [112] Reflect that you have obtained a vast wave of wisdom that is unobstructed, regardless of the meaning of the scripture.

2. Clear Wisdom

2. Establishing clear wisdom by means of speech

Then my body is filled with clear wisdom
in the aspect of orange nectar.
Every atom of nectar has the aspect of
Arapatsana[63] clearly radiating light.

The clear wisdom of the conquerors of the ten directions,
their sons
and daughters, dissolves into me as dhāraṇī mantras,
filling my body.
Please bless me to obtain clear wisdom
that discerns subtle difficult points without confusing them.

While visualizing this, recite the Miktsema praise.

Due to your strong devotion to Jé Rinpoché and his two spiritual sons, the clear wisdom of their three minds, which is clear realization, arises in the aspect of orange nectar-light and fills your body. Every atom of the nectar that has filled your body clearly appears in the aspect of the Arapatsana mantra. Countless rays of light radiate from the syllables OṂ A RA PA TSA NA DHĪḤ. All the clear wisdom of the conquerors of the ten directions and their sons and daughters arises in the aspect of countless Arapatsana mantras that fill your body.

Wisdom capable of discerning the meaning of any scripture you read is called [113] "vast wisdom." Wisdom capable of discerning subtle and extremely subtle difficult points without confusing them is called "clear wisdom." Reflect that you have attained such clear wisdom.

3. Swift Wisdom

3. Establishing swift wisdom by means of seed [syllables]

Then my body is filled with swift wisdom
in the aspect of orange nectar.
Every atom of nectar has the aspect of
orange DHĪḤ syllables clearly radiating light.

The swift wisdom of the conquerors of the ten directions, their sons
and daughters, dissolves into me as seed [syllables], filling my body.
Please bless me to obtain swift wisdom
that quickly eliminates misunderstanding, wrong conception, and doubt.

While visualizing this, recite the Miktsema praise.

The swift wisdom in the mindstreams of Jé Rinpoché and his two spiritual sons arises in the aspect of orange nectar-light and fills your body. Every atom of the nectar that fills your body clearly appears as the orange syllable DHĪḤ. They radiate countless rays of light, and all swift wisdom of the conquerors of the ten directions and their sons and daughters arises in the aspect of countless DHĪḤ syllables. They dissolve into you, filling your body.

Reflect you are blessed to obtain the swift wisdom [114] that quickly eliminates misunderstanding, misconception, and all doubt, as you recite Miktsema.

Reflect that you have obtained such blessings, and that this is called "the swift seed."

4. Profound Wisdom

4. Establishing profound wisdom by means of hand symbols

Then my body is filled with profound wisdom
in the aspect of orange nectar.
Every atom of nectar has the aspect of
texts and swords clearly radiating light.

The profound wisdom of the conquerors of the ten directions, their sons
and daughters, dissolves into me as hand symbols, filling my body.
Please bless me to obtain profound wisdom
that is inexhaustible and discerns the meaning of texts.

While visualizing this, recite the Miktsema praise.

The profound wisdom in the mindstreams of Jé Rinpoché and his two spiritual sons arises in the aspect of orange nectar-light, which fills your body. Atoms of nectar clearly appear as the hand symbols of Jé Rinpoché: a text proclaiming the entire path and a sword that eliminates ignorance. Each atom of nectar radiates rays of light that fill your body. Their radiance pervades the ten directions, and all the profound wisdom of the conquerors of the ten directors and their sons and daughters arises in the aspect of countless swords and texts. They dissolve into you and fill your body. [115]

Wisdom discerning the meaning of texts that is exhaustible is [wisdom] that comes to an end. When you think about the meaning of a text, at first you produce a minimum level of wisdom, but then gradually that wisdom declines and fades. This is called "the exhaustion of wisdom." But wisdom that is not like that—which is capable of extracting many different levels of understanding of each point of the text—is called "profound wisdom."

Reflect that you have obtained such profound wisdom. The instruction "Explanation, debate, and composition are established by texts, swords, and texts with swords" [given earlier] means that the wisdom of explanation is established by [visualizing] texts, the wisdom of debate is established by [visualizing wheels of] swords, and the wisdom of composition is established by [visualizing] texts and swords.

5. Wisdom of Explanation

5. Establishing the wisdom of explanation by means of texts

Then my body is filled with the wisdom of explanation
in the aspect of orange nectar.
Every atom of nectar has the aspect of
explanatory texts clearly radiating light.

The profound wisdom of the conquerors of the ten
directions, their sons
and daughters, dissolves into me as texts, filling my body.

Please bless me to obtain the wisdom of explanation that bestows supreme certainty of all words and meaning.

While visualizing this, recite the Miktsema praise.

The fifth is the wisdom of explanation. If you seek to establish the wisdom of explanation by means of texts, then again you make strong requests. Due to that, the wisdom of explanation of Jé Rinpoché and his two spiritual sons arises in the aspect of limitless nectar-light. The atoms of nectar that fill your body [116] are texts that are to be explained in this context. Students should visualize them in the aspect of whichever text they are studying, such as Vinaya, Abhidharma, Madhyamaka, or Prajñāpāramitā. Visualize that they radiate light, and that the wisdom of explanation of the conquerors and their sons and daughters in the ten directions arises in the aspect of separate texts. They dissolve into you, filling your body.

Reflect that the wisdom of explanation that bestows supreme certainty of all words and meaning has been obtained. Recite the Miktsema praise.

6. Wisdom of Debate

6. Establishing the wisdom of debate by means of wheels of swords

Again my body is filled with the wisdom of debate
arising in the aspect of orange nectar.
Every atom of nectar has the aspect of
a wheel of swords clearly radiating light.

The profound wisdom of the conquerors of the ten directions, their sons
and daughters, dissolves into me as swords, filling my body.
Please bless me to obtain the wisdom of debate
that is never overcome by the eloquence of evil adversaries.

While visualizing this, recite the Miktsema praise.

The wisdom of debate in the mindstreams of Jé Rinpoché and his two spiritual sons arises in the aspect of orange nectar-light and fills your body. The atoms of nectar that fill your body clearly appear as wheels of swords. They radiate light, [117] and all the wisdom of debate of the conquerors and their sons and daughters in the ten directors arises in the aspect of wheels of swords. They dissolve into you and fill your body.

Request blessings to obtain the wisdom of debate that can absolutely never be overcome by an opponent's arguments.

Due to this, you visualize the wheel of swords when you debate non-Buddhists. This is also the method of focusing on severing the tongues of opponents so that you are never overcome by the arguments of opponents.

7. Wisdom of Composition

7. Establishing the wisdom of composition by means of both

Since it is said, "Explanation, debate, and composition are established by texts, swords, and texts with swords," the wisdom of debate is established by wheels of swords. Here "establishing the wisdom of composition by means of both" means that the wisdom of composition is established by both texts and swords.

> **Again, my body is filled with the wisdom of composition**
> **arising in the aspect of orange nectar.**
> **The atoms of nectar have the aspect of**
> **texts and wheels clearly radiating light.**
>
> **The wisdom of composition of the conquerors of the ten directions,**
> **their sons and daughters, dissolves into me as texts and wheels, filling my body.**
> **Please bless me to obtain the wisdom of composition**
> **of excellent words and meaning that generate joy in the intelligent.**
>
> *While visualizing this, recite the Miktsema praise.* [118]

Visualize texts and wheels of swords. They radiate countless rays of light. All the wisdom of composition of the conquerors of the ten directions and their sons and daughters arises in the aspect of countless texts and wheels of swords. They dissolve into you and fill your body.

Jé Rinpoché spoke of "articulating speech with three valuable attributes." He stated that if the inner meaning is good, the words are less important, but if the meaning is excellent, and in addition the words ornament that meaning, [then] it is like a whitewashed house that appears whiter in the moonlight. Therefore you must also train in poetic speech. The words "excellent words and meaning" refer to excellent meaning, and if there are excellent words ornamenting [that meaning], they are capable of generating joy in the intelligent.

> ***Thus you should increase [your wisdom] through practicing these seven rounds of visualization.***

You should wash away impurities and remove ignorance and engage in the seven practices for establishing wisdom: the first four are vast, swift, clear, and profound wisdom, as well as the three wisdoms of explanation, debate, and composition. [119]

> ***Alternatively, you may take any object you desire as your main practice.***

For example, when it is important to establish the wisdom of composition, you may focus on that alone or make it your main practice.

> ***When I practiced for just a month with respect, faith, and clear visualization, I experienced definite increase in just that wisdom I sought to establish.***

[Pabongkha Rinpoché] Jé Dechen Nyingpo states that when he practiced for just a month with faith and respect in the qualities of Jé Rinpoché and a clear visualization of one of the focal objects previously explained, he "experienced definite increase in just that wisdom I sought to establish."

> ***You should recite the Miktsema praise as many times as you can according to the time you have available, without holding to a specific number of recitations in each session.***

When you have the time, you should recite the Miktsema praise as much as you can.

> ***Thus the focal objects for establishing wisdom have been properly explained.***

Venerable Mañjuśrī directly transmitted these focal objects for establishing wisdom to Jé Rinpoché, and these words were stated by Mañjuśrī. The focal objects for establishing wisdom can also be applied in conjunction with other special deities. [For example,] you can apply the focal objects for establishing wisdom in the context of Yamāntaka.

> ***Still,*** [120] ***there is different advice about how deities should be arranged, and endless variations of the lines recited in the Miktsema praise.***

There are many differences in the way the deities are arranged, the color of the deities, and their hand symbols. The special deity of each guru may be inserted [in the Miktsema praise], and previously it was said you may change the shape and color of the body of Mañjuśrī according to your need. Here they are included in the root words.

> ***Further, from statements such as "white for pacification, holding a white lotus; with the mudrā of supreme generosity, granting refuge," it seems there are countless ways to establish myriad activities.***

When primarily establishing peaceful activities in reliance upon Venerable Mañjuśrī, the deity has a white body, holds a white lotus, and demonstrates the mudrā of supreme generosity and granting refuge. When primarily establishing activities of increase, Mañjuśrī has a yellow body and holds a jewel and a vase. When primarily establishing activities of power, he has a red body and holds a hook and a lasso. When primarily establishing wrathful activities, he has a dark-blue body and holds a knife and a skullcup. The visualization can be adjusted according to the specific needs of the type of activity you practice.

> ***Since it is indescribable,*** [121] ***here you should understand it through the profound guidance of the oral transmission and the pleasing [instruction] of your guru. And you should come to understand any earlier instructions that were unclear by relying on your guru.***

It is indescribable because it would take a great mass of words to outline it. This is [the section on] establishing wisdom.

6. The Visualization for the Miktsema Praise

Explaining the specific stages of the visualization

> ***Now I will set out the specific stages of visualizations that are extremely secret and should be known orally. Further, there are five different stages of visualization in the five-line Miktsema praise:***

THIS PASSAGE STATES that these [visualizations] are extremely secret. "Known orally" means that they should be understood through oral instruction, for they are not written down. The specific stages of visualization will follow below. Jamyang Shepa[64] has stated that those who recite the Miktsema praise 100,000 times will certainly meet Jé Rinpoché directly, and it is this round of visualization that comprises the specific oral tradition. If you wish to practice according to the specific oral tradition, then there are five stages:

1. First Round of Visualization

The visualization in this context is explained below.

> ***When you recite, "Avalokiteśvara, great treasure of non-reifying compassion," the essential nature of the compassion of all the conquerors appears as Avalokiteśvara.***

In this context the great compassion and altruism of all the conquerors appears in the form of a deity, and that being is known as Ārya Avalokiteśvara. [122]

> ***Since the great Jé Rinpoché is also one in nature with [Avalokiteśvara], I praise him through reflecting that he is the embodiment of the compassion of all the conquerors.***

You should reflect on this when reciting the Miktsema praise in your normal practice.

> ***When you recite, "Mañjuśrī, master of stainless wisdom," [reflect that] the essential nature of the wisdom of all the conquerors is condensed in a single being, Venerable Mañjuśrī.***

Now you offer praise to Jé Rinpoché.

> ***Since Jé Rinpoché is Venerable Mañjuśrī in the aspect of a human being, I praise him through reflecting that he is the very essence of the wisdom of all the conquerors.***

In this context, if you desire to recite the four-line [instead of the five-line] Miktsema praise, there is no need to separately recite the name of the Secret Lord [Vajrapāṇi].

> ***When you recite, "Tsongkhapa, crown jewel of the scholars of the Land of Snows," the name of Vajrapāṇi does not need to be recited separately.***

Stating "Tsongkhapa, crown jewel of the scholars of the Land of Snows" fulfills this purpose.

> ***Since Jé Rinpoché himself is the Secret Lord, and since his name is equivalent to Vajrapāṇi's name, it has the specific attribute of fulfilling this purpose.***

Vajrapāṇi is called "Secret Lord," and since it is equivalent to the name of Vajrapāṇi that is applied to Jé Rinpoché, it has the specific attribute of fulfilling this purpose. Thus the four-line Miktsema praise may be recited [rather than the five-line one].

> ***Therefore, when the might, power, and potency of all the conquerors appears as a deity, it is Vajrapāṇi. Since Jé Rinpoché himself also has this nature,*** [123] ***I praise him by reflecting that he is the very might, power, and potency of all the conquerors.***

When you recite the Miktsema praise below, he should be praised by reflecting that his nature is that of the protectors of the three lineages.

> ***When you recite "Losang Drakpa, I make requests at your feet," place your mind undistractedly on the thought that the combined nature of the three lineages appears in the aspect of Jé Lama Tsongkhapa and his two spiritual sons in the space in front [of you].***

In this context there are different focal objects. When you pray to one who is the nature of the three lineages and state, "Losang Drakpa, I make requests at your feet," you place the mind single-pointedly on the thought that Jé Rinpoché and his two spiritual sons are the single nature of the three lineages.

> ***If your mind moves from that [image], change from the aspect of Jé Rinpoché to that of orange Mañjuśrī and place your mind on that.***

Change the image from Jé Rinpoché to that of Venerable Mañjuśrī with an orange-colored body, holding a text and a sword. Place your mind on that image.

> ***If your mind moves from that [image], change from the aspect of Mañjuśrī to that of your root guru and hold your mind on that [image].***

Then take that as your focal object, and remain there for some time. When the mind moves from that [image], change from the aspect of Mañjuśrī to that of your root guru [124] and hold your mind on that [image].

> ***If your mind moves from that [image], again change back to the aspect of Jé Rinpoché and touch your head to his lotus feet.***

Focus on the words "Losang Drakpa, I make requests at your feet." If your mind moves from Jé Rinpoché and his two spiritual sons, then change to the aspect of Mañjuśrī. If your mind moves from that [image], change to the aspect of your root guru. If your mind moves from that [image], change back to the aspect of Jé Rinpoché.

> ***When you recite "I make requests," you make a plea for your desired aim: "May all negativities and obscurations that I have accumulated from beginningless time be cleansed and purified."***

The focal object is different for each of the five rounds of visualization. In this, the first round of visualization, reflect that you make the entreaty: "Please cleanse and purify all negativities and obscurations accumulated by myself from beginningless time."

> ***When you recite ". . . at your feet," [visualize that] the three sites of Jé Rinpoché's body are marked with seed syllables and that Mañjuśrī resides at his heart.***

On Jé Rinpoché's crown is the syllable OṂ, at his throat is the syllable ĀḤ, and at his heart is the syllable HŪṂ. At his heart resides Mañjuśrī as previously visualized. Due to making such requests:

> ***He has a mind of compassion, a pleased expression, and his right hand holds the handle of his sword to his heart, with its tip placed at your crown aperture.*** [125]

When this request is made, Venerable Mañjuśrī displays a mind of compassion and a pleased expression. He holds the handle of his sword to his heart, and he places the tip of the sword at your crown aperture [the aperture of Brahmā].

> ***Within its internal pathway flows a stream of orange nectar-light with the nature of bodhicitta.***

Through the sword's internal pathway flows orange nectar-light with the nature of bodhicitta.

> ***It enters your crown aperture, filling [your body, down] to the soles of your feet. Every negativity and obscuration accumulated from beginningless time is expelled from all your sense doors and from every pore of your body.***

Visualize that all negativities and obscurations are expelled as a seething mass of black smoke and charcoal; all illness is expelled in the aspect of pus, blood, and lymph; and spirit harm and obstacles are expelled in the unattractive and unclean aspects of spiders, scorpions, and so on. They are expelled from such doors as the mouth, nostrils, lower orifices, and so forth.

> ***They sink seven levels below the surface of the earth and satisfy Yama, the Lord of Death, and obstructive spirits who take retribution.***

Yama, the Lord of Death, as well as māras who take retribution, abide with their mouths open with a hostile attitude toward you. Eighty thousand obstructive spirits [126] surround you and constantly think about when they can eat, coveting your life force. Your negativity, obscurations, and their imprints depart your body in countless unpleasant forms, such as spiders, scorpions, smoke, and charcoal. They enter the mouth of Yama, the Lord of Death, who abides seven levels below the earth with mouth open, and they enter the mouths of those coveting your life force. It satisfies Yama, the Lord of Death. Visualize that he closes his mouth and lies down, and that this is the supreme means of establishing long life. If there are obstructive spirits who harm you and bear hostility toward you, then this also satisfies all obstructive spirits. If there are spirits who take retribution or extract [karmic] debt, you should reflect that all retribution and debts have been repaid and that they are satisfied. You should reflect that they are pacified and tamed and that they bear no thought of harm or hostility. You should practice in this way.

> ***Your body becomes like solid crystal, free of any impurities, with the nature of limpid, clear light. Visualize that your mindstream becomes a suitable vessel.***

Reflect that your mindstream has been filled with the nectar of bodhicitta and that you become a vessel in which the realization of the path and its result may arise. This method of focusing on the purification of negativities, obscurations, and their imprints [127] is known as the first round of visualization.

> ***This is the first round of visualization of the Miktsema praise.***

This constitutes the first of the fivefold round of visualization of the specific oral tradition.

2. Second Round of Visualization

The words:

> **Avalokiteśvara, great treasure of nonreifying compassion,**
> **Mañjuśrī, master of stainless wisdom,**

> **[Secret Lord, destroyer of hordes of māras,]**
> **Tsongkhapa, crown jewel of scholars of the Land of Snows,**
> **Losang Drakpa . . .**
>
> ***are the same as before.***

When you recite "Avalokiteśvara, great treasure of nonreifying compassion," contemplate the nature of Avalokiteśvara, who is the single embodiment of the compassion of all the conquerors. When you recite "Mañjuśrī, master of stainless wisdom," contemplate the nature of Mañjuśrī. When you recite "Tsongkhapa, crown jewel of the scholars in the Land of Snows," contemplate the nature of the Secret Lord. When you recite "Losang Drakpa, I make requests at your feet," you should visualize all three—Jé Rinpoché and his two spiritual sons—in the aspect of your guru. If your mind moves from that [image], change from that aspect to Mañjuśrī. If your mind moves from that [image], change from that to your root guru. If your mind moves from that [image], change from that back to Jé Rinpoché and his two spiritual sons. Up to this point, the visualization is the same.

When you recited "I make requests" in the first visualization, you made the request: "Please cleanse and purify my negativities, obscurations, and their imprints." In the second visualization:

> *But there is a difference. When you recite "I make requests," you a make a plea for your desired aim: "In general, may all negativities and obscurations I have accumulated from beginningless time,* [128] *and in particular all negativities and obscurations I accumulated through*

> ***my body, be cleansed and purified. Please bestow on me the blessing of the vajra body."***

You make a plea for your desired aim, and having cleansed general distinct focal objects such as negativities, obscurations, and imprints, and in particular the negativities and obscurations of the body, you make the request: "May I be granted the blessing of the vajra body, and may my body be blessed with the nature of the vajra body."

Previously, when you recited "... at your feet," you visualized that Mañjuśrī held the handle of his sword to his heart and directed the tip of the sword toward you, and in that former visualization you envisaged a stream of nectar flowing from the wisdom sword at the heart of Venerable Mañjuśrī within [the heart of] Jé Rinpoché. [Now, the visualization changes.]

> ***When you recite "... at your feet," Jé Rinpoché reveals his compassion and delight. At this point white nectar-light radiates from the white syllable OṂ at his crown, striking your forehead, and your entire body is completely filled with white nectar-light. It cleanses and purifies general negativities and obscurations accumulated from beginningless time, and in particular negativities, obscurations, and imprints of the body. The blessing of the vajra body enters your body. Reflect that you have received the potent imprint to establish the vajra body. This is the focal object of the second Miktsema praise.*** [129]

When you say "I make requests," white nectar-light dissolves into your forehead and purifies general negativities and obscurations, and in particular negativities and obscurations of the body. The blessing of the vajra body enters your body, and you reflect that you have received the special potent imprint to establish the vajra body in future. This is the second [recitation] of the Miktsema praise.

3. Third Round of Visualization

Again, when you recite the third Miktsema praise:

Avalokiteśvara, great treasure of nonreifying compassion,
Mañjuśrī, master of stainless wisdom,
[Secret Lord, destroyer of hordes of māras,]
Tsongkhapa, crown jewel of scholars of the Land of Snows,
Losang Drakpa . . .

[it] is the same as before.

You make requests to that being who has the nature of three lineage [protectors] and who is in aspect Jé Rinpoché. If your mind moves from that [image], change to the aspect of Mañjuśrī. If your mind moves from that [image], change to the aspect of your root guru. If it moves from that [image], change back to the aspect of Jé Rinpoché. The process of changing [the image] is as before, and you offer the request: "I make requests at your feet."

When you recite "I make requests," you a make a plea for your desired aim: "In general, may all negativities and obscurations [I have accumulated from beginningless time], and in particular all negativities and obscurations I have accumulated through my speech, be cleansed and purified. Please bestow on me the blessing of vajra speech."

When you recite "... at your feet," Jé Rinpoché reveals his compassion and delight. At that point, red nectar-light radiates from the red syllable ĀḤ *at his throat, striking your throat, and your entire body is completely filled with red nectar-light. It cleanses and purifies general negativities and obscurations ...*

This refers to all negativities and obscurations you have accumulated from beginningless time.

and in particular negativities, obscurations, and [130] *imprints of speech. The blessing of vajra speech enters your speech. Reflect that you have received the potent imprint to establish vajra speech. This is the focal object of the third Miktsema praise.*

4. Fourth Round of Visualization

Again, when you recite the fourth Miktsema praise:

Avalokiteśvara, great treasure of nonreifying compassion,
Mañjuśrī, master of stainless wisdom,
[Secret Lord, destroyer of hordes of māras,]
Tsongkhapa, crown jewel of scholars of the Land of Snows,
Losang Drakpa ...

[it] is the same as before.

This is similar to the request in the earlier first round of visualization.

> ***When you recite "I make requests," you a make a plea for your desired aim: "In general, may all negativities and obscurations I have accumulated from beginningless time, and in particular all negativities and obscurations I accumulated through my mind, be cleansed and purified. Please bestow on me the blessing of vajra mind."***

> ***When you recite ". . . at your feet," Jé Rinpoché reveals his compassion and delight. At this point blue light radiates from the blue syllable HŪṂ at his heart, striking your heart, and your entire body is completely filled with blue nectar-light. It cleanses and purifies general negativities and obscurations accumulated from beginningless time, and in particular negativities, obscurations, and imprints of mind. The blessing of vajra mind enters your mind. Reflect that you have received the potent imprint to establish vajra mind. This is the focal object of the fourth Miktsema praise.***

In these rounds [of visualization], when you focus on purifying negativities and obscurations of the body, you purify general negativities and obscurations such as killing, stealing, and sexual misconduct, [131] and cleanse specific instances such as the body appearing to be ordinary and being conceived of as ordinary. You purify negativities and obscurations accumulated through your speech, such as lies, slander, harsh words, and so forth, as well as purifying specific instances, such as wind and mantra appearing to be distinct and being conceived of as distinct. You cleanse negativities and obscurations accumulated through your mind, such as greed, malice, and wrong view, as well as cleansing specific instances, such as the mind appearing to be ordinary and being conceived of as ordinary.

5. Fifth Round of Visualization

The focal objects of the fifth recitation of the Miktsema praise

The structure is the same as before, but there is a difference:

When you recite "Avalokiteśvara, great treasure of non-reifying compassion," visualize Ārya Avalokiteśvara, in nature the vajra body of all the buddhas and in aspect appearing as the white syllable OṂ at the crown of the three gurus in front [of you]—Jé Rinpoché and his two spiritual sons. A replica separates from them, transmitted through white light, like a flame passing from one lamp to another. As soon as it reaches your forehead, it turns to face outward and remains fixed at your forehead.

When you recite "Mañjuśrī, master of stainless wisdom," you visualize Venerable Mañjuśrī, in nature the highest-wisdom vajra speech of all the buddhas, and in aspect appearing as the red syllable ĀḤ at the throat of the three gurus in front [of you]—Jé Rinpoché and his two spiritual sons. [132] ***A replica separates from them, and it is conveyed by that red light until it reaches your throat. Then it turns to face outward and remains fixed at your throat.***

When you recite "Tsongkhapa, crown jewel of scholars of the Land of Snows," you visualize Secret Lord

Vajrapāṇi, in nature the vajra mind, or might and power of all the buddhas, and in aspect appearing as the blue syllable HŪṂ *at the heart of the three gurus in front [of you]—Guru Jé Rinpoché and his two spiritual sons. A replica separates from them, and it is conveyed through blue light until it reaches your heart. Then it turns to face outward and remains fixed at your heart.*

When you recite "Losang Drakpa . . . ," there is no new visualization different from the first recitation of the Miktsema praise.

When you recite "I make requests," you make a plea for your desired aim: "In general, may all negativities and obscurations I have accumulated from beginningless time, and in particular all negativities and obscurations I have accumulated through my body, speech, and mind, be cleansed and purified. Please bestow on me the blessing of the indivisible three vajras of body, speech, and mind."

When you recite ". . . at your feet," Jé Rinpoché reveals his compassion and delight. At this point the three external syllables at your forehead, throat, and heart dissolve separately and simultaneously into your three sites. White, red, and blue light, or the three syllables and their nectar, completely fill [your body], from your crown to the soles of your feet. [133] *It cleanses and purifies general negativities and obscurations accumulated from beginningless time, and in particular negativities, obscurations, and imprints simultaneously accumulated by your body, speech, and mind. They are expelled from your body through your lower doors, the soles of your feet, and so forth in the aspect of foul and repulsive forms such*

as smoke, charcoal, pus, blood, lymph, spiders, and scorpions, and you are cleansed and purified.

The blessing of indivisible vajra body, speech, and mind enters your body, speech, and mind. Reflect that you joyfully and respectfully receive the special potent imprint to establish the siddhi of indivisible vajra body, speech, and mind. This is the focal object of the fifth Miktsema praise.

First focal object [of the fifth round]: In general, the words "Avalokiteśvara, great treasure of nonreifying compassion" indicate that Avalokiteśvara embodies the compassion of all the conquerors. Reflect that Jé Rinpoché also has this nature, as he has in the rounds of visualization previously stated. Now, in this context, that which is by nature Ārya Avalokiteśvara, who is the vajra body of all buddhas, has the aspect of OṂ at his crown, [Mañjuśrī has] the aspect of ĀḤ at his throat, and [Vajrapāṇi has] the aspect of HŪṂ at his heart. Then, in accordance with the text "Visualize . . . OṂ separates . . . remains fixed at your crown," a replica white syllable OṂ separates from the [guru's] white syllable OṂ and approaches you in the aspect of light. At your forehead it turns to face outward, remaining fixed at your forehead without being absorbed.

Second focal object: For the second focal object, when you recite "Mañjuśrī, master of stainless wisdom," [134] you visualize that [the syllable ĀḤ] radiates red light, it is conveyed on that [light] path, and [it] abides [at your] throat.

Third focal object: This accords with the previous fourth round of visualization [explained above], where you visualize that [the syllable HŪṂ] radiates blue light, it is conveyed [to your heart] on that [light] path, and you recite: "Tsongkhapa . . ."

Fourth focal object: The three syllables OṂ, ĀḤ, and HŪṂ separately remain fixed at your three sites. When you recite "Losang Drakpa," you focus as before on the three gurus—Jé Rinpoché and his two spiritual sons. If your mind moves from the image [of Jé Rinpoché and his two spiritual sons], change to Mañjuśrī. If your mind moves from that [image], change to the aspect of your root guru. If your mind moves from that [image], change back to the aspect of Jé Rinpoché. This should be practiced as explained earlier. There is no new visualization [when reciting "Losang Drakpa" in this fifth round of visualization] different from the first Miktsema praise.

When you recite "I make requests . . ." [in this, the fifth round of visualization], you request to purify the negativities and obscurations of your body, speech, and mind separately, as in the first three focal objects [of the fifth round]. [So too,] as in the request made [earlier,] at the time of the fourth Miktsema praise, you may also visualize that you obtain the blessing of the vase empowerment corresponding to the second round [of visualization], that you obtain the blessing of the secret empowerment corresponding to the third round, that you obtain the blessing of the wisdom empowerment corresponding to the fourth round, and [in addition,] you [may now visualize that you] obtain the blessing of the word empowerment corresponding to the fifth round.

When you recite "I make requests . . ." and reflect that ". . . the indivisible three vajras . . . up to . . . dissolve," [135] the fixed [syllables] do not dissolve [immediately]. But when you state "at your feet," they dissolve simultaneously into the three sites [of your body].

"Fill [your body] from your crown to the soles of your feet" refers to the white syllable OṂ dissolving and white light radiating. So too, when the red syllable ĀḤ dissolves, red light radiates, and when the dark-blue syllable HŪṂ dissolves, dark-blue light radiates. Thus you visualize that your body is filled with white, red, and blue rays of light. Or the three syllables OṂ, ĀḤ, HŪṂ dissolve, and due to that white, red, and dark-blue nectar-light fills your body. Or the seed syllables OṂ, ĀḤ, HŪṂ and nectar-light fill your entire body to the brim. Or the seed syllables OṂ, ĀḤ, HŪṂ as well as nectar fill your entire body to the brim.[65]

"From beginningless time . . ." and so on refers to [blessings] entering you, and the body, speech, and mind of Guru Jé Rinpoché becomes indivisible in taste from your body, speech, and mind.

"Reflect . . . you receive . . . the siddhi [of indivisible vajra body, speech, and mind]" refers to the blessing of the vajra of indivisible body, speech, and mind entering your body, and you receive the potent imprint to establish the vajra body in the future.

> ***However many times you recite the Miktsema praise in a session, you should apply the first four rounds of visualization to the first four [recitations]. Then, from the fifth [recitation] on, you should only apply the fifth round of visualization and then count the [recitations].***

If you are counting Miktsema praises, you make requests for blessings by means of body, speech, and mind, as explained earlier, by stating, "holder of the jewel treasure of the body, sun illuminating speech, [136] and holder of the secret treasure of mind." Then, in the context of the focal objects of the practice cycle for establishing wisdom, you may practice any visualization. If you are counting Miktsema praises, first engage the first four specific focal objects and then, when counting Miktsema praises, count recitations after taking the fifth round of visualization as your main practice. This [completes the presentation of] the fifth round of visualization.

> ***If you recite 100,000 Miktsema praises while focusing on the fifth focal object in this way, I assure you, without doubt, that the great lord Jé Rinpoché himself will directly manifest and bless you. You will know how many extra recitations you can recite in the time you have available. I urge you to do a minimum of seven recitations each day while engaging this focal object.***

Ngawang Tsöndrü, the first Jamyang Shepa, gained a direct vision of Jé Rinpoché after employing this focal object. He said: "You will know how many extra recitations you can do from the free time you have. But I urge you to do a minimum of seven recitations [137] each day while engaging this round of visualization. If you recite it 100,000 times, you will gain a direct vision of Jé Rinpoché."

> ***This is unsurpassable advice on the secret practice derived from the stream of vajra speech of Omniscient Jamyang Shepa, and you should make it your standard practice.***

This is called "the focal object of the practice cycle for establishing wisdom" and "opportune visualization."

7. Requesting the Blessing of the Entire Path, Collectively

Now you engage in a concise review and request the blessings of the entire path, collectively. Serially engaging in a meditative review of the main points and reflecting "I have received such blessings" is called "requesting the blessings of the entire path, collectively."

1. First Round of Explanation

Regarding that, first there is the means of relying on your spiritual friend: the root of the path. Then, in terms of the stages of how to train your mind, there are three: small, medium, and great scope. In the context of great-scope practices, there are shared practices and unique mantric practices. Every practice is included in them.

Also, in terms of how to rely on one's spiritual friend who is the root of the path, there are (1) the characteristics of the guru on whom you rely, (2) the characteristics of the student who practices reliance, and (3) the means of how you practice reliance. [138]

Regarding the means of your practice of reliance, there is (1) training in faith as the foundation, and (2) training in respect that recalls your guru's kindness.

When training in faith as the foundation, you should view

the headings of [Paṇchen Losang Yeshé's] *Swift Path*, such as: Vajradhāra has explained that the guru is a buddha. In the past, when practical advice was given, students were guided by applying such headings.

First, the means of practicing reliance:

The single taste of the pristine wisdom of all the conquerors
within the expanse of reality appears as the guru himself.
With faith and respect that achieves heartfelt certainty in this,
bless me to establish the root of my collection of virtue.

Since all the conquerors share a single taste within the expanse of reality (*dharmadhātu*), since the pristine wisdom of great bliss appears as the guru, and since you achieve certainty that the guru is a buddha, this is called "training in faith as the foundation." "Respect" refers to respect that recalls the kindness [of your guru]. The benefits of relying on a spiritual guide and so forth arise from being blessed. You make the request, "Bless me to establish the root," and through making that request you reflect that various interferences are purified and various realizations arise in your mindstream.

Then you are urged to extract the essence of this basis of leisure:

Such leisure and endowment are found just once.
Since if I lose this opportunity it will be hard to find later,
bless me to extract the essence of this highly meaningful [basis]

by transcending [saṃsāra] by practicing Dharma continuously, day and night.

These words identify leisure and endowment, they indicate that leisure and endowment are hard to find, [139] and by the statement "found just once," we understand that [this basis] is highly meaningful.

The great purpose of [this basis with] leisure and endowment is expressed by the words "highly meaningful." [Just] as it is said, "Understand all mundane activities to be like winnowed husks," [so] you should put aside mundane activities, and by continuously practicing Dharma day and night, you can transcend [saṃsāra]. By that means you request to be blessed to extract the essence of leisure and endowment. You reflect, "Bless me to cleanse the stains obstructing the arising of the realization of leisure and endowment, and the special realization of leisure and endowment, in my mindstream."

Generating the mind seeking a future existence in the round of impermanence

To generate a mind seeking a future existence, you need to meditate on impermanence. Therefore you meditate on impermanence by contemplating that death is certain, the time of death is uncertain, and at the time of death nothing but Dharma is of benefit.

Age and youth are uncertain, and death occurs suddenly.
If I were to die today, what would I do?
Bless me to genuinely recall that there is no time to spare,
since there is no assurance that I will survive the night.

Contemplate that death is certain, the time of death is uncertain, and at the time of death nothing but Dharma is of benefit. From these three points, the mere thought that death is certain [140] occurs to most people. Still, you may think: "What is required here?" What is required is [to understand that] the time of death is uncertain. Therefore [the words] "Age and youth are uncertain, and death occurs suddenly" teach that the time of death is uncertain.

You need to quickly extract the essence of this physical basis. You may think that you can extract it later, but you do not have the time or leisure to do this. Therefore it is said, "Bless me to genuinely recall that there is no time to spare," for you must do it right now. At the time of death, nothing but Dharma is of benefit, and therefore you must practice Dharma. And it is certain that you must establish Dharma through contemplating that even this Dharma will certainly disappear. Since nothing but Dharma will be of benefit at the time of death, you must decide to practice pure Dharma and focus on such goals. It is said that you should contemplate the happiness or suffering that will be your two possible destinies in future lives. If you ask, "What will happen if I am born in an evil rebirth in my future life?" then:

My mind is heavy with negative karma like myriad Mount Merus,
the cause of evil rebirth in Avīci Hell alone—where else?
I am certain to proceed only to evil rebirths for billions of lives.
Ah, Guru, please bless me with your protection.

At this point, contemplate the sufferings of evil rebirth. When contemplating the sufferings of evil rebirth, do not view the suffering of evil rebirth as something distant, but contemplate: "When I die, [my negative actions] [141] are certain to be the cause of rebirth in evil realms. Aside from just [being reborn in] evil realms, I have a store of evil action as great as Mount Meru that will bring about rebirth in Avīci Hell not just once, but many hundreds of thousands of times. My mindstream is full [of such evil acts]. Not only will I progress from evil rebirth to evil rebirth billions of times, but I lack the means of becoming liberated. Since I lack the capacity to exhaustively purify these actions, I reflect, 'Who has this capacity?' It is the Three Jewels who are abodes of refuge who have this capacity. I take refuge, reflecting, 'Guru, please bless me with your protection.'"

Teaching the means of attaining future happiness requires training in karma and its result, therefore:

> **The slightest white or black karma greatly increases;**
> **just a speck produces a result like Mount Meru,**
> **and I alone experience its projected result:**
> **bless me to practice and discard what I should.**

[The first line] deals with how karma is definite. [The second two lines] indicate that you do not meet [the results of] karma not committed, and that committed [karma] does not lose its potency. These words reveal the headings: karma is definite, karma increases, you do not meet the results of karma not committed, and karma that is committed does not lose its potency. [The fourth line] deals with the round of karma and its results, and teaches both (1) generating the mind seeking liberation, and (2) the path progressing to liberation at the beginning of the path of those of intermediate scope. Among those two, generating the mind seeking liberation [142] requires contemplating the suffering of saṃsāra:

Even the glorious cakravartin, Lord Brahmā, is shaken
when tossed by the mountain-like waves of suffering due to karma and affliction.
What is the chance for happiness in saṃsāra?
Bless me to generate the intense wish to be liberated.

Saṃsāra that arises through the power of karma and affliction is likened to a vast ocean. While you abide in the ocean of saṃsāra, it is as though you are tossed by waves in this vast ocean. The waves are the three types of suffering that occur through the power of karma and afflictions. These waves are like mountains, and you are thrown about by them.

[The third line indicates] that until you are liberated from this samsaric abode, whatever good or bad rebirth you may take, you lack any chance for happiness and remain tormented by any of the three types of suffering. [The fourth line indicates that] you request to be "blessed to generate the intense wish to be liberated" from this saṃsāra. At this point you should reflect that you have cleansed the stains that obstruct the generation of the mind that seeks liberation, and that you have received the blessing to generate the intense wish to be liberated.

When contemplating the suffering of saṃsāra, you may contemplate it by means of the twelve links:

The root of the twelve links that is the mechanism of saṃsāra
can be abandoned through supreme wisdom.
Seeing this, in order to obtain liberation, my goal,
bless me to strive to establish the three trainings.

Where do the system of roaming in existence by means of the twelve links, the time of roaming in existence by means of the twelve links, [143] and the root of roaming in existence due to the twelve links converge? They converge in grasping at a self. The antidote to the ignorance of self-grasping is the wisdom realizing emptiness, which directly opposes the mode of apprehension of ignorance.

What is the path that obtains liberation? It is the wisdom realizing selflessness, which acts as the direct antidote to self-grasping, the main practice in the three [higher] trainings establishing the path of liberation. To generate the higher training of wisdom capable of abandoning self-grasping, you need stable concentration to support it. To generate stable concentration, you need its cause, which is the higher training of ethics that pacifies inner and outer distractions.

When you state "Bless me to strive to establish the three trainings," you should reflect, "I have been blessed to generate special realization of the three higher trainings, which pacifies every condition counter to the three trainings."

Now, in the stages of the path of the individual of great scope, first train in the generation of bodhicitta. Here the awakening mind is generated by means of the sixfold instruction on causation: (1) understanding that all beings have been your mother, (2) recalling their kindness, (3) repaying their kindness, (4) appealing love, (5) compassion, and (6) special intention. [144]

Understanding that all beings have been your mother

> **Since I have taken countless rebirths,**
> **all reincarnating beings have been my mother many times.**

Your births from beginningless time until now are countless, and if you tried to calculate those countless [births] by taking them as the basis of your investigation, that would take countless [lifetimes]. During that time, it is impossible that only one being acted as your mother; therefore you have needed countless mothers.

If the number of sentient beings and the number of times you have taken womb birth[66] were compared, your womb births would be more. But if each sentient being were to be your mother just once, there would not be enough sentient beings. Therefore each sentient being has been your mother countless times.

Recalling their kindness

> **When I experienced samsaric suffering, they kindly cared for me with love.**
> **By contemplating this, bless me to understand that they have been my mothers.**

Each time they were your mother, they cared for you with kindness, especially when you experienced suffering in saṃsāra. Every sentient being has only been greatly kind to you. Your food, clothing, bedding, and so forth necessarily arise in dependence upon sentient beings, but when they are your mother, they are even kinder. Through contemplating that they are kind to you even when not your mother, you should meditate on recalling their special kindness. Here the verse on understanding that all beings have been your mother has been slightly expanded. [145]

Reflect that you have purified negativities and obscurations that stop you from understanding [that all beings] have been your mother, and generate the special realization that they have been your mother.

Repaying their kindness, appealing love, compassion, and special intention

Once I have released my destitute aged mothers from suffering,
I will bear the great responsibility of establishing them in bliss.

"Once I have released my destitute aged mothers from suffering" teaches great compassion; "I will establish them in bliss" teaches love; "I will bear the great responsibility" teaches the special intention that you yourself will bear such a burden; understanding that they have been your mother and contemplating their kindness is recalling their kindness; and repaying their kindness is engaging in the means of fulfilling their desire to be free of suffering and their desire to possess happiness. Therefore these words literally teach all [six] stages, such as understanding them to have been your mother, recalling their kindness, and so forth.

The result of the six causes

Bless me to master uncontrived bodhicitta,
which seeks highest complete enlightenment for that purpose.

You should reflect: "Bless me to generate uncontrived bodhicitta in my mindstream in reliance upon these six causes." Reflect that by training in such focal objects and aspects,[67] you purify all obstacles to generating bodhicitta through the purifying descent of nectar, and that you are blessed with the generation of various special realizations. This constitutes the round of training in bodhicitta.

Such training has two parts: (1) the general round of training in the practice, [146] and (2) specific training in the latter two perfections as it occurs in lamrim.

General training in the practice

Having properly taken just these vows engaging the basis of training,
central to the path of all the conquerors and their sons and daughters,
bless me to strive conscientiously
to reach the farther shore of the ocean of practice.

Question: What is the central path upon which all the conquerors and their sons and daughters travel?

Reply: It is the need to take the vows of engaging [bodhicitta]. If you do not take the vows of engaging bodhicitta after generating aspiring bodhicitta, it will just remain a noble intention and you will not progress on the path. Therefore you must first take the vows of engaging bodhicitta and then train according to the instruction on engaging bodhicitta. "Conquerors and their sons and daughters" first took [the vows of] engaging bodhicitta, then trained in it. But they would not obtain the state of a buddha without training in it. Therefore the text states "Having properly taken just these engaging vows," emphasizing "just."

The practices of a bodhisattva are like an ocean, vast and multifaceted. But if summarized, they are included in the six perfections, such as generosity. "Bless me to reach the farther shore" of such practices refers to the general training in the practice. Reflect that a cleansing nectar descends, cleansing you of various obstacles and generating various realizations.

> ***If you wish to take engaging bodhicitta vows, then at this point you may take them by inserting the general liturgy: "Just as the tathāgatas of the past . . ."***

Take the engaging bodhicitta vows with the words "Just [147] as the tathāgatas of the past . . ." from the text of [Śāntideva's] *Bodhisattva's Way of Life*, quoted in the six-session guru yoga.

Specific training in the latter two perfections

How to train in calm abiding

> **Due to this mind being like a crazed, agitated elephant that cannot be stilled**
> **even for the time it takes to stretch a nipple when milking a cow,**
> **I can never progress on the grounds and paths of sūtra and tantra.**
> **Bless me to establish single-pointed absorption.**

Your mind lacks stable abidance and cannot be stilled even for the time it takes to stretch a nipple when milking a cow. It is like a crazed elephant that charges everywhere, and due to this you cannot progress on the grounds and paths of sūtra and tantra. Therefore it is important to establish the single-pointed mind of calm abiding. By stating "Bless me to establish" such calm abiding, reflect that faults obstructing the establishment of calm abiding have been cleansed, and that you are blessed to establish special absorption in dependence on the nine means of mental abidance, the four attentions, and the six powers.[68]

How to train in the higher training of wisdom

> **Absorption devoid of the view of selflessness**
> **may endure in a single session of equipoise for up to an eon.**
> **But it does not transcend existence in the least.**
> **Bless me to realize the reality of selflessness.**

Though stable absorption can endure for up to an eon, if it lacks the view of selflessness it cannot liberate from saṃsāra. For example, it is like the tīrthika Lakjö cited in the lamrim. [148]

If you have stable concentration, you may travel to the summit of existence and enter equipoise on the summit of existence. But when such prior projecting karma is exhausted, you may be reborn in the hells. And since such outcomes arise, it indicates [that such absorption] has not transcended existence in the least.

Regarding the nature of reality, you should generate the view free from the two extremes—which conforms to [that of] the glorious protector Ārya Nāgārjuna, who elucidated the intention of our teacher, Munīndra—for views influenced by eternalism and nihilism cannot benefit you. Then:

> **Prior to the dawn of the powerful sun, Losang,**
> **every scholar of renown was mistaken as to the profound meaning,**
> **and this Land of Snows was filled with evil views.**
> **Bless me to realize unmistaken dependent origination.**

Before Jé Rinpoché, most early Tibetan scholars had fallen into the extremes of nihilism and eternalism. Most followed the view of Hvashang,[69] and though the view of Hvashang was known by different names, it is said that the source of [extreme view] was the view of Hvashang.

This is an extremely important point, for it is said, "Bless me to realize the view" and "Bless me to realize unmistaken dependent origination." Also, the *Three Principal Aspects* states, ". . . therefore strive in the means of realizing dependent origination."[70] [149] If you realize unmistaken dependent origination in accordance with these statements, you can negate both the extremes of nihilism and eternalism in reliance on the reason of dependent origination. Therefore [here you] request, "Bless me to realize unmistaken dependent origination."

Further, it is important to identify the object of negation:

> **Through not finding the object of negation, the reasoning "free of one or many"**
> **will undermine dependent origination, and I will fall into the extreme of nihilism.**
> **Also, the object of negation does not appear to the innate afflicted view of the self.**[71]
> **Bless me to ascertain this mode of conception according to my own experience.**

Until the object of negation that is to be negated—the means by which something is established from its own side—appears [to mind], you should investigate whether something such as a vase is the same as or different from its basis of designation. If you think that prior to finding the vase it does not exist, this would be [the extreme of] nihilism, which undermines dependent origination. Therefore, first it is crucial to determine the object of negation.

Regarding that which is called the object of negation, both the generic image and the object itself appear to the innate afflicted view of the self, and they appear as though they are mixed. But the mere mode of appearance to the innate afflicted view of the self cannot be negated.

Stating "Bless me to ascertain the mode of conception" of the afflicted view of the self "according to my own experience" [indicates] the need to ascertain this according to your own experience. For example, you must ascertain through your own experience how you conceive "I" to be established by its own characteristics. Ascertaining this by your own experience [150] relies on the mode of grasping the self becoming clear for a brief moment when you are very joyful, extremely sad, or in great fear. It is said that you must recognize this at such times with penetrating conception. When you say "Bless me to ascertain [this mode of conception] according to my own experience," you should reflect that all obstacles and states counter to ascertaining the object of negation are cleansed and purified, and that you are blessed to ascertain the object of negation exactly as it is.

When I ascertain the object of negation, each proof possesses the capacity to annihilate self-grasping. Bless me to simultaneously eliminate both extremes through the unique king of reasons: dependent origination.

The proof of dependent origination is called "the king of reasons." It is called "the king of reasons" because, for example, though a minister acts when he engages in actions for the king, the minister acts in dependence on the king. So too, though there are many reasons establishing selflessness, the root of such reasons is dependent origination, and they rely on that reason. It simultaneously eliminates the two extremes. It eliminates the extreme of eternalism because "dependent" refutes that it is established self-sufficiently without depending on time, and it eliminates the extreme of nihilism because through "origination" [151] and "dependent" you understand that it is established or occurs in dependence on causes and conditions.

Since this proof can thus remove both extremes, at this time you reflect that in simultaneously eliminating the two extremes you purify obstacles, and you are blessed with simultaneous realization.

Question: What is that which is called "subtle dependent origination"?

Reply: It does not refer to dependent origination that is "the mere interaction of cause and result." This is something asserted by the lower schools, such as the Mind-Only School (Cittamātra).

It is not the mere interaction of cause and result, nor
mere establishment
in reliance on parts. Dependent origination means that
everything is projected by conception,
as subtle conventional states, and saṃsāra and nirvāṇa
are tenable.
Bless me to attain unmistaken ascertainment of this.

It is not said that by merely understanding the interaction of cause and result you realize dependent origination. It is not said that even the dependent origination asserted by the Autonomy School (Svātantrika)—that phenomena are merely established in reliance on their parts—is dependent origination.

Question: How should this be understood in the context of the Consequence School (Prāsaṅgika)?

Reply: When there is nothing in the least from the side of the basis of imputation, when any conventional state is merely projected [by conception], and when [every] act and process of saṃsāra and nirvāṇa are tenable, [then] this is said to be the realization of subtle dependent origination in the system of the Consequence School.

Reflect that various obstructive states have been purified, [152] and that you are blessed to generate special realizations.

Calm abiding and insight are established separately, and then the union of calm abiding and insight:

Due to unmistaken study and contemplation, stable single-pointed
equipoise derived from meditation engages the mode of abidance,
and such subtle analysis produces superior clear appearance.
Bless me to generate the union of calm abiding and insight.

The unmistaken means of resolving [philosophical] view is first to eliminate overestimation of [the mode of abidance of phenomena] through study, [then] actualize [that view] through contemplation, and then meditate single-pointedly on that mode of abidance. While in equipoise with such stable [wisdom] derived from meditation, clear appearance and pliancy arise due to entering analysis by means of that equipoise. When this happens it is called the "union of calm abiding and insight."

This is known as "training in the last two perfections," and this concludes the explanation on how to request blessings of the stages of the shared path, collectively.

The unique practice of the Vajra Vehicle

The [presentation of the] unique Vajra Vehicle begins from this point. In the Vajra Vehicle, first you must enter a maṇḍala and then practice the two stages through guarding the vows and commitments taken by entering the maṇḍala. [153] At the beginning,

> **Once I mature my mindstream within the great vajra maṇḍala**
> **and guard my vows and commitments like my life,**
> **bless me to obtain the generation stage, which brings**
> **birth, death, and the bardo into the three bodies of the path and the result.**

The words "Once I mature my mindstream within the great vajra maṇḍala" reveal that you do not become a vessel suitable to meditate on the maṇḍala through a small maṇḍala or through the jenang[72] of a specific deity. Thus you must become suitable vessels through the four empowerments [vase, secret, wisdom, and word] that are certain to plant the seeds of the four bodies, as found, for instance, in the initiations of [any of] the three deities: Guhyasamāja, Heruka, and Yamāntaka. Further, it is not permissible to simply obtain an initiation; you must [also] safeguard your vows and commitments even at the cost of your life.

Thus you should meditate on the two stages of the path while maintaining your vows and commitments.

Meditation on the generation stage

The main [practice] of the generation stage is birth, death, and the bardo,[73] called "the three bodies of the basis." The three bodies of the basis transform in nature into the three bodies at the time of the path, and the three bodies at the time of the result are established in dependence on the three bodies at the time of the path. This is called "bringing the three bodies into the path."

The main [practice] of the generation stage is to bring the three bodies into the path, and this transforms birth, death, and the bardo into the three bodies of the path and the result.

When "mixing death with the Dharma body," you meditate on clear light [154] and generate clear light in the nature of the path.

When "bringing the bardo into the path as the enjoyment body," [the bardo body] is transformed into the illusory body at the time of the path, where it is established as the substitute for the bardo [body]. The illusory body transforms into the enjoyment body. "Rebirth" refers to entering into the old aggregates at the time of the path or taking an emanation body to benefit disciples, and this is done at the time of the result. At the time of the result you establish the emanation body of a conqueror. The words "birth, death, and the bardo . . ." express this meaning. Reflect that the stains [impeding] generation of the special realization of the generation stage and the comprehension of how to bring the three bodies into the path have been cleansed, and various special potent imprints have been planted. Reflect that you have been blessed.

Meditation on the completion stage

It is said that meditation on the completion stage has five or six stages. If the five stages are summarized, there are (1) concentration of the three isolations, and (2) concentration of the two truths. Concentration of the three isolations is the vajra body physical isolation, vajra speech verbal isolation, and vajra mind mental isolation.

The concentration of the three vajra isolations
manifests the true, fundamental face of the mind itself.
Bless me to complete the illusory concentration
when I rise from that in the illusory-net body.

The words "the concentration of the three vajra isolations" [indicate] the completion stage of the three isolations. The words "manifests the true, fundamental face of the mind itself" [teach] [155] metaphoric clear light from among the completion stage of the two truths and, first, the manifestation of metaphoric clear light dependent on the concentration of the three vajra isolations. It manifests the true, fundamental face of the mind itself and replaces [the process that] establishes the bardo. When you rise from it, you are an illusory-net body, then, through arising as an impure illusory body, you are blessed by vajra-like concentration.

After entering the actual expanse of thusness,
I rise again in the pure vajra body.
Bless me to obtain learner's union by
entering equipoise on the mind of ultimate clear light.

When you enter equipoise on clear light again, the [impure] illusory body dissolves and you meditate on actual clear light. You enter the expanse of actual clear light, and when you rise from that, you rise again in a pure vajra body that is the pure illusory body, since you have already dissolved the previous, impure illusory body. This is called "the completion stage of the two truths." The completion stage of the two truths has two parts: (1) The first is called "the completion stage of the individual two truths." Now in this case, first clear light and then the illusory body are explained separately. (2) [The second] is called "the completion stage of the indivisible two truths."

The words "Bless me to obtain learner's union by entering equipoise on the mind of ultimate clear light" indicate that when you rise again [156] in a pure vajra body, you obtain the pure illusory body. At that time you obtain the union of abandonment, but since you have not attained the main union, you enter equipoise on the ultimate clear light once again, and through that you obtain the main union, which is the *union of realization*. Reflect that you purify hindrances to obtaining learner's union and that you obtain the special potency to obtain learner's union. Learner's union is called "concentration bravely proceeding to union." Clear light obtained through concentration bravely proceeding to union is the first of the ten grounds. Then the remaining nine grounds are obtained at the time of union.

> **The concentration bravely proceeding to union**
> **fulfills the great wave of accumulation on the tenth ground.**
> **Bless me to eradicate dualistic appearance from the root**
> **through the final vajra-like concentration of a learner.**

The collection [of merit and wisdom] is accumulated on the tenth ground. Through completing and fulfilling that collection, the final vajra-like concentration of a learner, which equals the final uninterrupted path of a learner in the context of the Perfection Vehicle, arises. It acts as the antidote to subtle dualistic appearance, and when the liberated path is obtained due to it, you obtain omniscience.

At that time, [157] both the enjoyment body possessing five certainties,[74] which is the result explained in the Perfection Vehicle, and the seven attributes [of embrace],[75] which are the result explained in the Vajra Vehicle, manifest, and they are identical.

> **Through obtaining a body possessing five certainties and seven attributes,**
> **I will swiftly establish all reincarnating beings on the ground of a buddha**
> **by emanating trillions of emanation bodies.**
> **Bless me to empty saṃsāra in an instant.**

Through obtaining such a body and obtaining the main enjoyment body, you will emanate many trillions of enjoyment bodies and emanation bodies and swiftly establish all reincarnating beings on the ground of a buddha. May you be blessed to empty saṃsāra in an instant.

At that time, reflect that all hindrances to establishing buddhahood are cleansed and that you directly accomplish buddhahood. Reflect that you are a buddha possessing the five certainties and seven attributes. As a buddha you emanate trillions of emanation bodies that teach Dharma to all sentient beings according to their specific capacities. First you set out the basis of the path; then you act as one's spiritual friend who teaches the path; and then, through training in the path, they serially accomplish every stage until you establish them in the state of union. Generate joy, reflecting, "I was able to establish them [in union]." This is called "taking the result as the path."

To definitely accomplish the entire noble path
in twelve human years, or in just three years and three months,
and to accomplish the special attributes of your teaching,
bless me so that not even the word "obstacle" arises.

Jé Rinpoché rectified [faults] through enduring many hundreds of hardships [158] in reliance on the instruction of Venerable Mañjuśrī. If you, from your side, can take on the entire noble path of sūtra and tantra and can take on austerities with fortitude, like Milarepa, then you can establish the state of union in twelve human years. But even more swiftly, you can accomplish such a state in just three years and three months.

If you can perform a concise review of the points conforming to the words and meaning of the text, and blend this with your mindstream, it is certain that you will plant special imprints of the entire path in your mindstream.

These words were stated by Jé Rinpoché, and they present the entire path, from the proper way to rely on one's spiritual friend up to the union of a nonlearner. If you can perform a concise review and blend this with your mindstream, you will certainly plant imprints of the entire sūtra and mantra [in your mindstream]. When we requested this commentary, we received the fourfold explanation in detail. In this case, though the explanation is not really extensive, it constitutes one round of explanation.[76]

2. Second Round of Explanation

Another [round of] explanation is that first one should rely on one's spiritual friend and then train in the actual path in reliance on one's spiritual friend. The person who trains in the path is of small, medium, [159] or great scope, and from among those three, first is the [path of] small scope.

In the context of the small scope, meditate on death and impermanence, cultivate refuge through contemplating the sufferings of evil rebirths, and contemplate how karmic results are certain in terms of black karmic results and white karmic results. Specifically, contemplate how to establish the causes for the eight qualities of maturation,[77] their nature, and their function. This constitutes the round of contemplation of a being of small scope.

In the context of a being of medium scope, first generate the mind seeking liberation and then determine the nature of the path that establishes liberation. To generate the mind seeking liberation from saṃsāra, you must contemplate the six,[78] eight,[79] and three types of suffering.[80] Then disappointment with saṃsāra arises through contemplating the twelve links of dependent origination.[81]

Question: Once the desire for liberation from saṃsāra has arisen, what is the basis that can achieve liberation from saṃsāra? And in what path must you train?

Reply: The basis is one who possesses the vows of individual liberation, and the path is training in the three higher trainings. It is said that, having trained in the three higher trainings, you can obtain liberation free from saṃsāra. This constitutes the round of contemplation of a being of medium scope.

In the stages of the path of a being of great scope, first you train in bodhicitta. Then, having trained in bodhicitta, [160] you take the vows of engaging [bodhicitta] and train in the practices [of a bodhisattva], and specifically in the last two perfections. When you have internalized the stages of such a shared path, you should enter the Vajra Vehicle. When you enter the Vajra Vehicle and then, in the presence of a qualified master, you take the four pure initiations, within a great maṇḍala, that certainly plant the seeds of the four bodies and mature your mindstream. Then, safeguard and do not discard the vows and commitments you have taken, [just] as you would your own life.

Such pure vows and commitments are the root. If your vows and commitments are not pure, then though you may meditate on generation and completion stage paths, realizations will not arise. You should practice the generation and the completion stages while abiding with pure vows and commitments. Further, when first practicing the generation stage, meditate on yourself as the deity. Merely generating yourself as a deity when in reality you are not actually a deity is called "the generation stage."

Question: What is the purpose of deity meditation?

Reply: It is to transform the basis to be purified—birth, bardo, and rebirth—into the three bodies of the path and the result. The nature of the path is to transform them into the three bodies; however, the main transformation occurs in the completion stage. Nevertheless, you meditate on the generation stage to mature your mindstream by bringing the three bodies into [161] the path during the generation stage. Once your mindstream has matured through [meditation on] the generation stage and you have completed the coarse and the subtle generation stages, you enter the completion stage. In physical isolation you practice gathering the winds in the central channel. In verbal isolation you practice releasing the channel knots of the central channel. In mental isolation you practice manifesting innate bliss through dissolving all the winds in the indestructible drop at your heart, as in the death process.

Such innate bliss is generated in the nature of the mind realizing emptiness. When clear light realizes emptiness through a generic image, it is called "metaphoric clear light." You arise from that in an illusory body of mere wind and mind, and this illusory body is equivalent to [the merit] collected for three countless great eons. This illusory body again enters equipoise on clear light, and due to this all the winds without exception dissolve into the indestructible drop at the heart, as in the death process, and the practitioner is able to generate [innate bliss], by nature the direct realization of emptiness. This is called "actual clear light."

When the practitioner enters equipoise on such actual clear light, even the previous illusory body dissolves, and its continuum of similar type ceases. The practitioner arises from that as the pure illusory body established from mere wind and mind. That pure illusory body is called "the vajra body." [162] Its continuum of similar type endures without ceasing and necessarily transforms into the nature of the complete enjoyment body of a buddha.

When the practitioner rises from that illusory body and re-enters [equipoise on] clear light, he or she obtains learner's union. When learner's union acts as the direct antidote to knowledge obscurations and to the appearance of subtle duality unique to mantra, it is called "the final vajra-like concentration of a learner." When the liberated path produced by it arises, the complete enjoyment body with five certainties and seven attributes is established. This constitutes the second explanation.

3. Third Round of Explanation

This has two [parts]: how to properly rely on one's spiritual friend, and how to serially train the mind. After [proper] reliance, how to serially train the mind also has [two parts]: the motivation to extract the essence of freedom and endowment, and the topic of freedom and endowment. How to extract the essence of freedom and endowment also has: small-, medium-, and great-scope beings [and so on]. The topic of a great-scope being has shared [practices]: renunciation, bodhicitta, and correct view. The unique [practices of] mantra have: having entered [mantra], first taking initiation, [then] maintaining vows and commitments, [and] then training in the two stages. The second stage has the establishment of resultant union in the body of Vajradhāra. This constitutes the third [round of] explanation. [163]

4. Blessings of the Four Initiations

> ***If you wish to receive the shared and unique blessings of the four initiations and so forth, it should be done at this point.***

In terms of the blessing of the four initiations, many blessings of the four initiations have already been received.

Shared blessings of the four initiations

Visualize that white light radiates from the syllable OṂ at [Jé Rinpoché's] crown, striking your forehead. Negativities and obscurations of your body are cleansed, and you obtain the vase initiation. Red light radiates from the syllable ĀḤ at his throat, dissolving into your throat. Negativities and obscurations of speech are cleansed, and you obtain the secret initiation. Blue light radiates from the syllable HŪṂ at his heart and dissolves into your heart. Negativities and obscurations of your mind are cleansed, and you obtain the wisdom initiation. White, red, and dark-blue nectar-light radiate simultaneously from the three syllables OṂ, ĀḤ, HŪṂ. Negativities and obscurations of your body, speech, and mind are cleansed, and you obtain the fourth, or word, initiation. This visualization exists in the *Guru Pūjā*:

> Through the force of having requested this three times,
> white, red, and dark-blue rays of nectar-light come forth
> from the guru's sites of body, speech, and mind.
> They arise in sequence and all at once, and dissolve
> in my three sites, in sequence and all at once.
> The four obscurations are purified, and I obtain the four
> pure initiations.
> I obtain the four bodies, and a replica of the guru
> happily dissolves into me, and I am blessed.[82]

The unique blessings of the four initiations

Kyabjé [Pabongkha] Dechen Nyingpo stated how to take the four initiations related to Heruka Cakrasaṃvara, and Paṇchen Losang Chögyan [Paṇchen Losang Chökyi Gyaltsen] presented the unique blessing of the four initiations related to

Guhyasamāja. If you have done the approximation practices of such deities, then safeguarding your vows and commitments and engaging in self-initiation will effectively produce [such blessings].

> ***If you desire to meditate*** [164] ***on the deity assembly of a specific lineage, then visualize the three sites and focus on each [deity's] seed syllable and mantra garland. You may apply this to any type of activity by changing to different peaceful or wrathful activities.***

If you have meditated on another deity and desire to engage in the approximation practices of another deity, then for each lineage, if there is such a lineage deity of the body, meditate on such a deity at Jé Rinpoché's crown and recite the mantra; meditate on the lineage deity of speech at the throat; and the lineage deity of mind at the heart. It is also acceptable to recite the mantra of each deity.

Moreover, as stated above, you can apply this [practice] to different peaceful and wrathful activities, and accomplish the activities of pacification, increase, power, and wrath. In earlier times, there were 108 yogic feats associated with the Miktsema praise, but through the decline of later times, now only twenty or so remain. The capacity for such yogic feats actually does arise. In our local monastery [in Tibet], we invoked the Miktsema yogic feat of preventing frost. Also during the six months of summer, in a [nearby] Bönpo area, five monks—a senior monk and four companions—would invoke the Miktsema yogic feat of preventing frost. [165] Since the weather was cold there, ice formed on the grass that grew outside, and when [the stems] were about to break, if you reached down with your hand to touch the grass in the field, it would still be warm. Many such applications exist.

> ***If you wish to train in the transference of consciousness, you should practice in accordance with instructions set aside for this.***

If you wish to train in transference of consciousness related to *The Hundreds of Deities [of Tuṣita]*, you should consult relevant commentaries found in Jé Rinpoché's writings.

8. Concluding Practices

In the final stage, [first] contract the merit field: With a sense of intense devotion, [visualize that] the two main disciples dissolve into Jé Rinpoché at the level of his two shoulders.

When we first generated the merit field of Jé Rinpoché and his two spiritual sons, Gyaltsap Rinpoché was generated in the nature of Avalokiteśvara, and Khedrup Jé was generated in the nature of the Secret Lord. Here they will dissolve into his right and left shoulders.

Visualize Avalokiteśvara and Vajrapāṇi as the lotus stems at his right and left shoulders.

Visualize that the right lotus stem is Avalokiteśvara and the left lotus stem is Vajrapāṇi, and through dissolving into his right and left shoulders, reflect that both spiritual sons have dissolved.

The thrones of the two supreme spiritual sons, along with their lotus and moon, dissolve into the throne and lotus of Jé Rinpoché. Then:

Both empty thrones where his two spiritual sons sat dissolve into the throne and lotus of Jé Rinpoché. Then, that which was previously generated in front and has remained there, from now on is taken as "the visualization of the Guru that enters your "heart." [166] First the guru remains in the space in front, but then you invite him to your crown.

> **My glorious and precious root guru,**
> **take your seat on the lotus in my heart.**
> **Please take care of me with your great kindness,**
> **and bestow on me the siddhis of body, speech, and mind.**

> ***By making this request, Guru Jé Rinpoché with his lion throne proceeds to your crown.***

From the heart of Venerable Maitreyanātha extends a white cloud, upon whose edge sits [Jé Rinpoché]. The edge of the cloud extends to your crown.

> ***He abides facing the same direction as you.***

You invite him to sit on your crown.

> ***Visualize that the central line of your body is straight and that the central channel exists in the normal way. Visualize that [Jé Rinpoché] abides precisely at your brahmā aperture. Or, if you cannot visualize him, have conviction that he is there.***

The length of the central channel is visualized differently according to need. Here it is visualized as empty, with an opening at the crown. Alternatively, if you do not visualize it, you should generate the conviction that it exists in that way. Jé Rinpoché sits right on the upper opening of the central channel.

Again recite:

My glorious and precious root guru,
take your seat on the lotus at my heart.
Please take care of me with your great kindness,
and bestow on me common and supreme siddhis.

By making this request, [167] *the lion throne and lotus enter your brahmā aperture.*

They enter the small brahmā aperture at the upper opening of your central channel and then descend.

They merge inseparably with the eight petals at your heart, melt into light, and transform into an eight-petaled lotus.

There is an eight-petaled channel wheel at your heart that has four petals in the cardinal directions and four in the intermediate directions. When the lion throne and lotus descend and dissolve, they become inseparable in nature with the eight channel petals [at your heart] and appear as an eight-petaled lotus.

Then also, the sun disc fully enters your central channel and merges with the red component of the indestructible drop obtained from your mother at your heart. It fully melts into light and transforms into a sun disc. Also, the moon disc enters your central channel and merges with the white drop obtained from your father at your heart. It fully melts into light and transforms into a moon disc.

The sun disc [and moon disc] descend and dissolve, and both the white and red constituents above the eight-petaled lotus transform into a sun disc and a moon disc.

Your guru also enters your central channel through your crown and merges with your extremely subtle wind and mind at your heart.

Within the drop, which exists as a sphere joining both constituents, abides a drop of extremely subtle wind and mind. The red and white constituents joined in the spherical drop transform into a sun disc and moon disc. Guru Jé Rinpoché dissolves into them and merges with the extremely subtle wind and mind.

He completely melts into light, and [168] *in dependence on the extremely subtle wind-mind acting as substantial cause and the body of your guru acting as the cooperative condition, you arise in your guru's body, white with a red hue, in essence a miraculous emanation indivisibly merging your guru's body and your body. At the same time, in dependence on the extremely subtle wind and mind acting as the substantial cause and the mind of your guru acting as the cooperative condition, reflect that you attain the clear-light Dharma body of great bliss, which indivisibly merges your guru's mind with your mind.*

Here the text reveals secret points of ultimate significance on the generation and completion stages.

> ***In dependence on the tone of the extremely subtle wind that is the subtle seed of speech acting as the substantial cause and the speech of your guru acting as the cooperative condition, reflect that you attain the vajra of speech, which indivisibly merges your guru's speech with your speech.***

It is said, "By dissolving into your body, speech, and mind, they become of one taste." Regarding "body, speech, and mind," "body" refers to extremely subtle wind, "speech" refers to the extremely subtle tone of the wind as it moves out and back, and "mind" refers to the mind that is one in nature with that.

> ***Thus the three secret states of your guru become inseparable from your three doors.***

They become inseparable from the three doors of your subtle body, speech, and mind.

> ***Taking the nature of the union of body and mind as the basis of imputation, and maintaining pride in the resultant state, is the special profound point of the illusory body arising internally.*** [169]

Reflect that you arise in that very body of the guru. While reflecting that the body of the guru is the nature of union, and with that as your basis of imputation, maintain the pride that "I am the actual body of union of the resultant state." This is the special profound point of the illusory body arising internally.

You may practice vajra recitation by relying on this. Indeed, you may practice clear light and the illusory body or engage in any other practice, such as the rounds of mixing.

In the future, when the illusory body has arisen internally, you may also meditate on the winds through vajra recitation in dependence on this advice from *The Hundreds of Deities of Tuṣita*. There are practices you may engage in, having arisen from the clear light as the illusory body. The three "rounds of mixing" refer to mixing death with the Dharma body, mixing the bardo with the enjoyment body, and mixing rebirth with the emanation body. Or [they can refer to] mixing sleep with the Dharma body, mixing dreaming with the enjoyment body, and mixing waking with the emanation body. We can apply [these practices] to any of the three types of mixing while awake.

There is no time to discuss this here, and if it were set out in great detail, doubt would arise, as in the case of a two-legged person in Tsūta. Therefore, for now, these issues remain secret.

The land of Tsūta is a place where people have just one leg. Therefore, if someone with two legs were to visit them, locals would say, "This being is not a human." So too, though many clear and profound points may be explained, [170] such points may be rejected due to being deeply profound, just as those in Tsūta doubt that a two-legged being is human. Therefore the author does not discuss these issues here, and they remain secret.

When Jé Rinpoché descends at the tip of the white cloud extending from the heart of Protector Maitreya to the center of our heart:

> ***Reflect that the subtle thread of white cloud connects Guru Jé Rinpoché, the mind in your heart, and venerable Guru Protector Maitreya in Tuṣita without being severed. This is a profound point of instruction.***

Through doing that, visualize the guru of the hundreds of deities of Tuṣita at the tip of the white cloud [issuing from] the heart of venerable Guru Maitreyanātha. Through that, you amass the [two] accumulations. When you invite him to the center of your heart, the tip of the white cloud enters your heart without being severed. Reflect that Jé Rinpoché in your heart and Jé Rinpoché in the heart of Protector Maitreya remain connected through the thread of white cloud. This is a special profound point of instruction, because at the time of death the thread of white cloud condenses upward [toward Tuṣita], ready for you to take rebirth there. This is a point of auspicious connection.

Then we practice the three rounds of visualization:

> ***Again recite:***

> **My glorious and precious root guru,**
> **take your seat on the lotus at my heart.**
> **Please take care of me with your great [171] kindness,**
> **and remain steadfast until I attain the essence of**
> **enlightenment.**

While you recite this, reflect that you request that Jé Rinpoché remains inseparable from your three doors until you attain the essence of enlightenment and the state of a buddha, and that Jé Rinpoché agrees to do this.

> ***If you wish to cultivate mahāmudrā visualizations, you may do it here.***

At this point you may cultivate mahāmudrā visualizations that focus on the conventional and the ultimate nature of the mind.

> ***Then the eight-petaled lotus at your heart grows larger, and within its closed petals your mind, as Guru Jé Rinpoché, abides like a vase body within the lotus.***

Reflect that the lotus seat mentally created earlier grows larger, and Guru Jé Rinpoché abides within it like a vase body. Reflect that Jé Rinpoché is seated on this expanded lotus, the lotus petals envelop him, and he is like a body within a vase. Then reflect:

> ***Inside, it is covered with five-colored rays of light, in essence the five types of pristine wisdom.***

Inside, the lotus is pervaded by rays of light of the five types of inner pristine wisdom, as though covered with plaster.

> ***Rays of light from the heart of your guru [form] the [upper] half of a blue five-spoked vajra at the top of your heart.***

[Jé Rinpoché] abides at your heart as a vase body on a lotus whose petals have closed [around him]. [Inside, the lotus petals] are seamlessly covered with five rays of light. [172] Rays of light radiate upward from the heart of your guru to the top of your heart, forming the upper half of a blue five-spoked vajra.

> ***It is extremely heavy and presses down with a weight like Mount Meru. Within its spokes and at its center is a blue syllable HŪṂ, the nature of Akṣobhya. Externally [the lotus] is surrounded by threads of light garlands and by beads of mantra garlands. Visualize that the vase body is encircled by the mantra "OṂ A RA PA TSA NA DHĪḤ" and the mantra "GURU SUMATI KIRTI ŚRĪBHADRA SIDDHI ADHIṢṬHĀNA ADHIṢṬHITA KURVANTU," which circle clockwise, and [also] by the Miktsema praise, which circles counterclockwise, binding it without gaps, like a ball of thread. Visualize that the central channel up to the crown is encircled by garlands of mantras like a ball of thread, so that it is bound firmly.***

You should reflect that the half-vajra above the enclosed lotus at the heart is extremely heavy, like Mount Meru. If you think that it presses down, this is beneficial in [preventing] soklung (*srog rlung*).[83] When soklung occurs, or when the mind engages in analysis, it is as though the heart rises up. But if you think that a heavy weight presses down, this helps to bring the winds down. Earlier, you visualized a blue vajra with the nature of Akṣobhya, or that the syllable HŪṂ had the nature of the guru. The closed petals of the lotus are circled by threads of light garlands and beads of mantra garlands, which circle clockwise. Arapatsana is [the mantra of] Mañjuśrī. [173] *Guru sumati kirti śrībhadra* refers to glorious Guru Losang Drakpa, *siddhi* [here] means blessing, and *adhiṣṭhāna* means benediction. Therefore this mantra means "Please bestow the benediction of your blessing."

Generate the conviction that the Miktsema praise circles the closed lotus petals within the central channel at your heart in a counterclockwise direction. It is said that you must visualize the mantra garlands from OṂ A RA PA TSA NA DHĪḤ up to [the syllable] HŪṂ, [and that] then you must visualize the encircling Miktsema praise, the sixteen vowels, and the thirty-four consonants.

When the lotus petals close upward, if they close abruptly the winds may be forced inside and harm the life wind. You must close the petals gently, for the inner winds should be permitted to escape outside. Such special visualizations exist.

> ***These are the seal of the heart, that which is extremely precious [within] the eight petals.***

The eight petals enclose the seal of the heart, which is covered internally with the five types of pristine wisdom.

> ***The seal of the five pristine wisdoms is that which pacifies the five poisons. The seal of the five-spoked vajra is that which cannot be destroyed by anything.***

The five-spoked vajra above presses down, since it is extremely heavy.

> ***The seal of the guru is the syllable HŪṂ, which stabilizes blessings.***

Reflect that your guru is the syllable HŪṂ within the spokes of the vajra, or reflect that the seal of the guru is the nature of Akṣobhya, as before.

The seal of the three mantras is the indivisibility of the three doors.

It is encircled externally by the three mantras: [174] OṂ A RA PA TSA NA DHĪḤ, which is the mantra of Mañjuśrī; GURU SUMATI KIRTI ŚRĪBHADRA SIDDHI ADHIṢṬHĀNA ADHIṢṬHITA KURVANTU, which is the name mantra of Jé Rinpoché; and the Miktsema praise.

The seal of the vowels and consonants is the union of method and wisdom.

Visualize that the central channel is externally encircled by the seal of the vowels and consonants.

Pray to the guru three times. This is the instruction.

Previously, you were instructed to recite the prayer to the guru, which exists in the root verses of Mañjuśrī, three times. Therefore you seal this practice through these seals by reciting the words "My precious and glorious root guru . . ." and so on.

The general prayer

By the might of making these offerings and requests
to my venerable guru, who is the source of all siddhis,
may Guru Mañjuśrī be pleased with me
and care for me in all my lives.

The specific prayer to be born in the field of Tuṣita:

May I accomplish the pure field of Tuṣita
through properly meditating on Ajitanātha
at the center of ten million marvels
in the field of Tuṣita formed from myriad jewels,
and be reborn there at the time of death.

In accordance with [your aspiration to attain] this pure field and to mature [the causes] for rebirth there, recite: ". . . accomplish the pure field . . ." and so on. [175]

May my mindstream be easily matured
by accumulating merit through offering the seven-limb prayer
to Guru Jé Rinpoché and his two spiritual sons
at the tip of the white cloud issuing from Maitreya's heart.

After generating the merit field, the wisdom beings dissolve into it. First, merit is accumulated by means of the seven-limb prayer, and prayers are made with resolute conviction [that the merit field] has the nature of the three lineage [protectors].

The prayer making requests with resolute conviction that [the merit field] has the nature of the three lineage [protectors], according to the means for accomplishing appropriate wisdom, is this:

May I quickly obtain every common and supreme siddhi
by making requests to those [who are] by nature the three lineage protectors,
guides who appear in the emanation bodies of union and who embody

the realization, compassion, and power of the buddhas of the three times.

The prayer cycle of propitiation for appropriate wisdom is this:

In particular, may the pure nectar-water of pristine wisdom
cleanse all negativities, obscurations, and ignorance of my three doors,
and may my intelligence come to equal that of Protector Mañjuśrī
in explanation, debate, and composition, and in discerning infinite objects of knowledge.

Visualize that through eliminating ignorance, impurities are cleansed. The rounds of visualization that are the means of accomplishing wisdom are seven: wisdom that is vast, clear, swift, profound, and the three wisdoms of explanation, debate, and composition. The words of the root text, "explanation, debate, and composition," also refer to the wisdom that is profound, clear, and swift. Thus you pray, "May my intelligence come to equal that of Protector Mañjuśrī in explanation, debate, and composition, and in discerning infinite objects of knowledge." [176]

May I be reborn among your first disciples
at the feet of Guide Siṃhanāda [Lion's Roar], in the marvelously arrayed
field in the northeast, and attain eternal transcendence
through studying, contemplating, and meditating on sūtra and tantra.

Jé Rinpoché is the Guide Siṃhanāda, and the buddha-field in which he will attain the state of a buddha is called "the marvelously arrayed field in the northeast," whose wealth surpasses even that of Sukhāvati. Guide Siṃhanāda will have a long lifespan and a large body that emits countless rays of light. His right hand is in the mudrā of explaining the Dharma and his left hand holds an almsbowl full of nectar. Within the almsbowl is a stūpa, and those who merely see this stūpa generate realizations of the path without needing to hear teachings on Dharma.

> **In brief, in this and all my lives, may I never be separated**
> **from Venerable Losang Drakpa and his two spiritual sons,**
> **and by holding every method of the victor's Dharma,**
> **may I strive in the great purpose of the teachings and**
> **reincarnating beings.**

> ***You should make such dedication prayers. You should not dissolve the body of Guru Jé Rinpoché, which represents your own mind at your heart, until death. Then you should rise in the aspect of whichever body is appropriate, such as Guhyasamāja, Heruka, [or] Yamāntaka, and cultivate the practices [of that deity].***

Until death, you should hold with resolute conviction that your mind is inseparable in nature from Jé Rinpoché. [177] Also, when you practice deities such as Guhyasamāja, Heruka, or Yamāntaka, [Jé Rinpoché] changes into the aspect of that deity. And [then he] again transforms into the aspect of Jé Rinpoché.

> *You should regularly pacify obstacles to virtue. [Visualize that] fine rays of light that possess the nature of love, compassion, and bodhicitta radiate from the body of the guru at your heart. Outside the body they expand and form rainbows for white virtuous states and domes of flames, unbearable to look upon, for black nonvirtuous states. These rays of light scorch and subdue all spirits and hindrances, like feathers incinerated in flames. The hindrances cannot be observed and become emptiness. Reincarnating beings are surrounded externally by vajra tents and domes and tents of the four elements and so forth, and you visualize that all are freed from every type of hindrance.*

When you master this visualization, you will be able to accomplish anything.

> *When you place the guru-deity at your heart as a witness, you are careful and diligent in all your actions. You offer all your enjoyments, such as bathing, food, drink, and clothes, to your guru-deity at your heart. You offer any homage or service you receive to your guru-deity at your heart. You should reflect that any blessing you give to others, and the elimination of obstacles and unfavorable conditions,* [178] *is performed by your guru-deity at your heart. And whatever arises, such as the three—appearances, sounds, and cognition—is the play of the three secret sites of your guru. Maintain your guru yoga as if it were your very life, and strive so that you may easily and swiftly accomplish the state of Guru Vajradhāra. Even*

though you may not always be able to practice these clear instructions completely in accordance with your obligations, you should understand the various modes of practice, beginning with the basis, that conform to the time you have available by expanding and abbreviating, or extending and contracting, your practice.

Conclusion

Those who are skilled and adept
at perpetually conceiving the extreme of self or other
think of just this appearance alone.
What is the difference between them and cows?

Although they are guided by expansive analysis
as they seek the perfect pure path,
for the most part they lack merit
and stray into false and misleading paths.

Losang Mañjuśrī himself has produced the pith-essence
of a thousand streams of nectar of eloquent explanation.
But those with the fortune of one hundred million Brahmās
remain unsated and do not have the merit to enjoy it.

Do not cast away this series of births ornamented
with this amazing jewel-like chance of such fortune, [179]
but apply yourself intensely to making strong prayers
with faith and respect, recalling the guru's kindness.

Therefore I dedicate any white [virtue]
I have produced through special intention and exertion

solely to the spread of these teachings
in myriad illusory pure fields.

In all our lives may we be
cared for by the conqueror Losang,
and may we swiftly attain the ground of omniscience
through this pure path alone.

This text, titled* Bountiful Advice Clarifying the Oral Transmission and Explaining the Deep Meaning of How to Practice the Profound Path of Yoga of the Hundreds of Deities of Tuṣita, Called "A Treasury of Precious Jewels," *was composed as follows. Previously, in Lhasa, Wangchuk Tsawa Jampa Thayé, a proponent of logic, had urged me repeatedly with silk khatas, and by offering his body, speech, and mind, to compose a guru yoga of the indivisibility of oneself and Jé Rinpoché, including a concise review of the entire path.

Although the guru [Pabongkha Rinpoché] did not state this earlier, some say the person who requested this practice was Tsawa Jampa Thayé, and that since he was a great scholar, the author included special advice.

Also, in Ganden Jampa Ling, near Chamdo, a government official called Gompo Sönam earnestly requested that I compose a work on the yoga of the hundreds of deities of Tuṣita including the oral transmission and essential advice,* [180] *while offering silk khatas and a body, speech, and mind maṇḍala.

I did not shy away from this task. Instead, I combined

these two works in a single text [and composed] an original work of breadth and clarity encompassing the oral transmission and special advice. This work was composed by the seventh Pabongkhapa in the fire-mouse year of the sixty-year cycle [1936], while staying in a small room in Köndor Labrang, called The Pleasant Grove of Kachö, in Ganden Jampa Ling Monastery, Chamdo.

May the purpose of reincarnating beings be enhanced through it. [181]

COURTESY OF CURTY PHOTOGRAPHY

His Eminence Chöden Rinpoché

Condensed Explanation of The Hundreds of Deities of Tuṣita, *Called* Opening the Door of Blessings *by H. E. Chöden Rinpoché*

1. Motivation

Setting your motivation

IT IS SAID that when you engage in virtuous practice, two things are important, one at the beginning and the other at the end. In the beginning it is important to set your motivation, and at the end it is important to conclude by dedicating your virtue. Your motivation is important at the beginning because, even though your act is [externally] virtuous [Dharma], if your motivation is for the happiness and fame of this life, your action will be non-Dharma since it does not become Dharma [or virtue] due to your motivation. Similarly, if your motivation is merely to be liberated from saṃsāra in your next life, your actions become Individual Vehicle Dharma. If your actions are motivated by the awakening mind, they become Mahāyāna Dharma. To attain the awakening mind, you first need love and compassion that focus on other sentient beings. To obtain the compassion that desires that others be free of suffering, you must [first] generate the mind that desires that you yourself be free from the sufferings of saṃsāra. Prior to that, [182] you must generate the mind that desires freedom from manifest sufferings such as the suffering of lower rebirths. Since you must serially reach these milestones on the path, you must start training your mind by realizing the difficulty of finding this [body with its] freedoms and endowments.

Contemplating the precious human rebirth

We have obtained such a special body with freedoms and endowments that is difficult to find and once found is greatly meaningful. We have encountered the precious Buddhist teachings that are hard to meet. At this moment of great fortune we should extract the essence of this noble basis of freedoms and endowments and not waste it.

The Bhagavān Buddha has said that attaining a human body with freedoms and endowments that is hard to find and encountering the Buddhist teachings that are hard to meet is similar to a blind turtle in the depths of ocean that comes to the surface once every hundred years, surfacing within the single opening of a golden yoke floating upon the ocean that is carried randomly here and there due to the force of the winds and waves. The example of a blind turtle is used because for us, the eyes that view what should be practiced and abandoned are obscured by ignorance, and it is as if we are blind. The turtle residing at the bottom of the ocean exemplifies how we [183] reside in lower rebirths since our thoughts and intentions are solely negative and nonvirtuous. The head of the turtle breaking the surface once every hundred years exemplifies how infrequently we attain a human body. The golden yoke with a single opening floating on the surface of the ocean exemplifies the Buddhist teachings. The Buddhist teachings do not remain in one specific location. First they spread in the central region (Magadha), then they were disseminated in the north, for the Buddha said: "They will spread from the north to the north." Thus first the teachings[84] were established in the central region [of India], then in Tibet to the north, followed by Mongolia further north. So too the teachings are now spreading in Europe. Therefore the fact that the Buddhist teachings do not remain in one specific location but instead are disseminated everywhere is exemplified by the yoke that does not remain in one specific location but is carried here and there. The fact that the yoke has only one opening exemplifies that there is only one gateway to enter the Buddhist teachings.

Now that we have obtained such a human body with freedoms and endowments that is hard to find and once found is greatly meaningful, we should extract its essence. [184] We have obtained this body by accumulating many causes on the basis of our previous [human] bodies, such as safeguarding the pure ethics that abandon the ten nonvirtuous actions, linking with [future rebirth] through faultless prayers, and practicing generosity and the restraint of ethics, and so forth. If we do not extract the essence in this life, the root of virtue that has been accumulated through our previous lives will go to waste. Therefore we should extract the essence. If we do not extract the essence, there is no other option but to be reborn in lower rebirths. For example, a monk has previously said:

> Your past precious life bestowed upon you
> your present precious rebirth.

The precious human body of this rebirth occurs through causes established by a previous precious rebirth.

> So, precious monk of the present,
> don't toss your future into the abyss.

This means, "Monk, if you do not act properly, in the future you will fall into lower rebirth" and it is like a personal rebuke.

Contemplating death and impermanence

We must practice Dharma the right way, for the time of death is uncertain and death is certain. It is definite that taking birth is the cause of our subsequent death, therefore it is certain that we will die. Not only is death certain but the time of death is uncertain because at any given time there is no guarantee we shall not die. At the time of death [185] nothing but Dharma is of benefit. Wealth, enjoyments, friends, relatives, and so forth are of no benefit. Finally, even this body that we have dearly maintained is of no benefit. Only awareness continues, much like a hair that is plucked out of butter, and therefore we must practice pure Dharma. Further, since death is certain, it is indispensable that we practice Dharma. Since the time of death is uncertain, we must practice Dharma right now. Since at the time of death nothing but Dharma is of benefit, we must set our minds to practice only Dharma.

Contemplating karma and its result

When we die without Dharma, we do not become nonexistent and we must take rebirth. In terms of where we take rebirth there are only two possibilities: lower and higher realms. Further, we have no control over where we go but must proceed according to where we are propelled by white and black karma. Therefore if we do not establish virtue on the basis of this present body, we shall be born in lower rebirths due to this great mass of nonvirtuous karma that we have accumulated from beginningless time.

Contemplating the lower rebirths

If we are born in the lower realms, there are the great hells, the surrounding hells, and so forth. The great hells consist of the [eight] hot hells and the [eight] cold hells. The surrounding hells consist of the Pit of Burning Embers, the Mire of Rotting Corpses, the Plain of Sharp Razors, [186] the Forest of Sword Leaves, and the Śālmala Grove. When beings are freed from the great hells, they then experience the surrounding hells. As the vision of having escaped from the great hells arises, they arrive [in the surrounding hells.] By merely placing their feet in the fast flowing Vaitarani river, their flesh and bones are stripped away. When they raise their feet, their flesh and bones are restored. In the Mire of Rotting Corpses, a great many insects congregate in the putrid odor, biting beings who experience the suffering of being trapped. The Pit of Burning Embers is filled with tongues of fire. When beings put their feet down, their flesh and bones are incinerated, when they raise their feet, their flesh and bones are restored, and they experience this repeatedly until their karma is exhausted. In the Field of Sharp Razors, they see green grassy fields and mistake them for green meadows. When they go there, upward-pointed razors slice into their flesh and bones as they put their feet down, to heal again when they raise them.

In the Forest of Sword Leaves they see what resembles trees and shade. When they go there and stand by a tree, the leaves turn into swords that fall and slice into their flesh and bones. [187] In the Śālmala Grove, when they stand near a tree and look up, they see their friends at the top. When they call them to climb up, the branches turn into iron spikes. When they climb up, the spikes turn downward, piercing their flesh. When they reach the top, their friends call for them to come down from the foot of the tree. When they descend, the tree spikes turn upward, and they experience unendurable suffering.

We possess the causes of such suffering, nothing is lacking, and if we do not practice Dharma it is certain that we shall experience it. We must generate fear that we will not be able to endure such suffering. Moreover, such suffering is experienced till the karma is completed, and only then does one die. Such great suffering would bring instant death in other [realms] but when one is born [in the hells] due to negative karma, such suffering must be experienced until the nonvirtue that is its cause is exhausted.

So too for hungry ghosts there are those with internal and those with external obscurations. Those with external obscurations are obscured as to food and drink. When they look at a great flowing river, they see just a dry riverbed. [188] When they look at a tree that is laden with fruit, they see just a barren tree. Alternatively, they see river water as pus and blood, or they see [fruit] as guarded by others, and these are external obscurations. Hungry ghosts with internal obscurations have bellies like a mountain, limbs like thin blades of grass, and throats [the width] of a horse hair. They do not find food, but should they find it, it cannot descend in their throats due to their internal obstruction. Should even a small amount descend, their hunger increases when it reaches their stomach, and it burns their stomach like fire. Such are their obscurations as to food and drink. [Hungry ghosts] must experience such suffering until their nonvirtue is exhausted and they have no means to bear it.

As for animals, those who live among humans have the least suffering. Nevertheless, there are many ways in which they are killed, even for sport, and we can see how they experience suffering. If we had to experience such suffering we should question whether we could bear it or not. But it is certain we could not bear it. Yet since many such nonvirtuous and negative [imprints] exist in our mindstream, [189] we should conclude with certainty that if we do not practice Dharma properly at present, we must experience [such suffering], for we are not different from those who currently experience it.

The causes of refuge

When the mind of fear and terror arises with regard to [such suffering], then the desire for refuge that protects from it will arise. One is led to taking refuge in this way. The two causes of taking refuge are (1) the mind of fear and terror of such suffering, and (2) convictional faith that the Three Jewels possess the capacity to protect from it. When the causes for taking refuge are properly established, you entrust your mind to the Three Jewels with fervent sincerity, and refuge is properly established. When these two causes are not well established, a genuine refuge will not occur. Therefore both the mind of fear and terror for such suffering and convictional faith in the [Three] Jewels' capacity to protect from it are the two main causes of taking refuge.

Question: The Buddha has already established the causes for giving refuge and lacks nothing, but we are left behind. How did this happen?

Reply: We are left behind because we have not sincerely directed our minds [to refuge]. [190]

Question: How is it that the Buddha has already established every cause, lacking in nothing?

Reply: Since he has already abandoned all afflicted and knowledge obscurations, he is free from those fears. Freed from his own fears, he is therefore skilled in the methods that free others from their fears. When someone is not skilled in the methods of freeing others from their suffering, they are not able to fulfill the purpose of others, but Buddha Śākyamuni is skilled in the methods of fulfilling the purpose of others since he teaches Dharma in accordance with the individual needs of disciples and thus fulfills their purpose. Therefore he is skilled in the methods of freeing others from their fears. Furthermore, even though someone is freed from his own fears and skilled in the methods of freeing others from their fears, if they did not possess unbiased compassion, it would be conceivable that they might fulfill the purpose of some but not of others. However, the Bhagavān is not like that, and his great compassion engages others equally and impartially. Although it is possible that someone might fulfill the purpose of those who are helpful and abandon those who are not helpful, the Bhagavān Buddha is not like that. When he fulfills the purpose of all, including those who are and those who are not helpful in terms of immediate material support, [191] he is complete in every way in terms of being a suitable object of refuge.

Therefore, when sincere entrustment arises from our side, it is impossible that the Buddha would not protect us. Thus, the entrustment that arises through both (1) fear and terror of the suffering of saṃsāra and the lower rebirths and (2) convictional faith in the Buddha's capacity to protect [us] from it, and the reflection, "Bhagavān, you know what happiness or suffering arises"—this is called *taking refuge*.

Whether someone is a Buddhist or not is delineated in terms of refuge, and for this reason refuge is always very important. Whatever spiritual training we undertake begins with taking refuge in the Buddha, the Dharma, and the Saṅgha, and we need actual [refuge], not something fabricated. Refuge is necessary at all times. For example, when you meditate on guru yoga, you must go for refuge with the conviction that the guru yoga you cultivate has the capacity to protect you from your fears, completely trusting in its protection. Similarly, when you meditate on self-generation as the yidam, you must go for refuge with the conviction that this yidam has the capacity to protect you from fear, fully trusting in its protection. Therefore refuge is important, since it is always necessary. [192]

Each day you should carefully examine how much your refuge relies on the two causes. From your own side, you think that if you have pure refuge and guard your morality that abandons the ten nonvirtuous actions, you will not be reborn in lower rebirths [more than] once or twice. But in general, there is no stable trustworthy state until you are liberated from saṃsāra. Even if you are reborn in a fine body, it is not trustworthy, for it must be discarded. Any wealth and resources you may accrue are not trustworthy, for in the end, after death, you must proceed and leave them behind. Thus there is nothing that is trustworthy.

The mind seeking liberation

If you do not apply the specific antidotes to samsaric environments, or to taking birth as a being inhabiting them, you will never be satisfied. You cannot say that you have not taken birth in a specific samsaric abode, or have not experienced a specific type of samsaric happiness. Even though you have experienced every type of happiness, still, however great the happiness, the greater the craving. It becomes merely a condition for affliction; one is never sated, nor does one reflect, "I have had enough." Further, you do not end the stream of births and deaths, since, until you are liberated from saṃsāra you must take rebirth and [this stream] will not cease. Moreover, when you die from this birth you take another birth, [193] and in this way you are reborn in saṃsāra. But if you cannot sever the root of saṃsāra, you will not be able to end the stream of births and deaths. This being so, you must be able to sever the root of saṃsāra.

Whichever samsaric abode you are born in is a place of suffering, and whatever you experience is the experience of suffering—this is the nature of saṃsāra. Currently, you experience many types of suffering, and this is the fundamental characteristic of saṃsāra. Because this is the nature of saṃsāra, you should attain certainty that it manifests in this way. For example, the nature of fire is heat and the nature of water is moisture, and to not assert that "fire burns" or "water moistens" would be senseless. In terms of saṃsāra, the nature of saṃsāra is the bringer of suffering, and one should not be too distraught. If you do not want it, you should abandon its cause.

Question: But what is its cause?

Reply: It is karma and the afflictions, and their root is the ignorance of self-grasping. By acting as their root, other afflictions are generated, and we cycle within saṃsāra under their influence. Samsaric suffering is known as the *truth of suffering*, [194] and its two causes—karma and afflictions—are known as the *truth of origin*. If you do not desire the result—suffering—you must abandon its cause—the origin of suffering. To abandon its cause, which is its origin, you must abandon self-grasping, and for that you must generate wisdom realizing selflessness. The wisdom realizing selflessness must have great power to directly oppose afflictions, and it must have calm abiding as its basis. To establish calm abiding, you must have pure morality as its cause. By practicing the path of the three trainings, you can sever the root of saṃsāra and attain liberation from saṃsāra. Therefore you should generate the mind that seeks liberation.

The Mahāyāna

One such as a solitary realizer trains in the path of the three trainings inspired by the mind seeking liberation, and taking the attainment of individual liberation as his or her main goal, obtains liberation. But merely this cannot be the goal of the Mahāyāna. Why is that? It is unacceptable to attain liberation for yourself alone. All sentient beings have been greatly kind to you without exception. Not only have they been greatly kind to you when they acted as your mother, they have also been greatly kind when they did not act as your mother. Even in terms of this life, whether it is food, drink, [195] clothes, shelter, and so forth, many sentient beings have worked hard [to provide them]. These things arise and endure in dependence upon the kindness of many sentient beings. In terms of future lives, you must safeguard the ethics that abandon the ten nonvirtuous actions to obtain higher rebirth. But safeguarding the ethics abandoning the ten nonvirtuous actions also arises in dependence upon the kindness of sentient beings. Even obtaining the ultimate state of a buddha depends on buddhas and sentient beings who are equally kind. You must rely upon the blessings of buddhas, but you also must rely upon the kindness of sentient beings. Also, when you meditate on compassion that wishes [others] to be free of suffering, the focal object of compassion is sentient beings. If there were no sentient beings there would be no meditation on love and compassion, and therefore even meditation on love and compassion depends upon the kindness of sentient beings. Therefore, whether it is from the perspective of this or future lives, you must rely on the kindness of sentient beings to obtain the state of a buddha. Thus, to abandon sentient beings who have been extremely kind and seek liberation for yourself alone is of no benefit; you must fulfill the purpose of others.

In terms of fulfilling the purpose of others, you state: "May all sentient beings have happiness" and "May they be free of suffering." [196] But making them happy by providing food, clothing, shelter, and so forth merely addresses their temporary happiness. Since afflictions arise even when such things are provided, they do not benefit sentient beings at a deep level. Sentient beings need to obtain stable happiness that is free from suffering. But since this will not happen until they obtain the state of a buddha, you must generate the awakening mind that reflects: "I will obtain the state of a perfect, complete buddha so that I may free aged mother sentient beings from suffering and establish them in happiness." This is how to adjust your motivation in the beginning.

Guru yoga

There are many types of guru yoga and self-generation as a yidam to meditate upon. Your yidam is like a friend when you are happy. Your guru is like a friend who helps you in your time of need. It is for this reason that guru yoga is extremely important. There are many practitioners who attained enlightenment in a single life and single body. They took guru yoga as the very life force of their practice, and by taking guru yoga as their main practice, as if it were their very life force, and supplementing this with yidam deity-approximation, they became enlightened. Therefore guru yoga is the most important element, like the life force of the path. [197]

Guru yoga is not the mere recitation of the verses of *The Hundreds of Deities of Tuṣita* or the verses of the *Six Session*

Guru Yoga. [A practice] is called guru yoga when it [includes] (1) training in faith as the foundation as explained in the lamrim, (2) generating respect that recalls [the guru's] kindness, (3) amassing [merit and wisdom] through the seven-limb prayer, (4) making requests, and (5) requesting blessings.

So too when you practice yidam deity-yoga you meditate on self-generation, the generation stage, and the completion stage. This must be done so that you actualize the state of that deity. If you take, for example, Vajrabhairava [Yamāntaka] as your yidam, then meditation on its self-generation and so forth is for the sake of actualizing the state of Yamāntaka, and for obtaining enlightenment in future as Yamāntaka. Similarly, meditation on any other deity is for the sake of attaining enlightenment as that deity. The method that actualizes the state of your guru is known as *guru yoga*. Similarly, *The Hundreds of Deities of Tuṣita* is guru yoga that relies on Guru Jé [Tsongkhapa]. Guru Jé [Tsongkhapa] imparted the oral transmission to just a few disciples, such as Khedrup Rinpoché, in his lifetime [198] without making it widely known. Later, Jé Gendün Drup, who was a direct disciple of Jé Rinpoché, said the following as an expression of his gratitude:

> It is as if I pursued the white cloud into the sky
> from the snow-capped eastern peak.[85]

"White cloud" refers to part of the instruction given in *The Hundreds of Deities of Tuṣita*. Later, he had two students who were both holders of the Vinaya, one with a lighter complexion called "Dülkarwa" and the other with a darker complexion called "Dülnakpa." Dülnakpa Palden Zangpo reflected that if the instruction of their guru was left [unrecorded], it would decline, and if it declined it would be a great loss. Therefore he composed the version of *The Hundreds of Deities of Tuṣita* that we currently recite.

2. The Six Preliminaries

IN EVERY SPIRITUAL practice there are three preliminaries that must precede [the main practice]. The first three [of the six] preliminaries are this: (1) clean your room and set out objects representing [the Buddha's] body, speech, and mind; (2) arrange offerings that you have obtained without deceit in an appealing manner; and (3) arrange a comfortable seat and infuse your mind with refuge and the awakening mind. Since these three preliminary practices must precede any spiritual practice of the Mahāyāna, [199] they must precede your practice of *The Hundreds of Deities of Tuṣita*.

First Preliminary: Cleaning Your Room

"Clean your room" refers to giving the room a good sweep and keeping it tidy. In terms of your motivation, then, for *The Hundreds of Deities of Tuṣita* you first invite Jé Rinpoché and amass [merit] through the seven-limb prayer. Since the place where you invite Jé Rinpoché is your room, you should clean your room with the motivation: "This room should be made clean so I can invite Jé Rinpoché." Also, as you sweep, consider the dust to be negativities and obscurations, and as you sweep it away, think that you are sweeping away negativities and obscurations. Further, you should visualize the broom or any other instrument you use to clean the place as the wisdom realizing emptiness, and visualize that the wisdom realizing emptiness acts as the antidote that sweeps away negativities and obscurations.

At the time of the historical Buddha, there lived an ārya called Small Path (Cūḍapanthaka) who initially was extremely dull witted. First he lived in the home of a Brahman, studying Brahmin lore, memorizing the syllables OṂ BHU. But when he uttered OṂ he would forget BHU, and [200] when he uttered BHU he would forget OṂ. After three months he still could not recite OṂ BHU and the Brahman expelled him. Then he lived in the house of a Vedic scholar who taught him the words SVĀSTI ŚUDDHAṂ. But when he uttered SVĀSTI he would forget ŚUDDHAṂ, and when he uttered ŚUDDHAṂ he would forget SVĀSTI. After three months he still could not recite the words and he was again expelled. Then he entered the teachings of the Buddha where he eventually became one of the Sixteen Arhats [or Elders]. Small Path (Cūḍapanthaka) was also known as Little Path (Kṣudrapanthaka), and he had an older brother called Great Path (Mahāpanthaka). After Great Path entered the ranks of the hearer Saṅgha [that is, became an arhat], he gave Dharma instruction to [Small Path], but he did not understand. The Bhagavān made him sweep as a means to purify his karmic obscurations. First the Bhagavān made him clean the dust left by the feet of the monks at the entrance door when they assembled. As he cleaned the dust left by their feet, his karmic obscurations diminished slightly. Next he was made to sweep the temple. When he swept the temple, he was taught to recite, "Abandon dirt, abandon stains," and he recited this as he swept. When he said "dirt," this meant he was abandoning the dirt of the afflictions, and when he said "stains," this meant he was abandoning their imprints. [201] But as he recited these words while sweeping, he would forget the second word while reciting the first, or forget the first while reciting the second. So the Bhagavān requested the entire hearer saṅgha to help him learn these two words while he swept. Finally, he purified his karmic obscurations through sweeping. Then, having purified his karmic obscurations, he reflected on the instruction of his older brother and immediately attained the state of an ārya. It is said that sweeping brings such great benefits.

Therefore if you sweep while reflecting that the [Guru] Jewel will be invited here, you gain such benefits. Also, sweeping your room has the benefit that your mind becomes clear, and even the minds of others become clear. But it is inappropriate to consider that it is for this purpose alone. If you do it to clear your own mind, it is inappropriate since that is a thought concerning this life. In terms of your motivation, if you reflect that you clean your room because you are inviting the Guru Jewel here, then various benefits arise, such as the minds of yourself and others become clear, you please the deities who delight in virtue, and they will remain near you, and so forth. If you do not clean your room and leave it dirty, deities who delight in virtue will [202] distance themselves from you since they avoid defilement. When they are near, you receive the benefit of their safeguard and protection. Also, it is said that you amass the karma to be beautiful. "Amassing the karma to be beautiful" refers to pure morality, and when you remove external filth, you [tend to] remove states incompatible with internal ethics due to the reality of interdependence. Thus it makes a difference in [generating] pure morality. Moreover, it can also mature your root of virtue that establishes the pure buddha field untainted by the truth of suffering, where you will become enlightened in the future. Therefore if you sweep your room with a positive motivation you can amass a vast amount of virtue.

Setting out objects representing the Buddha's body, speech, and mind

It is said that you should set out these objects in a place that has been cleaned. The way you set them out is that the main object is your guru, then the statue of your yidam, then the Buddha in the aspect of the emanation body, then bodhisattvas, hearers, solitary realizers, heroes, ḍākinīs, Dharma protectors, and guardians, without confusing their order. It is inappropriate to rank the objects as chief or secondary by their shine or the quality of their materials. Instead you should arrange them according to the words: "guru, yidam, heroes, ḍākinīs." [203] Some worldly beings take the protector on which they rely—who swiftly engages in enlightened activity—to be chief and place him above. Some place the statue of the Buddha below. But acting in this way is a sign of complete lack of refuge and this is inappropriate. When you practice *The Hundreds of Deities of Tuṣita*, the main representation of the body can be a statue of the great Jé Rinpoché and the basis of speech can be *The Great Exposition of the Stages of the Path*. If you do not have a stūpa, the vajra and bell become bases of the mind. You should set up objects representing [the Buddha's] body, speech, and mind in this way.

The words "set out objects representing the Buddha's body, speech, and mind" indicate the order in which you should arrange them when you set them out for the first time. Once arranged in their normal order, the words "set out objects representing [the Buddha's] body, speech, and mind in a place that has been cleaned" indicate that you shall meet them. Do not think that you are familiar with them, since they are already in your house. With the recognition that they are the actual bodies of buddhas, you request to meet them, and this is how you should understand the words "set out objects representing [the Buddha's] body, speech, and mind."

Second Preliminary: Arranging Offerings

Next, "arrange any offerings that you have obtained without deceit in an appealing manner." There are two types of deceit: deceit in terms of the material, and deceit in terms of the motivation. Deceit in terms of the material refers to the substances that you offer. You should offer what is of best quality [204] for it is not appropriate to include items in the substances you offer that you would not eat or drink.

Further, when obtaining offering substances, it is said that it is inappropriate to acquire them through the five types of wrong livelihood. The five types of wrong livelihood refer to hypocrisy, flattery, hinting, pressuring, and seeking reward through favors.

When offering substances are obtained through deceit and pretense they are obtained through wrong livelihood. If you are engaged in business and if you trade according to customary business practice at a specific time and place, then your profit is not unethical since it conforms with business practice. But if the offering substances were obtained by profit through lies and guile motivated by deceit and pretense, they are not suitable to be offered.

Hypocrisy refers to displaying abnormally good behavior in the presence of others, such as benefactors and so on. Flattery refers to making compliments for the sake of gaining something. The Bhagavān has permitted Dharma practitioners to beg for alms when they are impoverished. When impoverished they may beg, and when they beg they may beg directly. Hinting refers to speaking indirectly about something you wish to receive without speaking directly to the point. For example, [205] someone may say, "Last year one person gave me this and it was a big help. At that time my spiritual practice flourished."

Pressuring refers to someone who hears that a benefactor intends to make offerings to a good meditator, but wishing to receive those offerings himself, he speaks of the many faults of that person and receives the offering himself.

Seeking reward for favors may be explained in two ways. Here it may be understood as giving a small present as a means for receiving something much larger. These are the five types of wrong livelihood, and if you have obtained something by these means, it is inappropriate to offer it to the [Three] Jewels.

To "arrange them in an appealing manner" means arranging them attractively. You should not set out the offering bowls crookedly but in a straight line. They should not touch and the distance between them should be [the width of] a grain. When you fill them with water, they should not overflow nor should the level be too low. The water should be at an appropriate level. [206] "Arrange them in an appealing manner" means such offerings are pleasing to your mind when you see them.

Third Preliminary: The Seven-Point Vairocana Posture

The third preliminary refers to sitting on a comfortable seat with your body in the seven-point Vairocana posture, or in any comfortable position, and earnestly infusing your mind with refuge and the awakening mind. "Comfortable seat" means the back [of the cushion] is slightly raised. "The seven-point

Vairocana posture" means you sit in a posture similar to that of Buddha Vairocana, and all seven points of Vairocana's posture are present.

The seven points include (1) the feet are in the vajra position, (2) the hands are in the gesture of equipoise, (3) the lower back is straight and upright, (4) the head is bent forward slightly, (5) the eyes are directed to the tip of the nose, (6) the teeth and lips are in their natural position, (7) and the tip of the tongue touches the palate. When the feet, hands, lower back, head, eyes, and shoulders are held upright, and the teeth and tongue are counted as one, this is called the seven-point Vairocana posture.

It is said that placing the tip of the tongue in a way that it slightly touches the palate makes a difference in terms of avoiding a dry mouth or saliva escaping. "Directing the eyes to the tip of the nose" indicates that the eyes are neither fully open nor closed, but are downcast so that you can just see the right and left side of your nose. [207] It doesn't mean that you look at the tip of your nose. Having arranged your posture in this way, you should earnestly infuse your mind with refuge and the awakening mind.

First examine your motivation and if it is by nature neutral or virtuous, then you may establish your practice on that basis. If your motivation is nonvirtuous you should count your breaths to pacify it. To pacify the mind when it is controlled by attachment, hatred, and the like, you observe the breaths, reflecting "I exhale" when you breathe out and "I inhale" when you breathe in, and this constitutes one round. Alternately you can count inhaling and exhaling separately. While doing this it is as if the mind becomes distracted by counting the breaths, and it becomes a method of pacifying attachment and other manifest afflictions. When you pacify afflictions in this way and begin your practice, you should direct [your mind] toward virtue. It is said that it only takes twenty-one [breaths] to pacify the mind.

Then, though there are many ways to visualize the objects of refuge, here it is said you should follow the *Guru Pūjā* merit field because it is easy to practice. In the *Guru Pūjā* [the merit field] arises from a lotus stem, but here the difference is you visualize a lion throne and then eleven levels of lotus petals and so forth. [208] At the center of the first level of lotus petals, generate your root guru, who is indivisible in essence from our teacher Munīndra [Śākyamuni]. From his heart, light radiates in the four directions. Upon the light rays to his right is the lineage of extensive conduct, with Venerable Maitreya as the central figure. At the center of the light rays to his left is Venerable Mañjuśrī surrounded by the lineage of profound view. Upon the light radiated in front of him is the assembly of your root gurus who possess actual attainments and with whom you have a Dharma connection. Upon the light radiating to his back are the lineage gurus of blessed practice. This [configuration]—with your root guru at the center—is known as "the five classes of guru."

Visualize these objects of refuge in front of you. Then visualize that you are surrounded by all six types of reincarnating beings. Each is in the aspect of a human being experiencing their specific type of suffering. Then reflect "I and all mother sentient beings from beginningless time until now have experienced the suffering of saṃsāra and the lower rebirths many times. Having already experienced [such suffering], I cannot say I will not need to experience [more] suffering. Now that I have obtained a human body and I have met the Buddhist teachings, I must obtain the state of a buddha in this life. If I cannot achieve this, I will have to experience [209] various types of suffering in saṃsāra [in general] and of the lower rebirths [in particular.]" This is the first cause of refuge. Then cultivate convictional faith that the objects of refuge generated in front have the capacity to protect from suffering [the second cause]. Actual refuge is when you sincerely entrust your mind to the [Three] Jewels in dependence on these two causes.

Then intone the refuge [formula] by reciting either the verse "I and all mother sentient beings go for refuge . . ." or the usual verse "I go for refuge to the Guru . . . I go for refuge to the Saṅgha." You should go for refuge by focusing on the two causes and properly visualizing them. As you go for refuge, visualize that you act as the chant leader and that all sentient beings who pervade space go for refuge at the same time. When you recite refuge you should visualize that all sentient beings also recite loudly with you.

Further, if you are accumulating a set number of refuge recitations and are just accumulating recitations of the line "I go for refuge to the Guru," focus on the general objects of refuge. But specifically focus on the five classes of guru—the gurus [of the four directions] and your guru at the center—who radiate light as a purifying descent of nectar. As you make requests to these gurus, an endless stream of nectar flows from their bodies and enters the crowns of yourself and all other sentient beings. [210] Reflect that the negativity and obscurations we have all accumulated from beginningless time are cleansed. Reflect that light again radiates [from the gurus' bodies] entering [your bodies] and that you obtain every blessing of the gurus' body, speech, and mind.

Then when you recite "I go for refuge to the Buddha," focus mainly on the four classes of yidam and the Buddha in the aspect of the emanation body, and accumulate recitations of the line "I go for refuge to the Buddha." An endless stream of nectar flows from their bodies and enters the crowns of yourself and all other sentient beings. It cleanses negativity and obscurations of body, speech, and mind accumulated since beginningless time. Reflect that you have obtained every blessing of the Buddha's body, speech, and mind.

Then you recite "I go for refuge to the Dharma." The main Dharma Jewel is the truth of cessation and the truth of path existing in the mindstream of the objects of refuge. However, when you visualize the objects of refuge, you should reflect that their teachings are in front of them in the form of sacred texts. When you say "I go for refuge to the Dharma," you focus on the mindstreams of the main beings, and when the purifying nectar descends and purifies, their streams descend from that scriptural Dharma in the form of sacred texts. They enter the crowns of yourself and all other sentient beings [211] and purify negativities and obscurations of our body, speech, and mind. Reflect that every type of blessing of the Dharma Jewel has entered [your body.]

When you recite "I go for refuge to the Saṅgha," focus on bodhisattvas, solitary realizers, hearers, heroes and ḍākinīs, Dharma protectors and guardians. An endless stream of nectar issues from their bodies and cleanses negativity and obscurations. When you focus on Dharma protectors and guardians, reflect that all adverse conditions for practicing Dharma and every type of obstacle have been cleared away. Think that all blessings enter [your body] and the favorable conditions for practicing Dharma are excellent.

When you go for refuge there are different ways to purify what needs to be purified in relation to each of the [Three] Jewels. For example, when you recite "I go for refuge to the Guru," think that negative karma accumulated in your previous lives, such as belittling your guru or endangering his body, is cleansed. When you recite "I go for refuge to the Buddha," [reflect that you purify] negativity [committed] in relation to the body of the Buddha, such as selling statues of the Buddha and setting a selling price. It is inappropriate to discern a statue of the Buddha as a commodity to be sold and think "I will only pay that much for it," or to say "this statue is beautiful but that one is not," since it is inappropriate to see faults in the body of the Buddha. [212] If you say such things, they are faults related to the Buddha. Examples of [faults] related to scripture include placing texts on the bare ground unsupported or allowing them to become sullied with filth. For stūpas, [it is a fault] to tread on their shadow. These are faults in relation to the body, speech, and mind, and when you go for refuge you should think that these stains have been cleansed.

Then, in the context of the awakening mind, you must think, "I will cause all sentient beings to possess happiness and will free them from suffering." But this will not happen until you obtain the state of a buddha, and therefore you should strongly generate the thought "I will attain the state of a buddha for that purpose" and recite three times the formula for refuge and bodhicitta: "I go for refuge until I am enlightened to the Buddha, the Dharma, and the Supreme Assembly . . ." At the third recitation, generate strong faith in Munīndra, and by saying "May I become a buddha to benefit all sentient beings" generate the mind of enlightenment.

Consequently, a replica separates from the body of Munīndra and dissolves into you. You reflect, "I have become the body of Munīndra." This is known as "taking the result as the path," and this makes an important, auspicious connection. [213] When you have transformed into the body of Munīndra, Munīndras equaling the number of all sentient beings emanate from your body and take their place on the crown of each sentient being. From each Munīndra seated on the crown of each sentient being, a stream of nectar descends, purifying all the negativity and obscurations of body, speech, and mind of every sentient being. Reflect that you have placed every sentient being in the state of a buddha. Still, reflecting that you have placed every sentient being in the state of a buddha is merely a wish, for you actually have not placed them there.

[In terms of the four immeasurables,] the thought "May all sentient beings possess happiness and the cause of happiness" is immeasurable love; the thought "May they be separated from suffering and the cause of suffering" is immeasurable compassion; the thought "May they not be separated from happiness that is free of suffering" is immeasurable joy; and the thought "May they abide with equanimity that is free of partiality" is immeasurable equanimity. And the instruction "Make sure you infuse your mindstream with refuge, the awakening mind, and the four immeasurables" refers to the first three preliminary practices.

The special awakening mind

Then there is the special awakening mind. Earlier, you generated one type of awakening mind but now you enhance it further, thinking, "I will quickly and even more quickly obtain the precious state of a perfect buddha by every means [for the sake of] all mother sentient beings." [214] The expression "quickly and even more quickly" means "I will attain the state of a buddha in one short lifetime in this degenerate era, without relying on accumulating [merit] for three countless great eons." The thought "For that purpose, I will practice the profound path of guru yoga" is known as the *special awakening mind*.

Once you have generated the special awakening mind, the entire merit field dissolves into Munīndra. Munīndra dissolves between your eyebrows and you reflect that you have obtained every blessing as you contract these objects of refuge.

Fourth Preliminary: Visualizing the Merit Field

The fourth preliminary is visualizing the merit field and the fifth is offering the seven-limb prayer and a maṇḍala. In the case of *Guru Pūjā* you visualize the merit field with the words "Amid a cloud of Samantabhadra offerings in the vast divine path of indivisible bliss and emptiness . . ."[86] and make an extensive offering of the seven-limb prayer with the words "I prostrate at your lotus feet . . . ."[87] Although there is no actual description of the visualization of the merit field in *The Hundreds of Deities of Tuṣita*, you should visualize and invite the merit field. The offering of the seven-limb prayer is the same.

When you visualize the merit field, in front of you there is a cloud of offerings, the ground is composed of tiny jewels, and the cloud contains inconceivable offerings of victory banners, flags, butter lamps, garlands, and so forth. [215] In the space directly in front of you, at the level of your eyebrows, visualize three thrones: the throne in the center is slightly elevated, made of precious substances, and supported by eight great lions, while the two lion thrones to its right and left are slightly lower. They are supported by eight great lions because there are two lions at each corner. Each throne being supported by eight lions symbolizes that Jé Rinpoché and his two spiritual sons, who are seated on the thrones, possess the eight sovereign qualities in their mindstreams.

Upon each of the three lion thrones are variegated lotuses and [moon] and sun maṇḍalas. They possess variegated lotuses and [moon] and sun maṇḍalas because the lotus represents *renunciation*, the sun *correct view*, and the moon *bodhicitta*. Thus this symbolizes that they possess the three principal aspects of the path in their mindstreams.

Venerable Maitreya stated in *The Ornament of Mahāyāna Sūtras* that all conquerors are of one taste within the expanse of reality. For example, even though different types of water in this world have different tastes, when they merge in the ocean they become of one taste. So too, when [sentient beings] become enlightened, all merge in one taste, [216] and it is said that they attain a single mindstream. Therefore all buddhas possess the same mindstream. Your guru is Buddha, for Vajradhāra declared in many sūtras and tantras: "In the future I will come in the form of a guru; I will come in the form of a spiritual master." Therefore you should visualize your guru as indivisible from Jé Rinpoché, or look at him as the collective embodiment of all the buddhas.

Upon the central throne you should visualize Jé Tsongkhapa who embodies all the buddhas of the three times and who is indivisible from your root guru. His broad face is peaceful and smiling, with long eyelashes, prominent nose, and skin smooth and free of wrinkles. His body is white with a red hue. His two hands perform the mudrā of turning the wheel of Dharma at his heart. "His body is clad in robes with saffron hue" indicates he wears saffron robes but with slightly different colors. For example, his lower robe is red, his Dharma robe is orange, and his outer robe is more yellow. It is well known that the "paṇḍita hat on his head has a high peak."

You should visualize that he sits with his legs in the vajra posture. His hands form such a mudrā to show that the union of the two truths [217] and that the union of sūtra and tantra are not contradictory. He holds the stems of utpala flowers with thumbs and ring fingers of both hands, and their flowers fully open at the level of his right and left ear. Upon the right flower is the hand symbol of Mañjuśrī, the sword of wisdom. Upon the left flower is the text of the *Perfection of Wisdom in Eight Thousand Verses*, which proclaims its own subject matter. If you are meditating on the lamrim, visualize that the text is *The Stages of the Path*, which proclaims its own subject matter.

Upon the throne to the right is Gyaltsap Darma Rinchen, who appears somewhat advanced in age, slightly bowed in respect to Jé Rinpoché. Both spiritual sons are similar in wearing the three Dharma robes and paṇḍita hats, explaining Dharma with their right hands and holding a text with their left. Visualize that Gyaltsap Rinpoché is seated in a manner showing respect to Jé Rinpoché, while Khedrup Rinpoché is seated in an imposing manner, fearing no one. These days artists depict him seated in a manner showing respect to Jé Rinpoché, but this is incorrect. You should visualize him as young and seated in an imposing manner without fear, not intimidated by anyone. Khedrup Jé sits in this manner, with his body erect, because [218] when alive he would immediately repudiate any criticism of the teachings of Jé Rinpoché through logic and scripture.

When the disciples of Jé Rinpoché—all inconceivable scholars—were alive, they would proclaim Jé Rinpoché's assertions. Later, some who were great scholars would claim Jé Rinpoché's assertions to be their own. But Khedrup Rinpoché criticized those who behaved in this way and proclaimed that apart from himself no one else was allowed to speak of Jé Rinpoché's statements. When opponents to the teachings of Jé Rinpoché would arise he would repudiate them. Therefore you should visualize him as having an imposing manner.

It is said that the emanations of Jé Rinpoché reside in many pure fields such as Tuṣita, Kachö, and Śambhala. Here we invite him to come from the heart of Maitreyanātha in the Delightful Dharma Abode of Tuṣita. In terms of Jé Rinpoché's residence, it was prophesied many times while he was still alive by Mañjuśrī, by the mahāsiddha and mahāpaṇḍita Lhodrag Vajrapāṇi who had direct visions of Vajrapāṇi, and others, that in the future he would come from the Delightful Dharma Abode of Tuṣita. In accordance with that, [219] an emanation of Jé Rinpoché currently resides in the Delightful Dharma Abode of Tuṣita, and he is invited from that place.

It is said that the heaven of Thirty-Three is a divine abode 80,000 yojanas beyond our world, the heaven Free of Conflict is 160,000 yojanas beyond our world, and Tuṣita is 320,000 yojanas beyond our world. A yojana is 4,000 spans[88] and Tuṣita exists at a distance of 320,000 yojanas. It is said that if you repeatedly contemplate the design of Tuṣita field, you mature the root of virtue so that you shall be reborn there in the future. Therefore it is good if you visualize the design of Tuṣita as you say "Tuṣita" when you recite "From the heart of the protectors of the hundreds of deities of Tuṣita . . ."

Moreover, Tuṣita, which is the abode of Venerable Maitreya, has a golden foundation possessing a checkered inlay of lapis, lakes, ponds, pleasure groves, wish-fulfilling trees, and various birds that proclaim the sound of Dharma. When the wish-fulfilling trees stir [in the wind] they proclaim the melodious sound of Dharma. It is as if your eyes directly perceive the extraordinary array of qualities of this environment and its inhabitants. It is as if you are actually there and as if your nose registers the exquisite and sweet fragrances. [220] It is as if you can hear the melody of the teachings of Venerable [Maitreya]. In the midst of this field of purity is the Palace of Venerable [Maitreya], which is said to be a noble residence elevated by Dharma and [graced by] white victory banners. This is the main palace. In front of it is a pleasant grove where Venerable [Maitreya] teaches Dharma. It is said that he is seated in the noble posture with his legs extended, and you should think that this establishes a special auspicious connection for coming quickly in the future. His hands are in the mudrā of turning the wheel of Dharma and [a flowering stem] to the right supports a wheel, and to the left [there is] an anointing vase that has the [typical] shape of a vase. Visualize him wearing jeweled ornaments and silk robes.

In the future, Regent Maitreyanātha will come to this world. You should visualize his great altruistic compassion that cares for disciples in this world in the aspect of white clouds. Visualize that the three beings—Jé Rinpoché and his two spiritual sons—are seated in the midst of this billowing mass of white cloud of great altruistic compassion at the heart of Venerable Maitreyanātha, which cares for disciples in this world. Further, as earlier explained, Venerable Maitreyanātha and Jé Rinpoché share the same mental continuum as all the buddhas. [221] Jé Rinpoché is also an emanation of Maitreyanātha. This is established because the mahāsiddha Lhodrag, who always had visions of Vajrapāṇi and received teachings and instruction from him, stated that when Jé Rinpoché arrived in front of him, Vajrapāṇi told the mahāsiddha Lhodrag that he received the *Compendium of Training* in the presence of Maitreya. Stating that he received it in the presence of Venerable Maitreya is stating that he received it in the presence of Jé Rinpoché. Thus he is invited from the heart of Venerable Maitreyanātha.

> **From the heart of the Protector of the hundreds of deities of Tuṣita**
> **comes a cloud resembling a mass of fresh white curd.**
> **At its crest is Omniscient Losang Drakpa, king of the Dharma,**
> **and his spiritual sons. Please come to this abode. ||1||**

"From the heart of the Protector of the hundreds of deities of Tuṣita" does not indicate a definite number of just one hundred [deities]. Since Venerable Maitreyanātha resides as the protector or lord of the many deities of Tuṣita he is called "Protector of the hundreds of deities of Tuṣita."

From his heart "comes a cloud resembling a mass of fresh white curd" and this cloud is the great compassion in the heart of Venerable Maitreyanātha. Just as the color of curd or milk is white, [his compassion] has the aspect of a cloud resembling a mass of fresh white curd.

When you state "At its crest is Omniscient Losang Drakpa, king of the Dharma, and his spiritual sons," this refers to Jé Rinpoché and his spiritual sons, Gyaltsap Jé and Khedrup Jé. Further, you previously visualized [222] Jé Rinpoché and his two spiritual sons in front of you, marked with OṂ at their crowns, ĀḤ at their throats, HŪṂ at their hearts, SVĀ at their navels, and HĀ at their secret places. As you pronounce the five syllables—OṂ, ĀḤ, HŪṂ, SVĀ, and HĀ—light radiates from them, inviting all the conquerors residing in the myriad pure fields in the ten directions and their sons and daughters in the aspect of

Jé Rinpoché and his two spiritual sons. In particular this light invites Jé Rinpoché and his two spiritual sons, who reside at the heart of Maitreyanātha, in a cloud resembling a mass of white fresh curd.

When you state "Please come to this abode" you are making a request for them to descend. You should visualize that the light rays incite a response, and the white cloud that embodies the great compassion in the heart of Maitreyanātha extends downward in a continuous stream to join with the white cloud upon which Jé Rinpoché and his spiritual sons are seated in front of you. This constitutes the fourth preliminary, visualizing the merit field.

Fifth Preliminary: The Seven-Limb Prayer

The fifth preliminary is offering the seven-limb prayer, and then you offer a maṇḍala. In *The Hundreds of Deities of Tuṣita* you offer the seven-limb prayer after you have invited the merit field. The seven limbs are prostrations, offerings, confession, rejoicing, urging them to turn the wheel of Dharma, requesting them not to pass into paranirvāṇa, and dedicating the root of virtue toward complete enlightenment. [223] Just as a person is able to fully engage in any activity if all their limbs are complete, so too you can fully establish virtue when these seven limbs are complete; therefore they are called "the seven limbs." Here, first you invite Jé Rinpoché and then accumulate merit and purify obscurations by means of the seven-limb prayer.

1. Requesting Not to Pass into Paranirvāṇa

In this text the request not to pass into paranirvāṇa comes first, but in others it occurs as the seventh [limb]. Here, the request not to pass into paranirvāṇa is the following:

> **Venerable gurus with your white smiles of delight,**
> **seated on lion thrones, lotus, and moon in the space before me,**
> **please remain for hundreds of eons in order to spread the teachings**
> **as the supreme field of merit for my mind of faith. ||2||**

It comes first because it is important that the field in relation to which you accumulate merit remains for a long time. According to custom, when you invite someone like a king, you should request him to sit on a high throne. Therefore by stating "seated on lion thrones, lotus, and moon in the space before me" you understand that "venerable gurus" are seated upon lion thrones, lotus, and moon, and thus possess the [224] three principal aspects of the path in their mindstreams, since they demonstrate the three principal aspects of the path.

You state "Venerable gurus with your white smiles of delight." In general our thoughts and actions are solely negative, therefore we lack the means to please the minds of buddhas and bodhisattvas. However, when you meditate on guru yoga you should visualize that Jé Rinpoché is pleased with us and smiles at us with compassion.

When you state "Please remain for hundreds of eons in order to spread the teachings as the supreme field of merit for my mind of faith" you acknowledge that they are the basis of our faith and the field for the accumulation of merit. By analogy, the field represents the earth. Just as abundant crops mature when we plant seeds in the earth, the Three Jewels in general are the field for the accumulation of merit, and therefore, even if the offering substances are miniscule, the result that ensues is great. But among [the Three Jewels] the guru is the supreme field. Furthermore, if you make an offering to buddhas and bodhisattvas you only gain the benefit of making the offering, without the benefit of them accepting your offering. But if you make an offering to a guru who is alive, you gain both the benefit of making an offering and the benefit of him accepting it. Therefore the guru is the supreme field, [225] and moreover he is also the representative of all buddhas. For example, when the representative of an organization visits and the people treat them well, the good reception also extends to the organization [they represent]. So too, since all the buddhas have sent your guru as their representative, when you make offerings to him you please every buddha and you gain the benefit of making offerings to every buddha. Thus the text states "as the supreme field of merit."

You request [your guru] to remain as the basis of your faith and as the field for accumulating merit for hundreds of eons for the sake of spreading the teachings and the happiness of reincarnating beings. Further, the word "hundred" does not merely indicate "one hundred" but you should understand it indicates a large number. While making the request you should imagine that you offer a new lion throne and that this new throne dissolves into your guru's throne. If you reflect that your guru from his side also accepts your request to remain for hundreds of eons, it is said this creates an auspicious connection.

2. Prostration

In terms of Tibetan language, "prostration" is *chak tsal* (*phyag tshal*). Here *chak* means "I distance myself from negativity and obscuration," while *tsal* means "I desire to obtain the qualities of your mindstream." In brief, prostration is "paying obeisance with respect." [226] Prostration has three types: physical, verbal, and mental prostration. Physical prostration refers to *full prostration*, where the entire body touches the ground; *five-point prostration*, where the five limbs—both knees, both palms, and the forehead—touch to the ground; and the *squatting prostration* sourced in Vinaya, where you merely squat while holding your calves. There are some who still follow this tradition. Verbal prostration is proclaiming others' qualities. Mental prostration is said to be meditating on faith and acting with respect.

Then,

> **Your intelligent minds comprehend the full extent of objects of knowledge.**
> **Your eloquent speech is the ear ornament of the fortunate.**
> **Your beautiful bodies blaze with the glory of renown.**
> **I prostrate to you who are meaningful to see, hear, and recall. ||3||**

The words "Your intelligent minds comprehend the full extent of objects of knowledge" expresses the mental qualities [of Jé Rinpoché and his two spiritual sons]; the words "Your eloquent speech is the ear ornament of the fortunate" expresses their verbal qualities; and the words "Your beautiful bodies blaze with the glory of renown" expresses their physical qualities. The words "I prostrate to you who are meaningful to see, hear, and recall" indicate that merely by seeing their bodies, hearing their speech, and recalling their pristine wisdom, you purify negativity and obscurations, you are liberated from lower rebirths, you obtain a noble physical basis, you awaken the Mahāyāna lineage within you, and so forth. Many such benefits are said to arise from merely expressing the name of Jé Rinpoché. Jé Rinpoché himself had said:

> By merely pronouncing or remembering my name,
> may those tormented by the effects of negative karma
> attain [227] the glory of perfect happiness and
> ascend the steps of the supreme vehicle.[89]

This verse expresses the benefits of hearing the name of Jé Rinpoché. For this reason the text says "I prostrate to you who are meaningful to see, hear, and recall."

Their minds possess the qualities of realization, compassion, and power, but here the line "Your intelligent minds comprehend the full extent of objects of knowledge" explicitly teaches the quality of realization. The pristine wisdom that comprehends the two truths, just as they are, is found exclusively among buddhas, and since Jé Rinpoché is a manifestation of Mañjuśrī, he possesses this quality. Having been explicitly taught their quality of realization, you should also recall their qualities of compassion and power.

Further, unless you had amassed vast merit in the past you would not encounter the teachings of Jé Rinpoché. For such fortunate disciples the teachings of Jé Rinpoché are similar to an ear ornament, and thus the text states: "Your eloquent speech is the ear ornament of the fortunate." To [illustrate] how difficult it was [228] to meet with the teachings of Jé Rinpoché, in the past a Mongolian [student] asked Paṇchen Palden Yeshé for his blessing and protection, saying: "Please bless me to attain a human body in my next life." The Paṇchen Lama said that he would. The student further requested: "Please pray that I will meet with the Buddhist teachings in my next life," and the Paṇchen Lama said that he would. Again the student requested: "Please pray that I will meet with the teachings of Jé Rinpoché in my next life." This time the Paṇchen Lama replied: "I am not sure whether this will come about." Vast merit is required to support such an outcome; it will not happen by chance. Further, the teachings of Jé Rinpoché are teachings that have been exhaustively analyzed by Jé Rinpoché himself, and in addition he met Venerable Mañjuśrī, like two humans meeting, and removed all stains of misunderstanding and wrong conception. Thus his teachings are of highest quality and without rival. If from your side you generate the power of exertion, [these teachings] can establish buddhahood in just three [human] years; thus they are "the ear ornament of the fortunate." The fact that right now we can practice the teachings of Jé Rinpoché is also [the mark of] good fortune.

The words "Your beautiful bodies blaze with the glory of renown" teaches one part of Jé Rinpoché's name. Previously, in the first line the word *intelligent* (*blo gro*) [229] contained the syllable *lo* (*blo*); in the second line the word *fortunate* (*skal bzang*) contained the syllable *sang* (*bzang*); and in the third line the phrase *glory of renown* (*grags pa'i dpal*) are the words *drak pa'i pal*. Therefore, in brief, this verse contains Jé Rinpoché's name in full: Losang Drakpai Pal. Jé Rinpoché practiced secret mantra and attained high realization, but he did not engage in the unconventional conduct of siddhas, for he lived exclusively in the practice of Dharma Vinaya. Due to the power of his ethics he was handsome and automatically inspired faith in those who met him; therefore it is said, "Your beautiful body blazes with the glory of renown." Just as Jé Rinpoché lived in the practice of Vinaya, so too, his followers even today maintain an unsurpassed practice of Vinaya. Since Jé Rinpoché's ethics were impeccable, even the aristocracy at that time bowed at his feet.

The Chinese emperor sent an envoy twice to invite Jé Rinpoché to come. On the first occasion the envoy arrived after Jé Rinpoché had departed and they did not meet. Since Jé Rinpoché took no delight in riches, honor, and fame, he did not grant such meetings. [230] When the second envoy arrived, he met the envoy at the request of many high lamas and political leaders. But he merely agreed to send a representative on his behalf, and they were unable to invite him to come to China in person. He sent as his representative Jamchen Chöjé Shākya Yeshé, who later established Sera Thekchen Ling [Monastery]. In brief, his influence over others was due to his ethical qualities. It is said, "By your power, without intimidation, all reincarnating beings bow to you." Thus, without intimidation, he influences all reincarnating beings due to his ethical qualities, and these words praise him in terms of his ethical qualities.

It is said that when you prostrate you should visualize that you prostrate with many hundreds of thousands of bodies, each body having that many heads, and each head having countless tongues. Another mode of explanation is that you have taken birth in countless bodies from beginningless time, and if you prostrate by visualizing all these bodies in human aspect you obtain great benefit. Further, as to the benefits of prostration, it is said that you will gain the immeasurable merit to be reborn as a cakravartin king one thousand times the number of atoms beneath the ground you cover with your body [231] [with your prostration] to the depth of the great golden basis 80,000 yojanas below the earth. To take even one birth as a cakravartin king you must amass countless merit. When a cakravartin king is reborn in this world, every reincarnating being solely engages in the ten virtuous actions and none engage in nonvirtuous action due to the power of his merit. Thus immeasurable merit is required. When you prostrate, you amass the merit to be reborn as a cakravartin king, not just once but countless times.

Question: Then why are there are so few cakravartin kings when so many prostrate?

Reply: The Bhagavān has said that anger destroys the root of virtue, and thus it is important to continuously meditate on patience since anger possesses the great flaw of destroying the root of virtue.

3. Offering

The root text states:

> **I offer this ocean-like cloud of offerings actually arranged and mentally created to you, the supreme field of merit, such as pleasing water offerings, various flowers, fragrant incense, light, scented water, and so on. ||4||**
> [232]

"Pleasing water offerings" are perfumed water offered for drinking and clean and refreshing water used for bathing. "Various flowers" refers to divine and human flowers in the form of flower gardens, flower garlands, flower canopies, flower parasols, and so forth. "Fragrant incense" refers to incense and to various types of fragrance applied or innate, such as naturally fragrant aloe wood and so forth. "Light" refers to various types of bright light that illuminate, such as the light of the sun and moon, the light of gems, the light of lightning, the light of lamps, and so forth. "Scented water" refers to different types of naturally cooling water that removes the suffering of heat when applied to the body, such as water that is naturally imbued with camphor, sandalwood, and the like. "And so on" refers to food and music, such as divine food possessing hundreds of flavors and so forth, and music that removes mental anxiety when heard, such as the music of cymbals, drums, and the like. In brief, you make offerings as you say "pleasant water offerings, water for the feet, flowers, incense, light, scented water, and music." Other offerings include victory banners, flags, pleasant parks, beautiful mountains, [233] lakes and ponds decorated with lotuses, and so forth. You can offer anything that is beautiful. "Actually arranged" refers to offerings that you have set out in front of you, and "mentally created" refers to offerings that you visualize, thinking "I offer this and that." These are also called "Samantabhadra offerings." In the past, Bodhisattva Samantabhadra held a jewel in his hand from which light radiated producing many jewels, and these also radiated light, filling all of space. You should make offerings in this way, visualizing that light radiates from a single offering and that offering pervades all of space, and then apply this [technique] to flowers and so forth. "An ocean-like cloud of offerings" refers to clouds of offerings that are as vast as an ocean. The words "arrange an ocean-like cloud of offerings" is an expression of abundance, and when you offer something, imagining that you make countless offerings similar to the one you have, the benefit you gain is limitless. The meaning of "supreme field" has been discussed earlier.

It is inappropriate to offer objects of inferior quality when you possess objects of good quality. Even if you don't have fine or good quality objects, you should offer what you have so long as it is not poisonous. [234] For example, even though you only have cheap or weak incense, you should definitely offer it. Even though at the beginning your offerings are of inferior quality, by the power of offering them, you will come to make fine offerings later. The Kadampa Geshé Phuchungwa said, "First I offered valerian until it burned my nostrils." Valerian is a rhizome that grows in the mountains of Tibet. "But later I received four types of [aromatic] pill from which I made fragrant incense, and that I offered. Then, on another occasion, I offered twenty gold coins' worth of prepared incense. If you become familiar with making offerings, the quality of your offerings will improve."

If you do not have a proper vessel when making water offerings, you could clean your cup [or bowl] and use that. When Drupkhang Gelek Gyatso and the great siddha Longdol Lama were studying, they had few material possessions and were poor. Since they did not have offering bowls or other containers, they would clean their bowls and make offerings in them. When it was time to eat, they would request the [Three] Jewels to lend them the bowls and would eat. Once they cleaned and washed them, they would again make offerings in them. They say [235] that if you have faith and the wish to make an offering, you will never be short of things to offer or offering containers. For example, you can offer just water and use your bowl [or cup] as the container.

4. Confession

Whatever nonvirtuous actions of body, speech, and mind
I have accumulated from beginningless time, and
in particular this mass of transgressions of my three vows,
I confess individually, with sincere regret. ||5||

The words "Whatever nonvirtuous actions of body, speech, and mind I have accumulated from beginningless time" refer to the negativity [accumulated] from time without beginning. Your present human body has been obtained in dependence on the virtuous karma of a previous life, and that life was also established by karma accumulated in a life previous to that. If you calculate past [lives] in this way, your births have no beginning. During those lives you placed an incredibly large number of potent negative imprints in your mind. Some are purified as you experience their maturation while others are purified through confession. Otherwise, the vast majority of negativity accumulated from beginningless time remains in your mind.

We possess countless faults, including every nonvirtuous negative act committed by our body, such as killing; committed by our speech, such as slander; and committed by our mind, such as the mental actions of anger, malice, and wrong view; and "in particular this mass of transgressions of my three vows" [236] refers to [transgressions of] individual liberation vows, bodhisattva vows, and secret-mantra vows. We have taken many vows. When we attend great initiations we take both bodhisattva vows and the vows of secret mantra. The ordained take ordination vows and lay practitioners take lay vows for one day or for the duration of their lives. When the three types of vows are properly guarded, limitless benefits ensue, but when they are transgressed, the faults are also limitless. Therefore with specific focus on the three vows, confess [transgressions] with the words "In particular, this mass of transgressions of my three vows I confess individually, with sincere regret," for you must generate an intense sense of remorse.

When you lack strong regret, confession is ineffective. But if you have strong regret—like one who has previously ingested poison—this constitutes the opponent power of repudiation. When you have this and you engage in reciting dhāraṇī mantras, express the name of your [deity], make offerings, and so forth—which act as the antidote to negativity—this is the opponent power of fully applying the antidote. When you have strong regret for negativity and you think "I will not repeat it," this is the opponent power of not repeating the action. [237] Practicing refuge and the awakening mind in the beginning is the opponent power of the basis. It is said that if you practice confession and restraint properly, even karma certain to be experienced will be purified. What need is there to speak of karma not certain to be experienced?

The words "I confess individually" mean that you should confess and restore each of the three types of vows individually. If your vows of secret mantra have declined, you must confess by means of performing self-initiation, requesting initiation, and so forth. If your bodhicitta vows have declined, you should take the vows again. If your vows of individual liberation have declined, you should purify them by means of restoring them, and so forth.

5. Rejoicing

In general, rejoicing refers to cultivating joy in the virtue of yourself and others, but here you rejoice in the life and deeds of Jé Rinpoché.

Question: What were his life and deeds?

> **In this time of degeneration, you studied extensively and strove to practice.**
> **And by abandoning the eight concerns, your life of freedom and endowment**
> **became meaningful. From the depths of my heart I rejoice,**
> **O Protector, in the great waves of your deeds. ||6||**

"In this time of degeneration, you studied extensively and strove to practice." In favorable periods, many practitioners integrate study and meditation. However, in this time of degeneration, those who meditate belittle those who study, saying study is of no benefit for you must mainly engage in meditation, [238] while those who study belittle those who meditate without study, and so on. Great Jé Rinpoché did not hold study and meditation to be contradictory. He studied extensively and then put into practice the meaning of what he studied. Jé Rinpoché himself said:

> In the beginning I sought extensive instruction.
> In the middle all scriptural systems appeared as personal advice.

> In the end I practiced day and night.
> I dedicate everything to the spread of the teachings.[90]

He engaged in the extensive study of a vast number of scriptural systems, relying on many gurus. To address unresolved doubts he [engaged in practices to] accumulate [merit] and eliminate [obstacles]. Then, having removed every stain of distortion, he had a vision of Venerable Mañjuśrī and listened to him. After listening to his instruction he saw that attainments would not follow from effort alone, and he traveled to different places such as Ölkha and Chölung to practice accumulation and purification, thus completing the practice of accumulating [merit] and purifying obscurations. While making maṇḍala offerings with a flat stone, his arm bled from rubbing against the stone, and while prostrating, his hands left impressions on the stone due to sliding over it. You can still see the stones he used for making maṇḍala offerings. He practiced constantly, night and day, integrating meditation with accumulation and purification. [239] By the might of his practice he generated realizations in his mindstream and from then on he explained Dharma to others, and the eighteen volumes of his collected works remain a legacy to students of later generations.

The words "and by abandoning the eight concerns, your life of freedom and endowment became meaningful" mean that when virtue is influenced by the eight worldly concerns, it does not become a path. Thus he abandoned all types of worldly concern—black, white, and mixed—and made his life of freedom and endowment meaningful. An example of having abandoned the eight worldly concerns is that he did not travel to China despite being invited by the powerful, dominant, and unrivaled Chinese emperor.

"From the depths of my heart I rejoice, O Protector, in the great waves of your deeds" means that in general he removed the stains of misunderstanding, wrong conception, and doubt regarding the Buddha's teachings through the path of reason and scriptures, and illuminated the teachings of the Buddha like the sun. His two greatest works—from among the eighteen volumes of his collected works—are the *Great Lamrim* and the *Great Exposition of Mantric Stages*, and the great waves of his deeds performed for the Buddha's teachings are related to these two texts. [240] The meaning of these words is that you sincerely rejoice from the depths of your heart in the great waves of his deeds, and not just pay lip service.

The benefits of rejoicing are also extensive. When you rejoice in those whose realizations are similar to yours, you gain a similar benefit. When you rejoice in those whose realizations are inferior to yours, you gain higher benefit. When you rejoice in the virtue of buddhas and bodhisattvas whose realizations are higher than yours, you do not gain similar benefit but at least you gain a partial benefit. Regarding that part, even part of the root of virtue of buddhas and bodhisattvas is a great wave compared to the entire root of virtue we have amassed over thousands of years. Therefore it is said that rejoicing is a supreme method for gathering the root of virtue.

6. Urging to Turn the Wheel of Dharma

May a rain of profound and extensive Dharma fall
from the billowing clouds of wisdom and compassion
gathered in the sky of your Dharma body, venerable holy guru,
to care for disciples in any way appropriate. ||7||

For instance, just as clouds gather in the sky and then rain falls on the land, so too you urge that clouds of compassion and wisdom gather in the Dharma body of Jé Rinpoché [241] and a rain of profound and extensive Dharma falls in any way appropriate upon the mind of each disciple. His wisdom sees whether or not disciples are suitable vessels, and his compassion understands who needs to be taught Dharma so that others are benefited. Therefore wisdom and compassion determine the teaching of Dharma, and there is no way this can be done without them.

7. Dedication

After the limb of urging to turn the wheel of Dharma there is dedication of one's root of virtue, since the limb of requesting not to pass into paranirvāṇa has gone before.

> **May any virtue that I have accumulated**
> **benefit the entire teachings and all reincarnating beings.**
> **In particular, may the essence of the teachings of**
> **Venerable Losang Drakpa shed illumination for a long time. ||8||**

You dedicate your root of virtue with the words "May any virtue that I have accumulated benefit the entire teachings and all reincarnating beings." In general, the object of the dedication of the entire root of virtue you have already accumulated is to spread the Buddhist teachings and to benefit reincarnating beings. And specifically, since the teachings of Guru Jé Rinpoché are like the essence of the Buddha's teachings, you state, "in particular, may the essence of the teachings of Venerable Losang Drakpa shed illumination for a long time."

The teachings of Jé Rinpoché are called "the essence of the teachings" because they condense the essence of 84,000 aggregates of Dharma into sūtra and tantra so they can be readily practiced, and it is rare to find teachings like those of Jé Rinpoché. "May they shed illumination for a long time" comprises a dedication that these teachings spread [242] and shed illumination for a long time in the world. "May the essence of the teachings of Jé Rinpoché shed illumination" indicates both a prayer and a dedication through the virtue accumulated by the six preceding limbs. Therefore, when you pray by taking any root of virtue as your focal object, it becomes a dedication. If you pray saying "In all my lives may I meet with pure gurus . . ." without having this specific focal object, it is only a prayer. Therefore there is a slight difference between prayer and dedication. The dedication here is an example of that which is both a prayer and a dedication. It is said that something is a prayer without being a dedication when you make a prayer without having a specific substance to dedicate. Here, since it is both a prayer and a dedication, it is the seventh limb.

Sixth Preliminary: Offering a Maṇḍala

Then, offer a maṇḍala to Jé Rinpoché and perform a concise review of the entire path. You may base this on *The Foundation of All Qualities* or any of the many other texts that teach the entire path. [243] It is extremely beneficial to perform a concise review of the entire path, starting from the means of relying on your spiritual friend and concluding with the union of a nonlearner. Further, in the beginning [when you are about to meditate] on a subject such as the means of relying on your spiritual friend, offer a maṇḍala and make the request: "Bless me to generate the realization of the entire path." Next, cultivate the topics related to how to rely on one's spiritual friend. After [you have cultivated] these topics, nectar descends from Jé Rinpoché's body and you reflect that all obstacles that obstruct the generation of the realization of how to rely on your spiritual friend are purified, and that you are blessed to generate the correct realization of how to rely on your spiritual friend. Then [contemplate] leisure and endowment, impermanence, refuge, and karma and its result. After that, generate the mind seeking liberation, practice the path of the three [higher] trainings, and then train in the conduct of the six perfections—that forms the round of training in bodhicitta. At the end of each round you should visualize the descent of purifying nectar for each and think that you are blessed with the generation of various realizations. It is recommended that you perform a concise review of the entire path.

3. Actual Practice and Conclusion

1. Actual Practice of the Miktsema Praise

NEXT YOU should make requests by means of the Miktsema prayer:

> **Avalokiteśvara, great treasure of nonreifying compassion,**
> **Mañjuśrī, master of stainless wisdom,** [244]
> **Secret Lord, destroyer of hordes of māras,**
> **Tsongkhapa, crown jewel of scholars of the Land of Snows,**
> **Losang Drakpa, I make requests at your feet. ||9||**

Avalokiteśvara, Vajrapāṇi, and Mañjuśrī are called the protectors of the three lineages. Avalokiteśvara is the compassion of all the buddhas embodied as a deity, Mañjuśrī is the quality of their wisdom embodied as a deity, and Vajrapāṇi is their power embodied as a deity. Jé Rinpoché in essence combines all three protectors in one being, and any request to him is a request to all three lineage protectors.

When you say "nonreifying," you make a request while visualizing him as Avalokiteśvara, whose nature combines all compassion. The word "nonreifying" indicates that this is not mere compassion and that you should understand it as compassion that is influenced by the wisdom realizing the lack of true existence, free from what is targeted by grasping at true existence. You should understand that it possesses both method and wisdom. Therefore when you state "nonreifying" you should understand *wisdom*, and when you state "compassion" you should understand *method*. You make requests through reflecting that Avalokiteśvara by his very nature embodies compassion that possesses both method and wisdom. [245]

When "stainless" is applied to both method and wisdom, then "stainless" refers to wisdom that is free of the stain of self-interest. And "wisdom" refers to the power of [omniscient] wisdom that possesses both method and wisdom. When you state "Master of stainless wisdom," you make a request while visualizing him as having the nature of "Mañjuśrī," who embodies the wisdom of all the buddhas.

"Secret Lord" embodies the power and strength of all the buddhas who destroy the hordes of all māras, and he is "destroyer of hordes of māras." When you say that, you make a request visualizing that he has the nature of Vajrapāṇi.

"Scholars of the Land of Snows" indicates that when Jé Rinpoché appeared there were none among the scholars in the Land of Snows who did not bow at his feet, and therefore he is the "crown jewel" of scholars of the Land of Snows. "Tsongkhapa" is the name that reflects his birthplace; "Losang Dragpa" is his actual name, and thus: "Losang Dragpa, I make requests at your feet."

When a word commentary is given on the Miktsema, it is a vast commentary, and when a meaning commentary is given, it becomes a request to all the buddhas, since you are making requests to the protectors of the three lineages [who represent their] realization, compassion, and power. Therefore, even though it is a single verse, [246] both the word and meaning [commentaries] are vast. When Phürbuchok Ngawang Jampa was advanced in age, he was requested to give teachings. Those who sought teachings sent a message through his attendant stating that even if a great Dharma teaching could not be given, at least they would request a teaching on Miktsema. He immediately scolded them saying: "I having nothing greater to explain than Miktsema." Therefore this Miktsema [verse] is a great Dharma.

When you make the request, you reflect that the crowns of Jé Rinpoché and his two spiritual sons are marked with the syllable OṂ, in nature the vajra body; their throats are marked with the syllable ĀḤ, in nature the vajra speech; and their hearts are marked with the syllable HŪṂ, in nature the vajra mind. Then, as you make requests by means of the Miktsema, visualizing that the syllable OṂ on the crowns of Jé Rinpoché and his two spiritual sons is in nature the vajra body of all the buddhas, a stream of white nectar descends, entering your crown, completely filling your body. Negativities, obscurations, and their imprints accumulated by means of your body over beginningless samsaric lives are purified. You obtain the blessing of their body and [247] should reflect that you have received the potency to establish the vajra body.

Then you make requests visualizing that the syllable ĀḤ in the throats of Jé Rinpoché and his two spiritual sons is in nature the vajra speech of all the buddhas. Red nectar-light is emitted and dissolves into your throat. The negativities, obscurations, and their imprints that you have accumulated from beginningless time by means of your speech are purified. You obtain every blessing of their speech and should reflect that you have received the potency to establish vajra speech.

Again, you make requests visualizing that the syllable HŪṂ at the hearts of Jé Rinpoché and his two spiritual sons is in nature the vajra mind of all the buddhas. Blue nectar-light is emitted from the syllable HŪṂ at their hearts and dissolves into your heart. The negativities, obscurations, and their imprints that you have accumulated from beginningless time by means of your mind are purified. You obtain every blessing of their mind and you should reflect that you have received the potency to establish vajra mind.

If you are counting Miktsema prayers, you should first recite it a few times with the visualization described above. When you make the requests that you actually count, white nectar from the syllable OṂ on their crowns, red nectar from the syllable ĀḤ in their throats, and blue nectar from the syllable HŪṂ at their hearts, descend simultaneously. They purify the three sites of your body simultaneously. You obtain all their blessings of body, speech, and mind and should reflect that you have received the potency to establish the union of body and mind in the future. It is excellent to count most of your Miktsema prayers with this last visualization. [248]

If your main purpose in counting is for the sake of purifying negativities and obscurations, visualize that three hollow tubes of light emerge from the hearts of Jé Rinpoché and his two spiritual sons. They quickly merge as one and enter your crown as a single tube. White nectar, the color of milk, flows through it and fills your body. You should reflect that all the negativity, obscurations, and imprints you have accumulated in your beginningless samsaric lives are expelled from the doors of your senses and the pores of your body as blackness. Such negativity and obscurations are expelled [from your body] in the aspect of a seething mass of black smoke and charcoal. They enter the mouth of Yama, the Lord of Death who abides below the earth, coveting your life force. Visualize that it satisfies him and he closes his mouth and lies down. It is said that this is the supreme means of establishing long life. If there are obstructive spirits who harm you and bear hostility toward you, and spirits who take retribution or extract [karmic] debt, you should reflect that [whatever exits your body] enters their mouth, they are satisfied, and they bear no further thought of harm. This is the best long-life practice.

Otherwise, if your [main purpose is to] establish wisdom through this prayer, focus on the practices that establish wisdom and thus establish vast wisdom, clear wisdom that discerns subtle difficult points, swift wisdom that is capable of swift recollection, [249] and profound wisdom. You can also establish the wisdom for composing texts, for explaining Dharma, and for debating the meaning of texts. Lamas of the past have said that if your focus is good, you will experience these clearly within a month or two.

Various yogic feats can be achieved through the Miktsema praise, such as, for example, the capacity to cause rain to fall, protect from frost, and so forth. When the weather turns cold, frost and ice tend to form on grain crops that [subsequently] go to waste, and this practice benefits by preventing this from happening. In our Bönpo area, just five monks from our monastery would go to prevent frost. Ice formed on the grass that grew outside [the protected area] and the stems were about to break, but the grains inside the [protected] fields would remain warm. Therefore they say that there is no knowledge mantra that can compete with the Miktsema praise, and it is recited a lot. Therefore it is good to recite it continuously. [250]

2. Conclusion

Once you have finished the Miktsema praise, you should contract the merit field. When you contract the merit field, the two spiritual sons that you have visualized along with Jé Rinpoché will dissolve into his right and left shoulder. The thrones of the two spiritual sons dissolve into the throne of Jé Rinpoché. Next you focus on the body of Jé Rinpoché, who sits on a lotus, sun, and moon seat, and recite:

> **My glorious and precious root guru,**
> **take your seat on the lotus and moon on my crown.**
> **Please take care of me with your great kindness,**
> **and bestow on me the siddhis of body, speech, and mind.** ||10||

When you recite this for the first time, as you say "my glorious and precious root guru," you address Jé Rinpoché. You say "take your seat on the lotus and moon on my crown" [because] previously Jé Rinpoché was sitting facing you but now he comes to your crown and sits facing the same direction as you. When you recite "my glorious and precious root guru . . ." for the second time while he is seated in this way, you request him to abide at your heart. Generally [the indestructible drop at] your heart faces downward, but when you perform this meditation you reflect that you have turned it upward. You must think that it opens and transforms into an eight-petaled lotus. [251] Jé Rinpoché's lotus seat also descends and dissolves into your heart that is an eight-petaled lotus. Meditate that they become inseparable in nature. It is said that your consciousness resides within the sphere of the two conjoined constituents: the white drop that is the white component obtained from your father and the red drop that is the red component obtained from your mother. When the sun seat of Jé Rinpoché descends, it dissolves in the red component, and when the moon descends, it dissolves in the white component. Thus serially, the red portion transforms into a sun disc and the white portion transforms into a moon disc. Next you should think that Jé Rinpoché descends and becomes indivisible from your mind.

Jé Rinpoché is in nature indivisible from the protectors of the three lineages, and therefore you should think that the guru, the yidam, and your own mind have become indivisible in nature and reside internally at the center of your heart. You should think that the cloud that extends from the heart [of Venerable Maitreyanātha] is connected with the cloud in your heart where Jé Rinpoché resides, without being severed.

When you recite the verse "My glorious and precious root guru . . ." for the third time, you request Jé Rinpoché, who resides at your heart, to ". . . remain steadfast till I attain the essence of enlightenment." You request him to remain in the center of your heart until you attain the state of a buddha and should imagine that he accepts whatever you have requested. [252]

Then reflect that the eight petals of your heart close and Jé Rinpoché abides within. When the petals close they transform into the aspect of your heart. Looking at it from the outside, it is surrounded by threads of Miktsema and Arapatsana mantra garlands. At the top of your heart is the [upper] half of a blue five-spoked vajra, the nature of Akṣobhya. You should think that it is heavy and presses your heart down with its weight, and this is also beneficial in [preventing] heart ailments. At all times reflect that Jé Rinpoché resides at your heart and imagine that the thread of cloud remains, without being severed. This is a point of auspicious connection, so that at the time of your death you will be able to proceed to a pure land. Place Jé Rinpoché at your heart as a witness for all your physical and verbal activities. Think that you offer all your enjoyments, such as food, clothes, and accommodation, to Jé Rinpoché at your heart. Think that if you engage in any nonvirtuous activity, Jé Rinpoché at your heart becomes worried. When others offer homage to you, think that they are respectful to Jé Rinpoché at your heart. You should imagine all appearances that arise to be the body of Jé Rinpoché and all sounds to be the resonance of the Miktsema praise that proclaims itself. [253]

Dedication

It is said that two things are required at the beginning and the end: motivation at the beginning and dedication at the end. In conclusion, it is important to make dedication prayers. The final prayers are generally for the spread of the teachings and for the long life of great beings who are holders of Dharma. In this case, you should pray that in all your lives the great guru Jé Tsongkhapa will directly act as your spiritual friend so that you can generate the complete path of sūtra and tantra in your mindstream. Also, through the might of having meditated on the arrangement of the pure land of Tuṣita and on the thread of white cloud not being severed, you should pray that when you die, you will be reborn in the pure land of Tuṣita, meet directly Venerable Maitreyanātha and Jé Rinpoché, and hear their Dharma [teachings].

Final words of advice

Here I have offered a short commentary based on the root text of *The Hundreds of Deities of Tuṣita*. I have received these teachings from His Holiness the Dalai Lama and many other gurus. You should recite the Miktsema praise in relation to *The Hundreds of Deities of Tuṣita* while visualizing Jé Rinpoché, whose nature combines the protectors of the three lineages. In terms of your usual practice, although at present it is difficult to engage in tantric practice, you should consider refuge and karma and its result as the main things to safeguard [254] and then, if you can, it is good to meditate on love and compassion. In this way the purpose of all of us—the teacher who explained the Dharma and the students who listened to it—will be fulfilled. If in dependence upon our Dharma connection you have the thought that this was a special occasion, then that Dharma connection has been useful. We have spent a few days discussing Dharma, and since you requested all these teachings for the sake of practicing them, I urge you to practice well.

Appendix

The Hundreds of Deities of Tuṣita

From the heart of the Protector of the hundreds of deities
of Tuṣita
comes a cloud resembling a mass of fresh white curd.
At its crest is Omniscient Losang Drakpa, king of the Dharma,
and his spiritual sons. Please come to this abode. ||1||

Venerable gurus with your white smiles of delight,
seated on lion thrones, lotus, and moon in the space
before me,
please remain for hundreds of eons in order to spread the
teachings
as the supreme field of merit for my mind of faith. ||2||

Your intelligent minds comprehend the full extent of objects
of knowledge.
Your eloquent speech is the ear ornament of the fortunate.
Your beautiful bodies blaze with the glory of renown.
I prostrate to you who are meaningful to see, hear, and
recall. ||3||

I offer this ocean-like cloud of offerings actually arranged
and mentally created to you the supreme field of merit,

such as pleasing water offerings, various flowers,
fragrant incense, light, and scented water, and so on. ||4||

Whatever nonvirtuous actions of body, speech, and mind
I have accumulated from beginningless time, and
in particular this mass of transgressions of my three vows,
I confess individually, with sincere regret. ||5||

In this time of degeneration, you studied extensively and strove to practice.
And by abandoning the eight concerns, your life of freedom and endowment
became meaningful. From the depths of my heart I rejoice,
O Protector, in the great waves of your deeds. ||6||

May a rain of profound and extensive Dharma fall
from the billowing clouds of wisdom and compassion
gathered in the sky of your Dharma body, venerable holy guru,
to care for disciples in any way appropriate. ||7||

May any virtue that I have accumulated
benefit the entire teachings and all reincarnating beings.
In particular, may the essence of the teachings of
Venerable Losang Drakpa shed illumination for a long time. ||8||

Avalokiteśvara, great treasure of nonreifying compassion,
Mañjuśrī, master of stainless wisdom,
Secret Lord, destroyer of hordes of māras,
Tsongkhapa, crown jewel of scholars of the Land of Snows,
Losang Drakpa, I make requests at your feet. ||9||

My glorious and precious root guru,
take your seat on the lotus and moon on my crown.
Please take care of me with your great kindness,
and bestow on me the siddhis of body, speech, and mind.[91] ||10||

Notes

1. On Gyaltsap Jé and Khedrup Jé, Tsongkhapa's two heart disciples, or spiritual sons, see notes 25 and 26 below.
2. "Miktsema" is the abbreviated name given to the five-line praise of Jé Tsongkhapa in Tibetan: "dmigs med brtse ba'i gter chen spyan ras gzigs . . ." and so on. The abbreviated name comprises the first and third syllables with the suffix "ma" added
3. Published by Jamyang Publications, Choedhen Labrang, House No.4, Sera Jhe Monastery, 2005.
4. The Geden tradition (*dge ldan chos lugs*) refers to the early Gelukpa tradition (*dge lugs pa'i chos lugs*) founded by Jé Tsongkhapa (1357–1419).
5. Seals of secrecy (*bka' rgya ma*) refer to teachings that are restricted to certain lineage holders.
6. Pabongkha Rinpoché's commentary, which is reproduced here in bold, now appears in italics representing the change in the Tibetan text from large to small print. In general, small Tibetan print—here represented by italics—indicates that the author is giving instruction or commentary on the practice.
7. Machik Labdrön (Ma cig lab kyi sgron ma, 1055–1149) was a great Tibetan practitioner and teacher and many lineages of the practice of *chö (gcod)* are attributed to her.
8. Tsongkhapa, *For As Long As (Ji srid thub mchog ma)*. In *Chos spyod kyi lag len nyer mkho phyogs gcig tu bsdebs pa sogs*, 348–53, p. 2b. Accessed October 14, 2023. http://purl.bdrc.io/resource/MW1NLM4330_O1NLM4330_020. [BDRC bdr:MW1NLM4330_O1NLM4330_020])

9. Könchok Jigmé Wangpo, *How to Practice the Six Preliminary Practices: Essential Instructions on Mañjuśrī's Transmission of the Stages of the Path*, 228.
10. Wrong livelihood (*log 'tsho*) for the ordained refers to earning a living by means of hypocrisy, flattery, hinting, pressuring, and seeking reward through favors, and so on. For the lay, it refers to earning a living through butchery, trading flesh, both of animals and humans, and so forth.
11. Paṇchen Losang Chökyi Gyaltsen (Paṇ chen Blo bzang Chos kyi rgyal mtshan), *Guru Pūjā* (*Bla ma mchod pa*), verse 2.
12. The eight sovereign qualities (*dbang phyug brgyad kyi yon tan*) that are found exclusively in a buddha are (1) quality of body, (2) quality of speech, (3) quality of mind, (4) quality of enlightened activities, (5) quality of miracles, (6) quality of omnipresence, (7) quality of abode, and (8) quality of fulfillment of desire.
13. The three principal aspects of the path (*lam gtso rnams gsum*) are renunciation, bodhicitta, and correct view. See the chapter on "The Three Principal Aspects of the Path" in H. E. Chöden Rinpoché's *An Offering Cloud of Nectar.*
14. The Buddha is seated with his right hand touching the earth and his left hand resting on his lap facing upward in the gesture of meditation, holding a bowl of nectar.
15. The four māras are (1) māra of affliction, (2) māra of the aggregates, (3) devaputra māra, (4) māra lord of death.
16. The lineage of extensive conduct is led by Maitreya, surrounded by masters Asaṅga, Vasubandhu, and so on. The lineage of profound view is led by Mañjuśrī, surrounded by masters Nāgārjuna, Āryadeva, and so on. The lineage of blessed practice is led by Vajradhāra, surrounded by masters Tilopa, Nāropa, and so on. All three lineages originate from Buddha Śākyamuni.
17. This is part of an alternate rendering of this line of the verse.
18. Munīndra (Thub pa'i dbang po), or Lord of Sages, is an epithet for Buddha Śākyamuni.
19 Highest yoga tantra (*rnal 'byor bla med rgyud*) is also known as highest yoga mantra (*sngags bla med*).

20. Paṇchen Losang Chökyi Gyaltsen, *Guru Pūjā*, verse 5.
21. Jé Gungthangpa (Rje gung thang pa) is an epithet of Jé Milarepa, who came from the Gungthang region near the Tibet-Nepal border north of Kathmandu.
22. The object-aspect (*gzungs rnam*) is the object that is engaged by awareness, and the subject-aspect (*'dzin rnam*) is the awareness engaging that object.
23. In the mudrā (hand gesture) of turning the wheel of Dharma, or dharmacakra mudrā (*chos 'khor kyi chag rgya*), both hands are held against the chest, with the left hand facing inward, covering the right hand that is facing outward. The index finger and thumb of each hand form a circle, or "wheel."
24. The three levels of being (*sems dpa' sum brtsegs*) refers to the visualization that includes (1) the outer commitment being; (2) a deity, usually in the aspect having one face and two arms, at the heart of the commitment being, constituting the wisdom being; and (3) a seed syllable at the heart of the wisdom being, constituting the concentration being.
25. Gyaltsap Jé Darma Rinchen (Rgyal tshab Rje Dar ma rin chen, 1364–1432) was born in Tsang Province of central Tibet. He was one of the heart disciples of Jé Rinpoché, and became the first Ganden Tripa of the Geluk tradition and the second abbot of Ganden Monastery after Tsongkhapa passed away.
26. Khedrup Jé Gelek Pelsang (Mkhas grub Rje Dge legs dpal bsang, 1385–1438) was born in Tsang Province. He was the second heart disciple of Jé Rinpoché and became the third abbot of Ganden Monastery after Gyaltsap Jé, and the second Ganden Tripa. He was a prolific writer whose line of incarnations became known as the Paṇchen Lamas.
27. The twelve deeds of Buddha Śākyamuni (*mdzad pa bcu gnyis*) are (1) descent from Tuṣita, (2) entering the womb of his mother, (3) taking birth, (4) displaying skill in mundane arts, (5) enjoying his retinue of female companions, (6) becoming a renunciate, (7) practicing austerities, (8) sitting under the Bodhi tree,

(9) defeating the māras, (10) becoming enlightened, (11) turning the wheel of Dharma, and (12) passing into paranirvāṇa.

28. Tashi Lhunpo Monastery was founded in 1447 by Gendün Drup, the First Dalai Lama, close to Shigatse, Tibet. The monastery is the traditional seat of the Paṇchen Lamas.
29. Khensur Rinpoché Losang Wangchuk (Blo bzang dbang phyug, 1901–72) was the 65th abbot of Sera Jé Monastery.
30. *The Praise to Jowo Atiśa* was composed by Naktso Lotsāwa Tsültrim Gyalwa (Nag tsho lo tsā ba Tshul khrims rgyal ba, b. 1011).
31. Reting Monastery was established in 1057 by Dromtönpa in the Reting Tsampo Valley, north of Lhasa. It became one of the great centers of the Kadampa tradition, and later on became a Geluk monastery and the seat of Reting Rinpoché.
32. Lhodrag Namkha Gyaltsen (Lho brag nam mkha' rgyal mtshan, 1326–1401) was a Nyingma master and teacher of Tsongkhapa. It is said that when he met Tsongkhapa he saw him in the form of Mañjuśrī, while Tsongkhapa saw the master in the form of Vajrapāṇi. They gave each other reciprocal teachings.
33. After Lama Tsongkhapa passed away, the bereaved Khedrup Jé often asked him for guidance. On five occasions Jé Rinpoché appeared directly to him: (1) as a monk on a white elephant, (2) as a sixteen-year-old youth on a throne, (3) as the bodhisattva Mañjuśrī on a snow lion, (4) as a yogi on a tiger, and (5) as a monk blazing with light among clouds. During these visions Khedrup Jé received special instructions, encouragement, and empowerments. These five visions are traditionally the subjects of a set of thangkas called "The Five Visions of Khedrup Jé."
34. Kachö (Bkha' spyod, Khecara) is the pure land associated with the practice of Vajrayogini.
35. Śambhala is the kingdom in which Buddha Śākyamuni taught the Kālacakra Tantra.
36. The eighteen unique qualities of a buddha are (1–10) the ten powers (*stobs, bala*), (11–14) the four fearlessnesses (*mi 'jig pa, vaiśāradya*), (15–17) the three foundations of mindfulness (*dran*

pa nyer gzhag, smṛtyupasthāna), and (18) great compassion (*thugs rje chen po, mahākaruṇā*).

37. The "three isolations of mantra" refers to the physical, verbal, and mental isolation of the completion stage.
38. Taktsang Lotsāwa Sherab Rinchen (Stag tshang lo tswa ba Shes rab Rin chen) was born in Tsang in 1405 and became an important Sakya master. His written works include *Understanding All Tenets* (*Grub mtha' kun shes*), which criticizes many of the views of Jé Tsongkhapa and which, in turn, inspired the composition of Jamyang Shepa's *Great Exposition of Tenets*.
39. Jamchen Chöjé (Byams chen chos rje, 1354–1435) was a disciple of Jé Tsongkhapa. His actual name was Shākya Yeshé (Shākya ye shes) but he was conferred the title Jamchen Chöjé, or "Dharma Lord of Great Love," by the Chinese emperor Shunde in 1434. He founded Sera Monastery in 1419.
40. Tsongkhapa, *Great Exposition of Mantric Stages* (or *Mantric Stages, Sngags rim chen mo*). Not found.
41. *Blo bzang nyi mas mun pa stug po rnam par bsal ba yi// mkhas pa dag ni stong nyid khong du chud cing grol bar gyur*. Candrakīrti, *Entering the Middle Way*, 209b.
42. Khedrup Jé, *Glorious Three Grounds* (*Dpal ldan sa gsum ma*), in *Chos spyod rab gsal skal bzang skye bo'i mgul rgyal bzhugs so*, 382.
43. "Higher rebirth" (*sngon mtho*) refers to attaining rebirth as a human or a god, and "highest good" (*nges legs*) refers to attaining the state of liberation, or enlightenment.
44. The First Phürbuchok, Ngawang Jampa (Phur lcog Ngag dbang Byams pa, 1682–1762), was born in Chamdo, Kham, and trained as a monk at Sera Jé Monastery. As a renowned teacher, he is included in the close lineage of Mahāmudrā and lamrim. As an author he composed fifty-two works in three volumes and his texts remain standard works in the Sera Jé geshé curricula. In the early seventeenth century he established the hermitage at Phürbuchok Peak (*phur lcog ri*) from which his title is derived.

45. There is an uncommon tradition coming from Lama Tsongkhapa, containing instruction on Vajrayāna Mahāmudrā, *Guru Pūjā*, *The Hundreds of Deities of Tuṣita*, the Miktsema prayer, and six sādhanas of Mañjuśrī. These were revealed directly to Tsongkhapa by Mañjuśrī and are known as the uncommon close lineage or the ear-whispered transmission. There are two main lineages of that transmission, one known as the lineage of Ensa and another called Ségyü. Some scholars explain that one could also enumerate three major transmissions: Ségyü, Ensa, and Shungpa. The Ségyü lineage, originating from Tsang Province, stems from Jetsün Sherab Sengé, (1383–1445) and the Shungpa, from Central Tibet, also stems from Jetsün Sherab Sengé. The Ensa lineage stems from Khedrup Jé (see note 26 above) and his brother Baso Chökyi Gyaltsen.
46. Passage not found.
47. As the Buddha said, "Let monks and scholars accept what I say, not out of veneration for me, but after testing it well by burning, cutting, and rubbing." Burning, cutting, and rubbing were the traditional ways of testing whether something was gold.
48. The maṇḍala of thirty-seven heaps was composed by Chögyal Phakpa Lodrö Gyaltsen (Chos rgyal 'Phags pa, 1235–80), who was the fifth of the Five Sakya Patriarchs. It includes (1) Mount Meru, (2–5) the four continents, (6–13) the eight subcontinents, (14) the jewel mountain, (15) the wish-fulfilling tree, (16) the wish-fulfilling cow, (17) the crops that do not require sowing, (18–24) the seven royal symbols, (25) the vase of great treasure, (26–33) the eight offering goddesses, (34) the sun, (35) the moon, (36) the precious parasol, and (37) the royal banner victorious in all directions.
49. The five are Mount Meru and the four continents.
50. During the process of death, coarse awareness subsides and subtle states of awareness manifest naturally. At that time, these three states of mind, accompanied by internal and external signs, become evident. They culminate in the experience of the clear

light of death. During tantric practice, the meditator induces similar states of mind using various meditation techniques, aiming to manifest the subtlest state of clear-light mind. These three states are associated with conceptions and the winds that support them, and are considered to be knowledge obscurations.

51. There are different ways the meaning of the five middle syllables—A RA PA TSA NA—can be explained. For instance, the first syllable, A, indicates that all phenomena lack production (*ādy-anutpanna*), RA that they lack impurity (*rajas*), PA that their ultimate nature (*paramārtha*) is emptiness, TSA (or CA) that they lack activity (*cyavana*), and NA that they lack nominal existence (*nāma*). See Edward Conze, *The Large Sūtra on Perfect Wisdom with Divisions of the Abhisamayālaṅkāra*, 160.
52. A damaru is a small two-headed drum that is used in ritual practices.
53. Jé Tsongkhapa has no equal among worldly beings and manifests a form equal to that of transcendent beings such as Avalokiteśvara, Mañjuśrī, and Vajrapāṇi.
54. "Secret Lord" is an epithet for Vajrapāṇi, who is the keeper of all tantras.
55. Ngawang Losang Gyatso (Ngag dbang blo bzang rgya mtsho, 1617–82) was the first Dalai Lama to wield effective temporal power and unify central Tibet. As an independent head of state, he established diplomatic relations with China and also met with European explorers. His extensive writings comprise twenty-four volumes, and he is referred to as the Great Fifth.
56. Kumbum Monastery was founded in 1583 in a narrow valley close to the village of Lusar, in Amdo, Tibet. It was built around the Tree of Merit, which grew where the blood from the umbilical cord of Jé Rinpoché fell to the earth.
57. Rendawa Shönu Lodrö (Red mda' ba gzhon nu blo gros, 1349–1412) was born in Renda Khapsor, near Sakya Monastery. He extensively studied both sūtra and tantra and received teachings on lamrim and mind training from Gyalsé Thokmé Sangpo, the author of the *Thirty-Seven Practices of a Bodhisattva*. He became

the teacher of Jé Tsongkhapa, and through his extensive teachings and compositions, he is credited with restoring the popularity of Madhyamaka studies in Tibet.

58. Ensapa Losang Döndrup (Dben sa pa blo bzang don grub, 1505–68) was a Kadampa master born in Ensa, near the Tsang River. He achieved enlightenment in one lifetime and was posthumously recognized as the Third Paṇchen Lama. He was known to have spent more than twenty years meditating in isolated caves near the Himalayan mountains.
59. Longdol Ngawang Losang (Klong rdol ngag dbang blo bzang, 1719–94) was born in Kham. He was known for creating an encyclopedia of technical terms from all the disciplines of traditional Tibetan scholarship. He received monastic ordination from Phürbuchok (see note 44 above). He was known as Longdol Lama (Klong rdol bla ma) because of his long meditations at Nyetang Longdol cave. His collected works are in two volumes.
60. See note 45 above.
61. *Mañjuśrī Root Tantra* (*Āryamañjuśrīmūlatantra*, *Phags pa 'jam dpal rtsa ba'i rgyud pa*). Not found.
62. The eight great attainments (*grub chen brgyad*) are the siddhis of the sword, pills, eye medicine, speed walking, extracting the essence, flying, invisibility, and hidden treasures.
63. The mantra of Mañjuśrī is called the Arapatsana mantra; the name consists of the middle five syllables of Mañjuśrī's mantra. The fourth Tibetan syllable, TSA, reflects the Tibetan pronunciation of the Sanskrit syllable CA. The mantra may be recited with either pronunciation. See also note 50 above.
64. The Jamyang Shepas are a lineage of reincarnated lamas. The first Jamyang Shepa, Ngawang Tsöndrü, was born in Amdo. He studied at Drepung Monastery near Lhasa and later founded Labrang Tashikyil, one of the two great monasteries of Amdo, in 1708. He wrote a famous text on the Buddhist and non-Buddhist philosophical tenets.
65. In the first case, the three syllables melt and your body is filled

only with nectar. In the second case, the three syllables remain and your body is filled with syllables, nectar, and light. In the third case, your body is filled with syllables and nectar, but not light.

66. There are four types of birth: (1) birth from a womb, (2) birth from an egg, (3) birth from heat and moisture, and (4) miraculous birth.
67. The focal object and its aspect (*dmigs rnam*) refer to the focal object itself and the way it is apprehended. The "aspect" here refers to specific characteristics of the focal object that are apprehended.
68. The nine types of mental placement are (1) mental placement, (2) continuous placement, (3) firm placement, (4) close placement, (5) subduing, (6) pacifying, (7) close pacification, (8) single-pointed continuum, and (9) balanced placement.
69. *Hvashang* (Wade-Giles: *ho-shang*, Sanskrit: *upādhyāya*) means "a preceptor, teacher, or spiritual advisor." In this context it refers to the eighth-century Chan monk who was invited by King Trisong Detsen (Khri srong lde btsan, ruled 755–97) to Tibet to defend his view at Samye Monastery and settle the meaning of the true Dharma. He was defeated in the debate by the Indian scholar Kamalaśīla, and his view—a form of Chan Buddhism called "east-mountain Dharma gate" that expounded sudden or "all-at-once" enlightenment—was henceforth banned.
70. Tsongkhapa, *Three Principal Aspects of the Path*, 9.
71. Innate afflicted view of the self (*lhan skyes kyi 'jig tshogs la lta ba*; *satkāyadṛṣṭi*; literally, "innate view of the transient collection") refers to the view that focuses on the mind-body continuum (in other words, the transient collection of aggregates) and grasps a self.
72. Jenang (*rjes gnang*) translates as "subsequent permission" since it is a permission to visualize oneself as the deity subsequent to receiving an initiation. In that sense, a jenang strengthens what we have already received.
73. Bardo (*bar do*) refers to the intermediate state between rebirths.
74. Kirti Tsenshap Rinpoché, *Principles of Buddhist Tantra*, 363, states: "The definition of the *enjoyment body* is 'the ultimate

body endowed with the five certainties.' The five certainties are explained differently in tantra and sūtra. In sūtra the certainty of *time* refers to the certainty that the enjoyment body will abide till the end of cyclic existence. The certainty of *abode* refers to the enjoyment body abiding in the Akaniṣṭha pure land. The certainty of *entourage* is that it will be accompanied by ārya bodhisattvas. The certainty of *Dharma* is that it will teach Mahāyāna Dharma. And the certainty of *body* is that it will be a body endowed with the complete set of marks and signs."

75. Kirti Tsenshap Rinpoché, *Principles of Buddhist Tantra*, 438n540, states: "The seven attributes of embrace (*kha sbyor yan lag bdun*) are (1) the attribute of being the complete enjoyment body, (2) the attribute of embracing [the consort], (3) the attribute of being great bliss, (4) the attribute of being without essence, (5) the attribute of being completely filled with compassion, (6) the attribute of being an unbroken stream, (7) the attribute of not ceasing."
76. Though H.E. Chöden Rinpoché initially received the four modes of explanation of the commentary, just three are listed in his commentary.
77. The eight qualities of maturation (*rnam smin gyi yon tan brgyad*) are (1) long life, (2) excellent complexion, (3) excellent family lineage, (4) excellent wealth and power, (5) respected speech, (6) renowned authority, (7) being male, and (8) having strength.
78. The six types of suffering are the suffering (1) of uncertainty, (2) of dissatisfaction, (3) of discarding our body again and again, (4) of being conceived again and again, (5) of changing from a higher status to a lower one again and again, and (6) of having no companions.
79. The eight types of suffering are the suffering (1) of birth, (2) of aging, (3) of sickness, (4) of death, (5) of separation from what is dear, (6) of meeting what is unpleasant, (7) of not finding what we desire despite looking for it, and (8) of the five aggregates.
80. The three types of suffering are (1) the suffering of suffering, (2) the suffering of change, and (3) pervasive suffering.

81. The twelve links of dependent origination are those of (1) ignorance, (2) karmic formation, (3) consciousness, (4) name and form, (5) bases, (6) conduct, (7) feeling, (8) craving, (9) taking, (10) existence, (11) birth, and (12) aging and death.
82. Paṇchen Losang Chökyi Gyaltsen, *Guru Pūjā*, 54.
83. Life wind or soklung (*srog rlung*) refers to the subtle wind that potentially moves in the central channel as depicted in yogic physiology. It is central to supporting life. The term also refers to any imbalance of this wind.
84. The Buddhist teachings referred to here are the complete Vajrayāna teachings.
85. Gendün Drup, *Collected Works*, 9:41a.
86. Paṇchen Losang Chökyi Gyaltsen, *Guru Pūjā*, 9.
87. Paṇchen Losang Chökyi Gyaltsen, *Guru Pūjā*, 18.
88. One span (*'dom pa*) is the measure of the outstretched arms from fingertip to fingertip. A yojana therefore is roughly 8 kilometers.
89. Tsongkhapa, *For As Long As* (*Ji srid thub mchog ma*), page 99b.
90. This quotation is from Jé Rinpoché's *Destiny Fulfilled* (*Rtogs brjod mdun legs ma*), 4.
91. Other versions of the tenth verse exist, such as this: By the might of Victor Tsongkhapa directly acting as/my spiritual guide to the Supreme Vehicle in all my lives,/may I not be diverted for even a second/from this pure path praised by the conquerors. ||10|| *Necklace of Fortunate Beings Illuminating the Practice of Dharma* (Mundgod: Drepung Loseling Library Society, 2012), 5.

Glossary

actual clear light (*don gyi 'od gsal*). The fourth of the five levels of Guhyasamāja completion stage. It is also called *actual clear light of the fourth level* (*rim pa bzhi pa'i don gyi 'od gsal*). It refers to clear light that realizes emptiness perceptually or directly. *See also* clear light.

afflictions (*nyon mongs, kleśa*). Obscuring mental states such as attachment, ignorance, and hatred that are included within the six root and twenty secondary or branch afflictions. They hinder the generation of liberation.

aggregates. *See* five aggregates.

approximation (*bsnyen pa*). Meditation that establishes the proximity of oneself and the deity by functioning to draw one's mind as close as possible to the enlightened mind of the deity.

ārya (*'phags pa*). A person who has attained a direct (or perceptual) realization of emptiness.

aspiring bodhicitta (*smon pa'i sems bskyed*). Conventional bodhicitta that aspires to enlighten all sentient beings.

awakening mind (*sems bskyed*). This is the same as bodhicitta, the mind of enlightenment.

bardo (*bar do*). An intermediate state of existence that occurs after death and prior to rebirth.

black near-attainment (*nyer thob nag lam pa*). A subtle mind that experiences a vision of darkness. Black near-attainment naturally manifests at the third stage of the dissolution of the subtle mind at death, or it may be induced through meditation on the tantric path. Black near-attainment of the forward order is followed by clear light. Black near-attainment of the reverse order is preceded by clear light.

bodhicitta (*byang chub kyi sems*). Literally the mind (*citta*) of enlightenment (*bodhi*). It is the aspiration to attain enlightenment for the sake of all sentient beings. *See* aspiring bodhicitta *and* engaging bodhicitta.

body of union (*zung 'jug gi sku*). There are two: the body of learner's union and the body of nonlearner's union.

brahmā aperture (*tshangs bug, brahmarandhra*). Terminal cranial aperture.

calm abiding (*zhi gnas, śamatha*). Continuous single-pointed concentration. Calm abiding is established through serially progressing through the nine levels of mental placement.

Causal Vehicle (*rgyu'i theg pa, hetuyāna*). The Perfection Vehicle that engages the causal path to obtain the state of buddha by completing the thirty-seven states conducive to enlightenment, and so on.

clear appearance (*gsal snang*). The clear appearance of divine identity and its attributes to a practitioner's mental awareness.

clear light (*'od gsal*). In general this refers to an extremely subtle mind that experiences a vision of clear light. Clear light naturally manifests with the dissolution of black near-attainment of the forward order at the time of death. This is also called the clear light of death. Clear light may also be induced through meditation on the tantric path. It also refers to subtle blissful awareness that comprehends emptiness. It is of two types, namely, subject clear light and object clear light; or three types: (1) metaphoric clear light, (2) actual clear light, and (3) clear light of the final continuum.

commitment being (*dam tshig pa, samayasattva*). A visualized deity that might appear in front of oneself. A deity into which wisdom beings dissolve.

completion stage (*rdzogs rim*). The stage, or part, of highest yoga tantra following the generation stage where one engages in meditation to penetrate vital points of the body that is naturally complete in channels, winds, drops, and so on.

conqueror (*rgyal ba, jina*). One who has conquered or eliminated all afflictive and knowledge obscurations; a buddha.

cooperative condition (*lhan cig byed rkyen*). A cause that does not exist in the same substantial stream as its result.

dependent origination (*rten 'brel, pratītyasamutpāda*). Also dependent arising. Dependent origination refers to phenomena existing in dependence on other phenomena. It has three levels from coarse to subtle. The first is dependence on causes where impermanent effects arise in dependence on the accumulation of causes and conditions such as a sprout. The second is dependence on parts where permanent and impermanent phenomena exist through contingent relationship due to mutual reliance such as space and its parts. The third is dependence on conceptual designation, such as labelling a four-wheeled powered vehicle "a car."

desire realm (*'dod khams*). *See* three realms.

dharma (*chos*). With a capital *D*, refers to the liberating teachings of the Buddha. With a lowercase *d*, refers to any existent entity or phenomenon.

Dharma body (*chos sku*). The body of a buddha manifested for his or her own purpose. It has two types: the nature body (*ngo bo nyid sku*) and the pristine-wisdom Dharma body (*ye shes chos sku*).

eight leisures (*'dal ba brgyad*). The eight leisures, or freedoms that allow the practice of Dharma, are freedom from being reborn (1) as a hell being, (2) as an animal, (3) as a hungry ghost, (4) as a long-lived god, (5) as a human with wrong views, (6) as a barbarian in a remote place, (7) at a time when Buddhist teachings do not exist in the world, or (8) as a human with defective faculties.

eight worldly concerns (*'jig rten chos brgyad*). These are eight states that create like or dislike within us due to even a trifling benefit or harm. They consist of gain and loss, pleasure and pain, praise and criticism, and fame and ill repute.

empowerment (*dbang*). That which fully matures the mindstream through planting special seeds of the four resultant bodies. There are four main empowerments: (1) vase, (2) secret, (3) pristine wisdom, and (4) word.

endowment (*'byor ba*). Having the good fortune to enjoy conducive conditions for the practice of Dharma.

engaging bodhicitta (*'jug pa'i sems bskyed*). Conventional bodhicitta that engages in practices to enlighten all sentient beings.

final vajra-like concentration of a learner (*slob pa mtha'i rdo rje lta bu'i ting nge 'dzin*). Learner's union that acts as the direct antidote to knowledge obscurations and to the appearance of subtle duality unique to mantra. It induces a liberated path that is the state of a nonlearner.

five aggregates (*phung po lnga, skandha*). These are the aggregates of (1) form, (2) feeling, (3) discrimination, (4) compositional factors, and (5) consciousness.

five-line praise (*lnga skor*). The most common version of Miktsema prayer: "Avalokiteśvara, great treasure of nonobjectifying compassion,/ Mañjuśrī, master of stainless wisdom,/ Secret Lord, destroyer of hordes of māras,/ Tsongkhapa, crown jewel of scholars of the Land of Snows,/ Losang Drakpa, I make requests at your feet."

focal object (*dmigs pa*). An object focused on by the mind and its concomitant mental factors.

form body (*gzugs sku, rūpakāya*). A body of the buddha manifesting for the purpose of others. There are two types: the enjoyment body and the emanation body.

four empowerments (*dbang bzhi*). The four empowerments that authorize disciples to enter and practice highest yoga tantra: vase, secret, wisdom, and the fourth or word empowerment.

four māras (*bdud bzhi*). The four māras are (1) the māra of the afflictions, (2) Devaputramāra, (3) the Lord of Death, and (4) the māra of the aggregates.

four opponent powers (*stobs bzhi*). These are the powers of the basis, repudiation, fully applying the antidote, and not repeating the action.

generation stage (*bskyed rim*). A stage or part of highest yoga tantra where one generates oneself as the deity to mature the mind for the completion stage. There are two types: coarse generation stage and subtle generation stage.

generic image (*spyi don*). The superimposed image that appears to be like a specific object, when it is not that specific object, to the conception apprehending that specific object.

ground (*sa*). A basis that supports the generation of enlightened qualities.

ground of buddhahood (*sangs rgyas kyi sa*). The eleventh ground that arises after the tenth bodhisattva ground.

guru yoga (*bla ma'i rnal 'byor*). The means by which the mind of the student is trained in order to positively engage or link (*yoga*) with the mind of the preceptor (*guru*).

hearer (*nyan thos, śrāvaka*). One who seeks individual liberation by hearing or listening to the instruction of the Buddha or a disciple of the Buddha.

highest yoga tantra (*bla na med pa rnal 'byor gyi rgyud, anuttarayogatantra*). The fourth and highest of the four classes of tantra that is proclaimed for disciples capable of bringing the bliss of embracing a visualized deity into the path. Entry to this tantra requires four empowerments, namely, the vase, secret, pristine wisdom, and word empowerments.

illusory body (*sgyu lus*). A subtle body and advanced stage of the completion stage. It is established from the wind and mind of the metaphoric clear light of final mental isolation. It acts as the agent that purifies the intermediate stage and is the unique cause that establishes the resultant Form Body. It is emphasized in father tantras, such as Guhyasamāja.

imprints (*bag chags*, *vāsanā*). Factors imprinted on consciousness that are the dormant potency derived from the internal mind's familiarity with external positive, negative, and neutral objects.

indestructible drop (*mi shigs pa'i thig le*). A subtle drop located at the central channel at the heart composed of white and red substances derived from the parents. There are two types: the indestructible drop that remains for as long as one is alive, and the completely indestructible drop.

inherent existence (*rang bzhin gyi yod pa*, *svabhāvasat*). Existence by way of an essential nature that appears to inhere in an object.

initiation (*dbang*). *See* empowerment.

innate afflicted view of the self (*lhan skyes kyi 'jig tshogs la lta ba*; *satkāyadṛṣṭi*; literally, "innate view of the transient collection") refers to the view that focuses on the mind-body continuum, or in other words, the transient collection of aggregates, and grasps a self.

insight (*lhag mthong*, *vipaśyanā*). Wisdom comprehending its apprehended object, generally obtained during yoga without signs in the three lower tantras and during the completion stage in highest yoga tantra.

knowledge consort (*rig ma*). A female seal (*mudrā*) who is relied on by a yogi in the practice of mantra. *See also* seal.

knowledge obscurations (*shes sgrib*). Obscurations such as imprints of ignorance that mainly obstruct the obtainment of omniscience.

lamrim (*lam rim*). Literally, the "stages of the path." It refers to the systematic presentation of the important elements, or stages (*rim*), by which a person serially progresses on the internal path (*lam*) leading to enlightenment.

leisure (*'dal ba*). Freedom from rebirth under oppressive conditions.

mindstream (*rgyud*). The mental continuum.

mudrā (*phyag rgya*). *See* seal.

nine rounds of mixing (*bsre ba skor dgu*). The nine mixings constitute mixing death with the Dharma body, mixing the bardo with the enjoyment body, and mixing rebirth with the emanation body. These are practiced when awake, when asleep, and at the time of death.

nonlearner (*mi slob pa*). One who has attained the path of no-more-learning, the highest of the five paths.

nonlearner's union (*mi slob pa'i zung 'jug*). Union that exists in the mental continuum of a nonlearner who has attained the state of Vajradhāra.

object of negation (*dgag bya*). An object to be negated in order to develop realization.

oral tradition (*zhal shes, snyan brgyud*). Pith advice that must be understood in dependence on the oral instruction of a guru and so on.

path (*lam*). The genuine, uncontrived, and continuous thought to escape from cyclic existence.

phenomena. *See* dharma *and* selflessness of phenomena.

practice establishing wisdom (*shes rab sgrub skor*). A practice combining a series of visualizations and requests for the sake of establishing the seven types of wisdom that are the vast, clear, swift, and profound wisdom, as well as the wisdom of explanation, debate, and composition.

pristine wisdom (*ye shes, jñāna*). A type of exalted knowledge, or gnosis. In general there are five types: (1) mirror-like pristine wisdom associated with the form aggregate, (2) the pristine wisdom of equality associated with the feeling aggregate, (3) the pristine wisdom of individual analysis associated with the discrimination aggregate, (4) pristine wisdom accomplishing activities associated with the aggregate of formation, and (5) the pristine wisdom of the expanse of reality associated with the consciousness aggregate.

profoundly swift Ganden oral transmission (*dga' ldan snyan rgyud kyi zab pa'i myur khyad*). The profound oral transmission that has the potency to establish enlightenment in just twelve human years, or three years and three months.

purpose of sentient beings (*sems can gyi don*). This includes both their temporary purpose, which consists of the factors that generate ordinary happiness in this and future lives, and their ultimate purpose, which is the attainment of enlightenment.

red increase (*mched ba dmar lam pa*). A subtle mind that experiences a vision of radiant red appearance. Red increase naturally manifests at the second stage of the dissolution of subtle mind at death, or it may be induced through meditation on the tantric path. Red increase of the forward order is followed by black near-attainment. Red increase of the reverse order is preceded by black near-attainment.

renunciation (*nges 'byung*). The aspiration to leave or escape from cyclic existence that arises continuously, night or day.

Resultant Vehicle (*'bras bu'i theg pa*). The vehicle that engages the resultant aspect as the path in the present, to obtain the state of buddha, by visualizing celestial mansions, deities, and so on.

samaya (*dam tshig*). Sacred pledge of restraint not to engage in a specific action.

seal (*phyag rgya, mudrā*). *See also* ḍākinī. A symbolic representation manifesting as a gesture, consort, posture, reality, sign, axiom, commitment, bone ornament, and so on.

secret empowerment (*gsang ba'i dbang*). In highest yoga tantra, the first of the three higher supreme empowerments. It is conferred in the relative bodhicitta maṇḍala, purifies stains of speech, empowers one to meditate on the path of channel and wind yoga, and places imprints on the mental continuum for obtaining the enjoyment body of resultant vajra speech.

selflessness of persons (*gang zag gi bdag med*). This is the nonexistence of an independent, inherently existent self of the person. It is the emptiness of the person.

selflessness of phenomena (*chos kyi bdag med*). This is the nonexistence of an independent, inherently existent self of phenomena other than the person. It is the emptiness of phenomena.

seven-limb prayer (*yan lag bdun*). A prayer for accumulating merit and purifying nonvirtue through the limbs of (1) prostration, (2) offerings, (3) confession, (4) rejoicing, (5) requesting the buddhas to teach, (6) requesting the long life of our teachers, and (7) dedication.

siddhi (*dngos grub*). The attainment of a special capacity to accomplish a desired result in dependence on the advice of a preceptor. There are two types: supreme and common. The supreme siddhi refers to enlightenment itself, while common siddhis are generally categorized in eight types, namely: the siddhi of (1) the sword, (2) pills, (3) eye medicine, (4) fleet footedness, (5) extracting the essence, (6) flying, (7) invisibility, and (8) penetrating the ground.

six perfections (*phar phyin drug, pāramitā*). The perfections of generosity, ethics, patience, effort, absorption, and wisdom that are the main practices on the first six of the ten bodhisattva grounds.

six types of reincarnating beings (*'gro ba rigs drug*). The six types of reincarnating beings consist of those in the three lower realms, or unfortunate migrations—hell beings, hungry ghosts, and animals—and those of the three higher realms, or fortunate migrations—humans, demigods, and gods.

solitary realizers (*rang sangs rgyas*, *pratyekabuddha*). Those who strive for their own liberation from cyclic existence but, unlike hearers (*nyan thos*, *śrāvaka*), do not rely on hearing their teacher's instructions in the life in which they attain liberation.

substantial cause (*nyer len gyi rgyu*). A cause that exists in the same substantial stream as its result.

suffering. *See* three types of suffering.

summit of existence (*srid rtse*). The fourth level of the formless realm and the highest within saṃsāra.

ten nonvirtuous actions (*mi dge ba bcu*). These include three related to the physical activities of (1) killing, (2) stealing, and (3) sexual misconduct; four related to the verbal activities of (4) lying, (5) divisive speech, (6) harsh speech, and (7) gossip; and three related to the mental activities of (8) covetousness, (9) harmful intent, and (10) wrong views.

three lineage protectors (*rigs sum dgon po*). These are Avalokiteśvara, Mañjuśrī, and Vajrapāṇi.

three realms (*khams gsum*, *tridhātu*). The three realms of saṃsāra are the (1) desire, (2) form, and (3) formless realms.

three types of suffering (*sdug bsngal gsum*). These are the suffering of pain, the suffering of change, and pervasive conditioned suffering.

three types of training (*bslab pa gsum*). These are training in ethics, concentration, and wisdom. They are also known as the three higher trainings.

tīrthika (*mu stegs pa*). A follower of non-Buddhist religion or philosophy.

two accumulations (*tshogs gnyis*). The accumulations of merit and pristine wisdom that are the causes for attaining enlightenment. Merit is accumulated through practicing the first five perfections, while pristine wisdom is accumulated through the perfection of wisdom.

Vajra Vehicle (*rdo rje thegs pa*). The Tantra Vehicle or the Secret-Mantra Vehicle.

vase empowerment (*bum dbang*). An empowerment common to all four classes of tantra. It is conferred in a colored-sand or painted-cloth maṇḍala and so on, purifies stains of the body, empowers one to meditate on the path of deity yoga or the generation stage, and places latent imprints on the mental continuum for obtaining the emanation body of the resultant vajra body.

winds (*rlung*). In the three tantric categories of channels, winds, and drops, winds are the energy winds that circulate in the body's subtle network of channels. There are ten winds explained in the *Guhyasamāja*: the five main winds and the five secondary winds.

wisdom being (*ye shes sems dpa', jñānasattva*). A visualized deity that appears in front of oneself. A deity that dissolves into the commitment being.

wisdom empowerment (*shes rab ye shes kyi dbang*). The second of the three higher supreme empowerments exclusive to highest yoga tantra. It is conferred in the *bhaga* maṇḍala, purifies stains of speech, empowers one to meditate on the path of clear light of the completion stage, and places latent imprints on the mental continuum for obtaining the dharma body of resultant vajra pristine wisdom.

word empowerment (*tshig dbang*). The third of three higher supreme empowerments exclusive to highest yoga tantra. It is conferred in the ultimate-bodhicitta maṇḍala, purifies stains of body, speech, and mind combined, empowers one to meditate on the path of union of the completion stage, and places latent imprints on the mental continuum for obtaining the nature body of resultant vajra pristine wisdom.

yidam (*yi dam*). Deities with the status of buddhas or bodhisattvas who are cultivated in tantra as personal or "tutelary" deities.

Bibliography

Kangyur (Canonical Scriptures)

Confession of Downfalls. Ltung bshags. 'Phags pa phung po gsum pa zhes bya ba theg pa chen po'i mdo. In *Chos spyod rab gsal skal bzang skye bo'i mgul rgyan*. Losel Literature Series, vol. 14. Mundgod, India: Drepung Loseling Library Society, 2012.

General Confession. Spyi bshags. In *Chos spyod rab gsal skal bzang skye bo'i mgul rgyan*. Losel Literature Series, vol. 14. Mundgod, India: Drepung Loseling Library Society, 2012.

Heart Sūtra. Bhagavatī-prajñāpāramitā-hṛdaya. Bcom ldan 'das ma shes rab kyi pha rol tu phyin pa'i snying po. Toh 531, rgyud *na*.

Mañjuśrī Root Tantra. Āryamañjuśrīmūlatantra. Phags pa 'jam dpal rtsa ba'i rgyud pa. Toh 543, rgyud *na*.

Perfection of Wisdom in Eight Thousand Verses. Aṣṭa-sāhasrikā-prajñāpāramitāsūtra. 'Phags pa shes rab kyi pha rol tu phyin pa brgyad stong pa. Toh 381.

Reciting the Names of Mañjuśrī. Mañjuśrījñānasattvasya-paramārtha-nāma-saṃgīti. 'Jam dpal ye shes sems dpa'i don dam pa'i mtshan yang dag par brjod pa. Toh 360, rgyud *ka*.

Tengyur (Canonical Treatises)

Candrakīrti (Zla ba grags pa). *Entering the Middle Way. Madhyamakāvatāra-nāma. Dbu ma la 'jug pa.* Toh 3861, mdo 'grel *'a*.

Maitreyanātha (Rje btsun byams dgon). *Ornament of Mahāyāna Sūtras. Theg pa chen po'i mdo sde'i rgyan gyi tsig le'ur byas pa. Mahāyānasūtrālaṅkāra.* Toh. 4020.

Śāntideva (Zhi ba lha). *Bodhisattva's Way of Life. Bodhicaryāvatāra. Byang chub sems dpa'i spyod pa la 'jug pa.* Toh 3871, mdo 'grel *la.*

———. *Compendium of Training. Śikṣāsamuccaya. Bslab pa kun las btus pa'i mngon par rtog pa* (abbr. *Bslab btus*). Toh 3939, dbu ma *khi.*

Tibetan-Language Works

Author unknown. *Dākiṇī Long Life Pūjā. Mkha' 'gro brtan bzhugs.*

Chöden Rinpoché, Kyabjé (Skyabs rje Chos ldan rin po che, 1931–2015). *Opening the Door of Blessings of the Extensive and Abbreviated Explanation of* The Hundreds of Deities of Tuṣita *to Enhance the Practice of Beginners with Limited Intelligence. Dga' lha rgyas pa dang bsdus pa'i bshad pa blo dman las dang po ba la 'khyer bder spel ba byin rlabs kyi sgo 'byed.* Mysore, Bylakuppe: Jamyang Publications, Chos ldan rin po che'i bka' khrid rtsom sgrig sde tshan nas dpar skrun, 2005.

Collected Works of the Kadam / Collected teachings and stories of Lord Atisha and his disciples on the precious practice of bka' gdams pa buddhism. Bka' gdams glegs bam / Jo bo yab sras kyi gsung bgros pha chos rin po che'i gter mdzod/ byang chub sems dpa'i nor bu'i phreng ba rtsa 'grel sogs. Sarnath: Kalsang Lhundrup, 1974.

Dülnakpa Palden Sangpo ('Dul nag pa Dpal ldan bzang po, 1402–73). *Hundreds of Deities of Tuṣita. Dga' ldan lha brgya ma.* In *Chos spyod phyogs bsgrigs lam bzang gsal ba'i sgron me*, vol. 1. Lhasa: Bod ljongs mi dmangs dpe skrun khang, 1999.

Gendün Drup (dGe 'dun grub pa, 1391–1475). *Collected Works. gSung 'bum dge 'dun grub.* Ser gtsug nang bstan dpe rnying 'tshol bsdu phyogs sgrig khang, 2011. Buddhist Digital Resource Center (BDRC), purl.bdrc.io/resource/IE1KG14505. [BDRC bdr:IE1KG14505]

Khedrup Jé Gelek Palsang (Mkhas grub Rje Dge legs dpal bzang, 1385–1438). *Glorious Three Grounds, the Prayer of Jé Rinpoché's Biography. Rje tsong kha pa'i rnam thar gsol 'debs dpal ldan sa gsum ma* (abbr. *Dpal ldan sa gsum ma*). In *Chos spyod rab gsal skal bzang skye bo'i mgul rgyal bzhugs so*. Mundgod, India: Drepung Loseling Library Society, 1995.

Jamyang Shepa ('Jam dbyangs bzhad pa, 1648–1721) *Great Exposition of Tenets, Sun of the Land of Samantabhadra Brilliantly Illuminating All of Our Own and Others' Tenets and the Meaning of the Profound [Emptiness], Ocean of Scripture and Reasoning Fulfilling All Hopes of All Beings. Grub mtha' chen mo/ grub mtha'i rnam bshad rang gzhan grub mtha'i kun dang zab don mchog tu gsal ba kun bzang zhing gi nyi ma lung rigs rgya mthso skye dgu'i re ba kun skong.* Mussoorie: Dalama, 1962

Könchok Jigmé Wangpo, the Second Jamyang Shepa (Dkon mchog 'jigs med dbang po, 1728–91). *How to Practice the Six Preliminary Practices: Essential Instructions on Mañjuśrī's Transmission of the Stages of the Path. Lam rim dmar khrid 'jam dpal zhal lung gi sngon 'gro sbyong ba'i chos drug nyams su len tsul.* Blab rang par ma, vol. 8. Bla brang bkra shis 'khyil: Bla brang dgon pa, 1999. TBRC Volume Number: 5266. TBRC Work Number: 2122.

Naktso Lotsāwa Tsültrim Gyalwa (Tshul khrim rgyal wa, 1011–64) *Naktso's Praise/ The Eight Verses of Praise to Jowo Atiśa. Nag tsho'i bstod pa / Jo bo rje'i bstod pa brgyad cu.* In *Blo sbyong nyer mkho phyogs bsgrigs.* Lan kru'u: Kan su'u mi rigs dpe skrun khang, 2003.

Pabongkha Dechen Nyingpo (Pha bong kha pa bde chen snying po, 1878–1941). *Bountiful Advice Clarifying the Oral Transmission and Explaining the Deep Meaning of How to Practice the Profound Path of Yoga of the Hundreds of Deities of Tuṣita, Called "A Treasury of Precious Jewels." Zab lam dga' ldan lha brgya ma'i rnal 'byor nyams su len tshul snyan brgyud zhal shes lhug par bkod pa'i man ngag rin chen gter gyi bang mdzod.* In *gSung 'bum bde chen snying po*, 2:467–512. Lha sa. Accessed October 13, 2023. http://purl.bdrc.io/resource/MW3834_AB6534. [BDRC bdr:MW3834_AB6534]

Paṇchen Losang Chökyi Gyaltsen (Paṇ chen Blo bzang Chos kyi rgyal mtshan, 1570–1662). *Guru Pūjā. Zab lam bla ma mchod pa'i cho ka bde stong dbyer med ma dang tshogs mchod bcas bzhugs so* (abbr. *Bla ma mchod pa*). Dharamsala, India: Sherig Parkhang, 1992.

Paṇchen Losang Yeshé (Pan chen Blo bzang ye shes, 1663–1737). *Swift Path: Essential Instructions on the Stages of the Path. Lam rim dmar khrid myur lam* (abbr. *Lam rim myur lam*). 1 vols. sKu 'bum: sKu 'bum byams pa gling, 1990–1999. Accessed October 13, 2023. http://purl.bdrc.io/resource/MW1KG472. [BDRC bdr:MW1KG472]

Necklace of Fortunate Beings Illuminating the Practice of Dharma. Chos spyod rab gsal skal bzang skye bo'i mgul rgyan. Mundgod: Drepung Loseling Library Society, 2012.

Taktsang Lotsāwa Sherab Rinchen (Shes rab Rin chen). *Understanding All Tenets. Grub mtha' kun shes*. Beijing: Mi rigs dpe skrun khang, 2000.

Tsongkhapa Losang Drakpa (Tsong kha pa blo bzang grags pa, 1357–1419). *Essential Explanation of Interpretive and Definitive Meaning. Drang ba dang nges pa'i don rnam par phye ba'i bstan bcos legs bshad snying po* (abbr. *Drang nges legs bshad snying po*). Sarnath, India: Dge ldan spyi las khang, 1973.

———. *For As Long As. Ji srid thub mchog.* Je Tsong Kha pa Chen po'i gSung 'Bum bZhugs so. Vol 2. Ser gTsangs Nang bsTan dPe rNying 'Tshol bsDu Phyogs sGrig Khang gis bSgrigs, 2012.

———. *Great Exposition of Mantric Stages* (*Mantric Stages / Stages of the Path of Secret Mantra*). *Rgyal ba khyab bdag rdo rje 'chang chen po'i lam gyi rim pa gsang ba kun gyi gnad rnam par phye ba* (abbr. *Sngags rim chen mo*). Collected Works, vol. *ga*. Lhasa: New Zhol Par-khang. Toh 5281.

———. *Great Lamrim*(*Great Stages of the Path / Stages of the Path of the Perfection Vehicle*). *Khams gsum chos kyi rgyal po tsong kha pa chen pos mdzad pa'i byang chub lam gyi rim pa chen mo* (abbr. *Lam rim chen mo*). Collected Works, vol. *pa*. Lhasa: New Zhol Par-khang. Toh 5392.

———. *Three Principal Aspects of the Path. Lam gtso rnam gsum.* In

Blo sbyong nyer mkho phyogs bsgrigs. Lan kru'u: Kan su'u mi rigs dpe skrun khang, 2003.

English-Language Works

Chöden Rinpoché, H. E. *An Offering Cloud of Nectar*. Translated and edited by Ian Coghlan and Voula Zarpani. Melbourne: Awakening Vajra Publications, 2012.

Conze, Edward (trans.). *The Large Sutra on Perfect Wisdom with Divisions of the Abhisamayālaṅkāra*, Berkeley, CA: University of California Press, 1975.

Csoma de Kőrös, Alexander. *Sanskrit-Tibetan-English Vocabulary*. [*Mahāvyutpatti, Lo pan mang pos mdzad pa'i bye brag tu rtogs byed chen mo.*] In 3 vols. Calcutta: Asiatic Society of Bengal, 1834, 1910, 1944. In 2 vols. Delhi: Sri Satguru, 1980–82.

Dalai Lama, Tenzin Gyatso. *The Union of Bliss and Emptiness: Teachings on the Practice of Guru Yoga*. Translated by Thupten Jinpa. Boulder, Colorado: Snow Lion, 1988.

Hopkins, Jeffrey. *Meditation on Emptiness*. London: Wisdom Publications, 1983.

Kirti Tsenshap Rinpoché. *Principles of Buddhist Tantra*. Translated and edited by Ian Coghlan and Voula Zarpani. Boston: Wisdom Publications, 2010.

Lamotte, Etienne. *History of Indian Buddhism: From the Origins to the Śaka Era*. Translated from the French by Sara Webb-Boin. Louvain: Institut Orientaliste, 1988.

Monier-Williams, Sir Monier. *A Sanskrit-English Dictionary*. Delhi: Motilal Barnarsidass, 1899, 1995.

Pabongka Rinpoche. *Liberation in the Palm of Your Hand: A Concise Discourse on the Path to Enlightenment, New Revised Edition*. Edited in the Tibetan by Trijang Rinpoché. Translated into English by Michael Richards. Boston: Wisdom Publications, 2006.

Rigpa Shedra Wiki. http://www.rigpawiki.org.

Rigzin, Tsepak. *Tibetan-English Dictionary of Buddhist Terminology*.

Dharamsala: Library of Tibetan Works and Archives, 1984.

Roerich, George N., trans. *The Blue Annals of 'Gos Lo tsa ba [Deb ther sngon po]*. Delhi: Motilal Banarsidass, 1976.

Snellgrove, David. *Indo-Tibetan Buddhism*, 2 vols. Boston: Shambhala, 1987.

Thurman, R., ed. *Life and Teachings of Tsong Khapa.* Dharamsala: Library of Tibetan Works and Archives, 1982.

Treasury of Lives. http://www.treasuryoflives.org

Tsongkhapa. *The Splendor of an Autumn Moon: The Devotional Verse of Tsongkhapa.* Translated and introduced by Gavin Kilty. Boston: Wisdom, 2001.

Index

A

A Treasury of Precious Jewels (Pabongkha Rinpoché), 1, 3, 9, 11, 195
Ajitanātha. *See* Maitreya
Atiśa, Jowo Jé. *See* Stainless Sky, 54, 56–57, 74, 98
Autonomy School. *See* Svātantrika, 164
Avalokiteśvara, 2, 5, 7, 49, 95–99, 100–109, 112, 118, 131–32, 137–38, 140–45, 179, 251–52, 262
Avalokiteśvara, four-arms (external form), 49, 96, 105
awakening mind. *See* bodhicitta, 32–34, 37–39, 74, 88, 155, 201, 212, 215, 220–21, 225–27, 244

B

bardo, 165–67, 172, 184
basis of imputation, 164, 183
bodhicitta. *See* awakening mind, 4, 13, 24–5, 34, 46, 69, 77–80, 88, 93, 98, 135–37, 155–59, 172, 174, 193, 225, 228, 244, 250
Bodhisattva's Way of Life (Śāntideva), 159
body of union, 70, 85–6, 183
Brahmā, 83, 97, 154, 194
brahmā aperture, 136, 180–81
bringing the bardo into the path as the enjoyment body, 166
bringing the three bodies into the path, 166, 172
Buddha Akṣobhya, 43, 65, 187–88, 257
Buddha Amitābha, 65
Buddha Indraketu, 18
Buddha Ratnasambhava, 110
Buddha Vairocana, 6, 24, 65, 220–21

C

cakravartin, 154, 240
calm abiding, 159, 164–65, 210
central channel, 39, 95, 173, 188–82, 187–89
Chöjé Yakpa Shuwa, 80
Cittamātra. *See* Mind Only School, 163
clear light, actual, 26, 68, 70, 84–85, 107, 167–68, 173, 182, 184
clear light, metaphoric, 85, 167, 173
commitment being, 48–50, 52, 61–62, 113
completion stage, 84, 166–68, 172–73, 183, 213
completion stage of the individual two truths, 168
completion stage of the indivisible two truths, 168

concentration being, 48, 50
concentration bravely proceeding to union, 170
concentration of the three isolations, 167
concentration of the two truths, 167
concise review, 21, 149, 170, 195, 249–50
Confession of Downfalls, 75
Consequence School. *See* Prāsaṅgika, 164
continuum of similar type, 173
cooperative condition, 182–83
Cūḍapanthaka [Small Path], 216

D

ḍākinī. *See* seal, 27, 68, 96, 218, 224
Ḍākinī Long Life Pūjā, 86
Dalai Lama 1st, Gendün Drup, 2, 11, 213, 282n31
Dalai Lama 5th, Ngawang Losang Gyatso, 227, 271n55
death, 58, 73, 151–52, 165–66, 171, 173, 184–85, 190, 192, 204–5, 206, 209–10, 258
deceit in terms of motivation, 23, 219
deceit in terms of the material, 23–24, 219
deity meditation, 172
Delightful Dharma Abode, 52, 54–5, 60, 230
dependent origination, 15, 17, 39, 46–47, 81, 160–64, 171
desire realm, 52
Dharma body, 62, 65, 83–84, 107, 166, 182, 184, 247–48, 262
doubt, 2, 17, 21, 64, 115–16, 121–22, 148, 184, 246–47
Dromtönpa, 56–57, 268n31
dualistic appearance, 92, 168–69
Dülkarwa, 2, 11, 213
Dülnakpa Palden Sangpo, 2, 11, 213

E

eight worldly concerns, 79, 246
emanation body, 56, 101, 166, 184, 218, 223
Ensa, 86, 109–10
Ensapa Losang Döndrup, 109, 272n58
Entering the Middle Way (Candrakīrti), 51, 82
essence-seal of secrecy, 12
Essential Explanation of Interpretive and Definitive Meaning (Tsongkhapa), 16
eternalism, 14, 160–63
external offerings related to the vase empowerment, 69
extremely subtle wind and mind, 70, 182–83

F

faith, 16–17, 19, 28, 63, 127, 149–50, 194, 207–8, 213, 223, 225, 234–36, 239, 242, 261
field of refuge, 23, 38
final vajra-like concentration of a learner, 168, 173
five certainties. *See* seven attributes of embrace, 169, 174, 274n74
five types of pristine wisdom, 43, 186, 188
For As Long As (Tsongkhapa), 19, 265n8, 275n89
form body, 70, 86
four empowerments (vase, secret, wisdom, word), 4–5, 71–2, 95, 101, 165

four opponent powers (basis, repudiation, fully applying the antidote, never committing that fault again), 74

G
Ganden oral transmission, 12, 37
garuḍa, 96, 108
Geden tradition, 12, 265n4
General Confession, 75
generation stage, 84, 101, 165–66, 172–73, 213
Glorious Three Grounds (Khedrup Jé), 82, 269n42
Gompo Sönam, 195
great bliss, 38, 44, 70, 83–4, 115, 150, 182, 274n75
Great Exposition of Mantric Stages (Tsongkhapa), 249, 285n57
Great Exposition of Tenets (Jamyang Shepa), 269n38
Guhyasamāja, 165, 176, 192
Guide Siṃhanāda (Lion's Roar), 99, 191–92
Gungthangpa, 41, 267n21
Guru Pūjā (Paṇchen Losang Chökyi Gyaltsen), 24, 27, 44, 75, 175, 222, 227, 266n11, 267n20, 270n45, 275n82, 275n86
guru yoga, 1–6, 8, 11, 19, 21, 28, 38, 159, 193, 195, 208, 212–13, 227, 234
guru, five classes, 30, 222–23
Gyaltsap Rinpoché Darma Rinchen, 2, 49–50, 62, 179, 229, 232, 265n1, 267nn25–26
Gyalwa Gyatso (secret form of Avalokiteśvara), 96, 104–05

H
heaven Free of Conflict, 52–53, 230
heaven of the Four Great Kings, 52
heaven of Thirty-Three, 52–53, 55, 230
heaven of Tuṣita, 2–3, 52
Heruka Cakrasaṃvara, 165, 175, 192
Hevajra, 81
highest yoga tantra, 37, 84, 115
Hvashang, 161, 273n69

I
illusory body, 68, 84, 104, 115, 166, 168, 173, 183–84
illusory body, impure, 85, 167–68
illusory body, pure, 85, 167–68, 173
illusory-net body, 167
immeasurable aspiration, 35
immeasurable equanimity 34, 226
immeasurable joy, 36, 226
immeasurable love, 35, 226
immeasurable prayer, 35
immeasurable request, 35
immeasurable special intention, 35
immeasurables, four, 4, 34–35, 226
impermanence, 151, 171, 204, 250
indestructible drop, 173, 181, 256
Indra, 55, 83, 97
inner offerings related to the secret empowerment, 69

J
Jamchen Chöjé Shākya Yeshé, 79, 239, 269n39
Jamyang Shepa 1st, Ngawang Tsöndrü, 131, 148, 269n38, 272n64

K

Kadampa, 98, 242, 268n31
Kāntamatī, 97
karma, 19, 35, 152–54, 160, 204–6, 210, 217, 224, 237, 243–44, 250, 259
Karmavajra, mahāsiddha, 57
Khedrup Rinpoché Gelek Palsang, 2, 49–50, 60, 62, 82, 179, 213, 229, 232, 265n1, 267n26, 268n33, 269n42, 270n45
knowledge obscuration, 92, 173, 207
Kṣudrapanthaka [Little Path], 216
Kumbum Monastery, 99, 271n56
Kyabchok Palsang, lotsāwa, 80

L

leisure and endowment, 150–52, 250
Lhodrag Namkha Gyaltsen, mahāsiddha. *See* Stainless Light, 54, 57, 230–31, 268n32
liberated path, 169, 174
liberation, 19, 25, 29, 36, 73–74, 109, 153–55, 171, 209–12, 243–44, 250
lineage of blessed practice, 27, 30, 266n16
lineage of extensive conduct, 27, 30, 222, 266n16
lineage of profound view, 27, 30, 222, 266n16
Longdol Lama Ngawang Losang, 109, 242, 272n59
Lord of All the Conquerors. *See* Vajradhāra, 16–18, 68, 109
Lord of Sages. *See* Munīndra, Śākyamuni, 33–34, 38–39, 42, 266n18
Lord of Speech. *See* Mañjuśrī, 12
Losang Chögyan, Paṇchen Rinpoché [1], 175
Losang Wangchuk, Khensur Rinpoché, 56, 268n39

M

Machik Labdrön, 18, 265n7
mahāmudrā, 107, 186, 269nn44–45
Mahāpanthaka [Great Path], 216
Mahāsattva bodhisattva. *See* Tsongkhapa, 18
Maitreya, 18, 45, 54–55, 58–61, 61–62, 182, 185, 187, 190, 222, 228, 231–32, 266n16
Maitreyanātha, 2, 45, 54–55, 61–62, 187, 224, 230, 232–34, 281n24, 289n94. *See also* Ajitanātha
maṇḍala of thirty-seven heaps, 90–91, 270n48
maṇḍala of twenty-three heaps, 90–91
maṇḍala offerings, 89, 93, 246
Mañjunātha. *See* Tsongkhapa, 20–21, 45, 78, 87, 108
Mañjuśrī, 2, 5, 7, 12, 15, 18, 20, 47–49, 52, 64, 78, 80, 82, 95, 97–110, 112–14, 116, 118–19, 128, 132, 134–35, 137–41, 143, 145–46, 170, 189, 191, 194, 222, 229–30, 237–38, 246, 251–52, 262, 266n16, 268nn32–33, 270n45, 271n53
Mañjuśrī Arapatsana, 95, 187, 272n63
Mañjuśrī, external form, 95, 100, 102, 104, 112
Mañjuśrī, internal form, 95, 96, 100, 104, 112
Mañjuśrī, Lord of Speech, 12
Mañjuśrī, orange body, 12, 48, 96, 132, 134

Mañjuśrī, red body, 96
Mañjuśrī Root Tantra, 18, 114
Mañjuśrī, secret form, 80, 95, 96, 100, 104, 112
Mañjuśrī, yellow body, 129
Mañjuśrī, youthful, 46
Mañjuśrīgarbha, 12, 54, 56
māra, 2, 26, 99, 101–10, 118, 136, 138, 140, 141, 251–52, 262
Middle Way, 13, 18
Miktsema praise, 2, 5, 7, 20–21, 89, 99–101, 109–10, 118–22, 124–28, 131–33, 137, 139–48, 176, 187–89, 251, 255–56, 258–59
Milarepa, 170, 267n21
Mind Only School. *See* Cittamātra, 163
mixing death with the Dharma body, 166, 184
Mount Meru, 52–53, 90–91, 152–53, 187, 270n48
Munīndra. *See* Lord of Sages, Śākyamuni, 12–13, 25–27, 30, 54–55, 208, 222, 266nn16–18, 267n27, 268n35

N

nāga tree, 54, 56
Nāgārjuna, 16, 160, 266n16
nihilism, 13–14, 160, 161, 163

O

object of negation, 14, 46, 161, 162, 283
offering of suchness, 66, 70, 71
offering, secret, 66, 68, 69, 70
offerings, external, 66, 69, 71, 72
offerings, inner, 66–67, 69, 71, 72
offerings, inner related to the secret empowerment, 69
Ölkha, 75, 89, 246
oral tradition, 3, 5, 6, 7, 21, 131, 137, 283
ordinary appearance, 99, 115
Ornament of Mahāyāna Sūtras (Maitreyanātha), 18, 45, 228, 289

P

Pabongkha Rinpoché Dechen Nyingpo, 1, 3, 4, 5, 6, 8, 9, 11, 21, 127, 175, 195, 196, 265n6, 291
Perfection of Wisdom, 54, 57, 229, 289
Phürbuchok Ngawang Jampa, 86, 253, 269n44
Prāsaṅgika. *See* Consequence School, 164
profound and vast, 51, 84
prostrations, 65, 66, 75, 233
prostrations, multiplying mantra, 65

R

rebirth, 6, 28–29, 36, 52–53, 83, 152–55, 166, 171–72, 185, 190, 201–4, 208–9, 211, 222–23, 237, 269n43
Rebirth, mixing with emanation body, 184
red drop, 181–82, 257
refuge, 4, 6, 23–25, 27–33, 38–39, 74, 82, 92, 93, 109, 128, 129, 153, 171, 207–9, 216, 218, 220, 221–27, 244, 250, 259, 261
refuge, uncommon Mahāyāna, 32, 33
Rendawa Shönu Lodrö, 2, 80, 99, 271n57
Reting Monastery, 57, 268n31

S

Śākyamuni. *See* Lord of Sages, Munīndra, 33, 34, 38, 39, 42, 109, 160, 222, 225–27, 266n15
Samantabhadra, bodhisattva, 44
Samantabhadra, offerings, 43, 45, 91, 227, 241
Sarasvatī, 96
seal of secrecy, 12, 265n5
seal of the five pristine wisdoms, 188
seal of the five-spoked vajra, 188
seal of the guru, 188
seal of the heart, 188
seal of the three mantras, 189
seal of the vowels and consonants, 189
seal. *See* ḍākinī, 68–69, 72
Secret Lord. *See* Vajrapāṇi, Sun of Speech, 2, 5, 7, 49–50, 57, 95–110, 112, 118, 132–33, 138, 140–41, 143–45, 179, 230–31, 151–52, 262, 268n32, 271n53, 271n54
Secret Wisdom ḍākinī, 96
Ségyü lineage, 109–10, 270n45
seven attributes of embrace. *See* five certainties, 169, 274n79
seven attributes of Vairocana, 6, 24, 220–21
seven-limb prayer, 2, 4, 7, 41, 63, 85, 213, 215, 227, 233
siddhi 15, 187, 272n62, 285
siddhi, common, 109, 115, 181, 190, 285
siddhi of body, speech, and mind, 180, 256, 263
siddhi of increase, 115, 176
siddhi of pacification, 115, 176
siddhi of power, 115, 176
siddhi of wrath, 115, 176
siddhi, supreme, 15, 109, 115, 145, 147, 182, 190, 285
Siṃhanāda, 99, 191–92
Six Preliminary Practices (Könchok Jigmé Wangpo), 6, 23, 216, 266n9
soklung, 187, 275n83
Stainless Light. *See* Lhodrag Namkha Gyaltsen, mahāsiddha, 54, 57
Stainless Sky. *See* Atiśa
substantial cause, 182–83
subtle duality, 173, 280
Sukhāvati, 43, 192
Sumati, 113–14, 187, 189
Sun of Speech. *See* Secret Lord, Vajrapāṇi, 49
Svātantrika. *See* Autonomy School, 164
Swift Path (Paṇchen Losang Yeshé), 150, 292

T

taking the result as a path, 34, 169, 225
Taktsang Lotsāwa Sherab Rinchen, 79, 269n38, 292
Tārā, 109
Tashi Lhunpo Monastery, 55, 268n28
The Eight Verses of Praise to Jowo Atiśa (Naktso Lotsāwa Tsültrim Gyalwa), 57, 268n30
three bodies at the time of the path, 165–66
three bodies at the time of the result, 167–66
three bodies of the basis, 166
three great purposes, 91–92

three levels of being (commitment, wisdom, concentration being), 49–50, 59, 96–97, 267n24
Three Principal Aspects (Tsongkhapa), 161, 266n13, 273n70, 292
three rounds of mixing, 166, 184
three trainings, 155, 210, 211, 250
threefold examination/analysis, 15, 16, 88, 270n47
Tölung, 80
transference of consciousness, 177
Trijang Rinpoché, 4, 8, 293, 302
truth of cessation, 27, 31, 224
truth of path, 27, 224
Tsongkhapa Losang Drakpa. *See* bodhisattva Mahāsattva, Mañjunātha, 2, 18–21, 45, 61, 78, 80, 87, 99–102, 104–10, 118, 133–34, 138, 140–41, 144, 146, 187, 192, 232, 238, 248–49, 251, 261–62, 280, 292, 265nn1–2, 265n4, 265n8, 267n25, 268nn32–33, 269nn38–39, 269n40, 270n45, 271n53, 272n57, 273n70, 275n89, 275n91, 280, 290, 292, 294
Tuṣita, city, 52–53

U

Understanding All Tenets (Taktsang Lotsāwa Sherab Rinchen), 269n38
uninterrupted path of a learner, 169
union of a learner, 167–68, 173, 278, 280
union of a nonlearner, 92, 170, 250, 278, 283
union of abandonment, 168
union of calm abiding and insight, 164–65
union of realization, 168

V

vajra body, 5, 42, 65, 97, 104, 106–8, 139, 140, 143–45, 147, 167–68, 173, 183, 253, 287
vajra mind, 5, 42, 65, 97, 142, 144–45, 147, 167, 183, 254
vajra position (of the channels, winds, drops, and bliss and emptiness), 48, 50
vajra seal of secrecy, 12, 265n5
vajra speech, 5, 42, 65, 97, 141, 143–45, 147, 167, 183, 253, 284
Vajrabhairava. *See* Yamāntaka, 42–43, 213
Vajradhāra. *See* Lord of All the Conquerors, 17, 48–50, 68, 76–77, 109, 111, 113, 150, 174, 193, 228
Vajradharma (internal form of Avalokiteśvara), 96, 105
vajra-like concentration, 169–71, 176
Vajrapāṇi fierce (internal form), 96–98, 108
Vajrapāṇi Mahācakra (secret form), 97, 107
Vajrapāṇi. *See* Secret Lord, Sun of Speech, 5, 7, 49–50, 57, 95–98, 100, 103, 106–8, 112, 132, 133, 144, 145, 179, 230–31, 251–52, 268n32, 271nn53–54, 286
Vajrasattva, 76–78
Vehicle, Causal, 46, 88
Vehicle, Great, 32, 203, 212–13, 217
Vehicle, Individual, 201
Vehicle, Perfection, 47, 89, 169

Vehicle, Resultant, 46, 88
Vehicle, Supreme, 19, 237, 275n91
Vehicle, Vajra/Mantra, 18, 47, 88, 165, 169, 172
Vijaya Palace, 53, 55
Vinaya, 46, 124, 213, 236, 239
Virūpa, mahāsiddha, 81
vows and commitments, 165–68, 172, 174, 176
vows, bodhisattva, 73–74, 75, 76, 158, 159, 172, 243–44, 262
vows, individual liberation, 73, 74, 75, 76, 171, 243, 244, 262
vows, tantric, 73–74, 75, 76, 243, 244, 262

W

Wangchuk Tsawa Jampa Thayé, 195
white cloud, 2, 58–59, 61, 180, 185, 190, 213, 231, 232, 233, 257–58
white drop, 182, 257, 282
wisdom being, 42, 48–50, 52, 59, 61–62, 76, 88, 190, 267n24, 279, 287
wisdom of composition, 5, 115–16 123, 125–27, 191, 283
wisdom of debate, 5, 115–17, 123–25, 127, 191, 283
wisdom of explanation, 5, 115–16, 123–25, 127, 191, 283
wisdom, clear, 5, 20–21, 116, 120–21, 127, 191, 255, 283
wisdom, profound, 5, 20, 116, 122–23, 125, 127, 191, 255, 283
wisdom, swift, 5, 20–21, 116, 121–22, 127, 191, 255, 283
wisdom, vast, 5, 20, 116, 118–20, 127, 191, 255, 283
wrong livelihood, 23, 219–20, 266n10

Y

Yakpa Shuwa, Chöjé, 80
Yama, Lord of Death, 136, 255
Yamāntaka. *See* Vajrabhairava, 42–43, 128, 165, 192, 213
yogic feats, 20, 176, 255

About the Contributors

H. E. Chöden Rinpoché was born in 1931, in Kham, Tibet. At the age of three he was officially recognized by Reting Rinpoché as the reincarnation of the previous Lama Chöden of the Rongpo Rabten Monastery, himself a candidate for the reincarnation of the Twelfth Dalai Lama. Once recognized, he was tutored by an uncle until he entered the monastery. At the age of seven, he took novice ordination from Pabongkha Rinpoché, who named him Losang Gyalten Jikdrel Wangchuk. He subsequently received many teachings from Pabongkha Rinpoché. At the age of fifteen, following the advice of Pabongkha Rinpoché, he traveled to Central Tibet and entered Sera Jé Monastery. He received debate instructions from some of the greatest scholars in the monastery, including Geshé Loga and Geshé Losang Wangchuk, while studying in the same class as Geshé Sopa, Geshé Ugyen Tseten, and Geshé Legden. During the course of the study of the five major treatises he continued to receive instruction from Pabongkha Rinpoché, as well as Trijang Rinpoché, Bari Rinpoché, and Ling Rinpoché. He received numerous empowerments and oral transmissions, as well as pith instructions on ear-whispered advice that enabled him to develop realizations of the teachings. As a result of his lengthy training with many renowned lineage holders he mastered the five treatises and earned the title of *paṇḍita*. Upon completing his studies he did not sit his final exam but instead repeated the *lharam* class for many years, focusing on Vinaya.

When the Chinese occupation began to seriously disrupt life and study in the monastery, Rinpoché commenced a *chulen* ("taking the essence") retreat but this was soon also interrupted by the restrictions imposed on the practice of Dharma by the occupation. He lived in Lhasa until 1964, engaging in the practice of Guhyasamāja, Yamāntaka, and Heruka, and when possible he gave teachings. As the situation worsened during the Cultural Revolution, he stopped all outer practices completely. He lived in the house of a relative, determined not to engage any activity that would contradict Dharma. He remained there in a small, dark room for the next nineteen years without going out and without cutting his hair. He was often visited by the Chinese, who kept checking on him. He practiced in a concealed manner, in a room devoid of *thankas*, statues, or other ritual objects. He only had a small mala that he kept hidden in a secret pocket of his robes. Without performing any external offerings or rituals, he remained contemplating the stages of the path and the generation stage practices of the Guhyasamāja, Yamāntaka, and Heruka tantras. Then in 1979, three years after Mao Tse Tung died, it became possible for Rinpoché to give private teachings in his room to small groups of lamas and geshés.

In 1985 he obtained a passport and traveled to India, escaping the Chinese oppression. At the request of the Dalai Lama, he continued to teach at Sera Jé Monastery, his own center in California, and around the world, giving tantric initiations and instructions on the main subjects of geshé studies, as well as on poetry and grammar. He was considered a Vinaya Holder due to his extensive knowledge and pure morality. Chöden Rinpoché passed away on September 11, 2015.

IAN JAMES COGHLAN (Jampa Yigyen) trained as a monk at Sera Jé Monastic University, completing his studies in 1995, and holds a PhD in Asian studies from La Trobe University. Currently he is a research associate at the School of Philosophical, Historical and International Studies, Monash University, and a translator for the Institute of Tibetan Classics, the American Institute of Buddhist Studies, Wisdom Publications, the Khenpo Appey Foundation, and the Juniper Foundation.

VOULA ZARPANI holds a double master's degree from the Agricultural University of Athens and graduated from the first Lotsawa Rinchen Zangpo Translator Program in Dharamsala, India, in 1995. She continues to translate for various Tibetan lamas.

About Awakening Vajra

Awakening Vajra is an international nonprofit organization founded in 2010 by Venerable Geshé Gyalten in order to fulfill the dreams of His Eminence Chöden Rinpoché to teach and preserve the five branches of study from the Nālandā spiritual tradition. Its ultimate goal is to awaken the roots of compassion, love, and wisdom in the hearts of students for the benefit and welfare of all beings.

The five branches of study are

1. Buddhadharma
2. Linguistics
3. Healing Arts
4. Fine Arts
5. Astrology and Feng Shui.

To learn more about Awakening Vajra and its projects, please visit our website:

www.awakeningvajra.org
or contact us at:
Awakening Vajra, Inc.
PO Box 6356
San Jose, CA 95150–6356 USA
Telephone: +1 408 490 1911

Thank you

What to Read Next from Wisdom Publications

Mastering Meditation
Instructions on Calm Abiding and Mahāmudrā
His Eminence Chöden Rinpoché
Foreword by His Holiness the Dalai Lama

"Kyabjé Chöden Rinpoché was more kind to me than all the three times' buddhas. His teachings are not just words but come from a learned mind—and from experience." —Lama Zopa Rinpoche

Extremely Secret Dakini of Naropa
Vajrayogini Practice and Commentary
Pabongkha Rinpoche
Translated by David Gonsalez

A commentary to the practice of Vajrayogini composed by Kyabje Pabongkha Rinpoche—as revealed to him directly by Vajrayogini herself.

Middle Length Treatise on the Stages of the Path to Enlightenment
Tsongkhapa
Translated by Philip Quarcoo

"It is thrilling at long last to have a complete translation of the *Middle-Length Treatise on the Stages of the Path to Enlightenment*. Philip Quarcoo's accurate and readable rendering brings Jé Rinpoché's lucid presentation alive." —Roger R. Jackson, John W. Nason Professor of Asian Studies and Religion, emeritus, Carleton College

About Wisdom Publications

Wisdom Publications is the leading publisher of classic and contemporary Buddhist books and practical works on mindfulness. To learn more about us or to explore our other books, please visit our website at wisdom.org or contact us at the address below.

Wisdom Publications
132 Perry Street
New York, NY 10014 USA

We are a 501(c)(3) organization, and donations in support of our mission are tax deductible.

Wisdom Publications is affiliated with the Foundation for the Preservation of the Mahayana Tradition (FPMT).